London : Humphrey Milford.   Oxford University Press

Georges Lemaitre

From Cubism to Surrealism
in French Literature

Cambridge, Mass., Harvard University Press, 1941

To
Dr. C. E. Fryer, F. R. Hist. S.

. . . and nothing is
But what is not.
        Macbeth, I. iii

Preface

I wish to express my sincere gratitude to Dr. C. E. Fryer, F. R. Hist. S., for his unfailing kindness in providing me, throughout the composition of this book, with encouragement and helpful advice. I have further to express my thanks to Mr. J. Gaillard Fryer for his very much appreciated services in assisting me to arrange the final draft of this volume for publication.

I am also indebted to Miss Janet Oswald, of Montreal, for her very invaluable secretarial collaboration, and to Dr. Walter Heil, Director of the De Young Memorial Museum of San Francisco, for his kind assistance in gathering important information about the material used for the illustrations included in this book.

I want to acknowledge the courtesy of the Museum of Modern Art, New York, for providing me generously with most of the photographs of the paintings presented here, and for allowing me very liberally to make use of its extensive collection of modern works.

For similar courtesy in permitting me to reproduce paintings which they own, I want to thank Mrs. Charles J. Liebman and Mr. Sidney Janis of New York, the Columbus Gallery of Fine Arts of Columbus, Ohio, the Bignou Gallery of New York, and the Dalzell Hatfield Galleries of Los Angeles.

G. L.

Stanford University
September, 1941

Contents

Introduction   15

I. The Forerunners 19

Rationalism and Realism in French literature. The influence of J.-J. Rousseau. Occultism in pre-revolutionary France. The mystic trend in Romanticism. Gérard de Nerval, the poet of a "super-naturaliste" revelation. Victor Hugo, the prophet of an apocalyptic beyond. Charles Baudelaire: his longing for an Absolute; his belief in universal correspondence and harmony; dislocation of the elements composing our visible world and their rearrangement according to a new order. Arthur Rimbaud, "révolté" and "voyant." The enigma of the Comte de Lautréamont; *Les Chants de Maldoror,* an epic of Evil. Symbolism. Stéphane Mallarmé; his attempt to reach the Absolute through the sheer power of words. Impressionism; conventional modes of vision are discarded; the apparent solidity of Nature is broken up into a multiplicity of separate fragments. The stage is set for sweeping changes in man's conception of the world.

II. The Breakdown of the Old Conception of Reality   51

Scientific discoveries bring about a complete disruption of all accepted ideas about the structure of the universe. Science fails to reduce the part of mystery in the world. The philosophy of Bergson; criticism of discursive intelligence; the value of intuition and of instinct. Alfred Jarry; his hectic, disjointed existence; *Ubu-Roi,* a virulent satire of modern society; Jarry becomes a living symbol of revolt against present-day conditions. The innovations of Cézanne. Fauvism; the painters no longer strive to imitate Nature, but attempt to express solely their own emotions and dreams. Henri Rousseau, "le douanier"; a case of candid and genuine primitivism. Widespread desire to attain something deeper and truer than external reality.

III. Cubism   **71**   The "bateau-lavoir" on the Rue Ravignan. Artistic Bohemia in Montmartre at the beginning of the twentieth century. Pablo Picasso. Introduction of Negro art. Braque and the first Cubist paintings. The theory of Cubism: reduction of the universe to its geometrical framework; systematic dislocation of outside forms and shapes; revelation of the mystic soul of the Cosmos; ideal suggestion of pure spirituality. French and Spanish trends within Cubism. Evolution towards decorative art. The vogue of Montparnasse. Guillaume Apollinaire: erratic education; ramblings throughout Europe; *Le Festin d'Esope;* leadership of the Cubist groups; crusade for "L'Esprit Nouveau." The necessity of breaking away from a stale tradition; efforts towards an entirely new type of Realism: *Les Mamelles de Tirésias, drame surréaliste.* Max Jacob; his close friendship with Picasso; subversive, grotesque clowning combined with profound religious rapture; unrestrained and devastating verbalism. André Salmon; his respect for hard facts. Pierre Reverdy, his predilection for hazy dreams. The frivolity of Jean Cocteau. Futurism; its decided stand against Nature; apotheosis of the artificial; glorification of speed. Paul Morand. Blaise Cendrars. In search of an Absolute.

IV. Dada   **155** Moral influence of the World War of 1914–18; general disgust and despair. Humor considered as a means of defense against the cruel stupidity of the modern world. "Sic." "Nord-Sud" and the theory of the meaningless work of art. Jacques Vaché; his challenge to all rules of rational thought and sensible behavior; his dramatic suicide. Formation of the group "Littérature" in Paris. Tristan Tzara in Zurich. Dada. Systematic destruction through blatant nonsense. Provocative and insulting attitude towards the general public. Intentional absurdity of Dadaist productions. Dissatisfaction within the Dadaist group; André Breton asks for the convocation of a "Congrès de l'Esprit Moderne"; violent opposition on the part of Tristan Tzara and his friends. Internal dissensions and controversies bring about the end of Dadaism.

V. Surrealism   **179** André Breton has a most startling psychic experience. Breton and Soupault try to reproduce the circumstances of the original phenomenon. *Les Champs magnétiques.* Diffusion of Einstein's

12

theories on relativity. The influence of psychoanalysis. Growing prestige of Rimbaud and Lautréamont. Constitution of the Surrealist school. Its tribulations and vicissitudes. Surrealist view of man's mental evolution: the magic realm of childhood; disastrous consequences of rational education; disjunction of the world of imagination and the world of reality; resultant mediocrity of outlook, dullness, inevitable suffering. The proposed remedies: liberation of the suppressed potentialities hidden in man's subconscious mind; criticism, through humor, of all forms of conventional thinking. The true essence of Surreality. Rehabilitation of our imaginative faculties. Transcendent revelation provided by dreams. The purpose of literature and art. Surrealist method of automatic dictation. Excursions into the domain of clinical insanity; the point of view of Salvador Dali. The works of André Breton. Paul Eluard's metaphysical anguish. Robert Desnos' eroticism. Tristan Tzara's chaotic display of exuberant energy. René Char. Philippe Soupault; poetical evocation of an opalescent dawn. Louis Aragon; the rumblings of an impending catastrophe. Fundamental weakness of Surrealist productions. Conclusion.

Bibliography   **219**

Index   **241**

Illustrations

Henri Rousseau 54 *Le Rêve* (1910)
By courtesy of Mr. Sidney Janis, New York.
Photo. Museum of Modern Art, New York

Pablo Picasso 72 *Les Demoiselles d'Avignon* (1907)
By courtesy of the Museum of Modern Art,
New York. Photo. Museum of Modern Art

Juan Gris 80 *Portrait of Picasso* (1912)
By courtesy of the Bignou Gallery, New
York. Photo. Museum of Modern Art, New
York

Pablo Picasso 90 *Portrait Arrangement with the Words
"J'aime Eva"* (1910)
By courtesy of the Columbus Gallery of
Fine Arts, Columbus, Ohio. Photo. Colum-
bus Gallery

Fernand Léger 112 *Composition No. 7* (1925)
By courtesy of the Museum of Modern Art,
New York. Photo. Museum of Modern Art

Gino Severini 148 *Train Blindé en Action* (1915)
By courtesy of Mrs. Charles J. Liebman,
New York. Photo. Museum of Modern Art,
New York

Max Ernst 172 *La biciclette* [sic] *graminée garnie de
grelots les grisons grivelés et les échino-
dermes courbants* [sic] *l'échine pour
quêter des caresses* (c. 1920)
By courtesy of the Museum of Modern Art,
New York. Photo. Museum of Modern Art

André Masson 180 *Bataille de Poissons* (1927)
By courtesy of the Museum of Modern Art,
New York. Photo. Museum of Modern Art

14   **Yves Tanguy**   **190**   *Extinction des Lumières inutiles* (1927)
                                            By courtesy of the Museum of Modern Art,
                                            New York. Photo. Museum of Modern Art

            Salvador Dali   **208**   *Endless Enigma*
                                            By courtesy of Salvador Dali. Photo. Dalzell
                                            Hatfield Galleries, Los Angeles

Introduction

The object of the present essay is to offer a comprehensive survey and discussion of the main "modernistic" tendencies which have recently intrigued — and even more than a little puzzled — all the lovers of contemporary literature and art. The ambitions and vicissitudes of the various schools — from Cubism to Surrealism — have been presented in their original setting, in the midst of the familiar haunts of picturesque Parisian Bohemia: Montmartre and Montparnasse. Indeed the most important "vanguard" movements, with the exception of Futurism, have sprung up and have grown essentially on French soil. Even Futurism, which was an Italian offshoot of Cubism, eventually became almost completely integrated in the general development of French thought. Very rapidly, it is true, these divers theories spread to the other countries of Europe and to America. The minor variations they underwent in the process did not alter to any marked degree, however, the fundamental principles set forth in France by their first originators.

Literature rather than art has been taken as a center of perspective for the consideration of the complex new doctrines. Although in this particular field the aggressive works put on exhibition by artists have all but monopolized the attention of the general public, the ideas behind these works have been, more often than not, elaborated by writers. In fact, the spiritual influence of inspired poets is nearly always discernible at the origin of the most decisive innovations in contemporary art. Moreover, very few modern painters have ever given definite clues as to the meaning of their disconcerting productions. Any attempt to ascertain their deeper views necessarily implies a large measure of personal, and therefore debatable, hypothesis. Many writers, on the contrary, have themselves supplied abundant information about their beliefs, their methods, and their goals. At times it is thanks only to their explanations that we are able to understand, indirectly, the intents of the painters with whom they usually associated. When trying to elucidate the problems presented by modernistic trends of thought, we find in literary works an evidence which is at once closer than any other to the original source of inspiration of these movements and infinitely more explicit about their aims.

There is no question, however, of arbitrarily dissociating modern literature and modern art. These two aspects of our culture have been for many years, and are still at the present moment, almost inextricably interwoven. Every change in one domain is inevitably accompanied by correlated transformations in the other. Consequently, even though literature as a rule provides more reliable guidance as to the spiritual orientation of any particular school, the testimony of the plastic arts must also be invoked, especially in order to give an adequate account of the most outstanding traits of the newly inaugurated technique.

Further, neither Cubism, nor Futurism, nor Dadaism, nor Surrealism has unfolded in a vacuum. All these movements are closely associated with the essential forms of our modern existence, and many of their characteristic features are absolutely incomprehensible if detached from their moral and material environment. Hence the necessity of showing their relationship to the general evolution of the society in which they developed, of tracing their historical filiation from certain responsible precursors, and finally of ascribing to them their proper place in the midst of the great currents of contemporary thought.

In the light of these broader phenomena, the bewildering "modernistic" conceptions will perhaps appear less as figments of the imagination of a few queer, isolated individuals than as typical products of our troubled, unbalanced epoch.

Thus, whatever opinion may be held about the intrinsic
worth of their achievements, it will at least be possible to
understand fairly clearly — in spite of certain inherent, intentional obscurities — the fundamental purposes and the claims
of the most enigmatic artists and writers of our generation.

I. The Forerunners

Throughout their history, the French have with almost complete consistency displayed a willing and steadfast allegiance to the rules of logical reasoning and to the primary importance of existing realities. Indeed, it is part of the mental discipline of any normal Frenchman to seek deliberately to discover in the welter of impressions, observations, emotions, and ideas that surge upon him a definite, coherent, and orderly pattern. The French mind delights in adopting this pattern, even being ready, for the sake of intellectual conformity, to reinforce boldly any uncertain detail or blurred outline. Further, more often than not, the French manifest an instinctive distrust of wild imaginings and outbursts of fancy. In their view, natural human actions or feelings are the proper substance to provide the basic material for any enduring literary and spiritual structure. To most of them it seems that outside the tangible world of positive experience loom only the vain shadows of self-delusion and folly.

These two fundamental trends, the need for a logical conception of life and a feeling of reverence for the objective aspects of the world — in effect, rationalism and realism — are to be found linked together in almost every phase of French cultural development. Sometimes one tendency may predominate for a while over the other, but more often the two exist side by side, limiting and complementing each other. Thus the richest epoch of literary creation in France, the classical period of the seventeenth century, proceeded from a perfect union, harmony, and balance between these two essential elements of French thought.

There have been times, however, when the omnipotence of reason and the tyranny of reality have not been accepted without protest and challenge. This has occurred repeatedly in periods of grave social disintegration or of profound moral and spiritual unrest. On such occasions, the intellectual theories that have been propounded to explain the trouble have appeared so absurdly inadequate, and the underlying circumstances have resisted so implacably any rational interpretation, that not a few people have been tempted to seek, above mere intellect and fact, an answer to their questionings.

Until very recently, however, such anxious quests beyond the limits of accepted reason and of everyday reality have failed to engage the attention of the majority. Only a few individuals, some endowed with a special power of mystic insight, others simply driven to rebellion by adverse circumstances, have ventured along these unknown and dangerous paths. As a rule they could expect little understanding and still less response from the general public. When they dared to present their strange discoveries, they were usually met with the condemnation and scorn of that countless host, the upholders of *le bon sens*.

Thus these bolder spirits remained in most cases isolated and ineffectual. A rapid review of their efforts will not reveal any consistent and continuous "school" of writers or artists systematically striving to attain to a truth of a higher order behind the screen of logic and apparent reality. Very often the protests of the rebels, being the outcome of personal maladjustments, were all but submerged under the great current of "sensible" thought that was still moving powerfully onwards. During the last half century, however, as the state of contemporary civilization grew more and more troubled and as cases of maladjustment multiplied everywhere, the individuals so affected gradually became aware that they held aspirations in common. The ties and associations which were almost automatically formed among them took the direction of the movements known as Cubism, Futurism, Dadaism, Surrealism — movements which have created so many eddies,

crosscurrents, and whirlpools in the general flow of contemporary art and literature.

The first important challenge to the hegemony of rationalism in France was delivered by J.-J. Rousseau in the latter
part of the eighteenth century. The *Ancien Régime* was then
nearing the brink of revolution; forces of disintegration were
at work undermining not only the outworn traditional social
order but the whole structure of abstract conceptions which
had constituted the intellectual framework of the great
"classical" age. When Rousseau appealed to intuition and
sentiment, he was not trying to destroy the whole basis of
confidence in human reasoning. He simply felt that the
"heart" was a richer source of inspiration; he wanted to show
that morally also it was a safer guide. By so doing, however,
he emphasized implicitly the relative failure of the rationalistic process, and prepared the way for further doubt concerning the intrinsic value of the type of conclusion that pure
reason is capable of reaching.

Rousseau himself seems to have been carried by the power
of his own inspired intuition into a magic realm, far beyond
the limits that rational thinking can ever hope to attain. In
Les Rêveries du promeneur solitaire, particularly, he has
recorded moments of ineffable ecstasy during which he felt
his soaring spirit actually entering into blissful communion
with the whole universe: "Durant ces égarements, mon âme
erre et plane dans l'univers sur les ailes de l'imagination dans
des extases qui passent toute autre jouissance" (1). In this
blissful state he would lose contact with the world of everyday
experience; objects that make reality, that men can see, feel,
and apprehend, would cease to exist for him; or, rather, they
would acquire a transcendent existence within the great

(1) J.-J. Rousseau, "Les Rêveries du promeneur solitaire," *Œuvres
complètes* (Paris: Hachette, 1909–12), IX, 374.

Whole — within a higher mystic totality. When a man's soul succeeds in attaining such dizzy, intoxicating heights, then, says Rousseau, "alors, tous les objets particuliers lui échappent; il ne veut, il ne sent rien que dans le Tout" (2).

About the time that Rousseau was recording these almost superhuman trances, there appeared in France a number of curious, daring spirits likewise intent on penetrating, by some means or other, into the mysteries of the unknown. Occultism, esoterism, mysticism flourished then in great abundance. The movement did not grow up, to be sure, under the influence of Rousseau's ideas, but it represented a set of kindred efforts towards the discernment, through the medium of inspired transports, of a sublime reality hidden behind the disappointing actualities proffered by our reason and our senses. It was perhaps something more than a mere coincidence that the Château of Ermenonville, where Rousseau spent the last period of his life, was also the most important rendezvous for the devotees of "Illuminism" on the eve of the French Revolution.

The impact of the French Revolution, however, dispelled all these phantasms. The necessity for clear-cut decisions, the exigencies of hard facts, asserted themselves for the time being with overwhelming force. The Goddess of Reason was enthroned in Notre-Dame during the Terror; later, Napoleon hunted down "ideologists," lumping together under that term of contempt all those who were unable to recognize the imperious claims of the immediately real.

After Waterloo, however, the grip of reality was loosened again; once more it was permissible to dream. The Romantic movement, expressing the feelings of youth during that unbalanced and trying period, brought back — with an added tinge of despair due to the stress of the times — many of Rousseau's essential themes, coupled with a more intense

(2) *Ibid.*

nostalgic longing for a mysterious supernatural realm, inaccessible to the minds of the vulgar, the *bourgeois*, the uninitiated. But at the same time Romanticism also represented a spontaneous, vital reaction after years of suppression and suffering — a reaction tingling with a new zest for life, throbbing with enthusiasm for art and for the beauty of the world. This latter aspect of the movement gained force steadily as general conditions improved. Ultimately it prevailed over the other, more morbid, visionary trend, obliterating the magic vision of introspective mysticism. Nevertheless flashes of the inner light can be perceived in many a great Romantic writer. Thus Nodier, Sainte-Beuve, Aloysius Bertrand, Balzac, at times show strange, deep affinities for the supernatural. But the most definite signs of that half-obscured strain of mysticism are to be found undeniably in Gérard de Nerval and in Victor Hugo.

Gérard de Nerval was the son of a military surgeon attached to Napoleon's armies in the field. From his infancy he was entrusted to the care of a great-uncle living in the little village of Mortefontaine, not far from Ermenonville — that center of occultism in pre-revolutionary days. The old gentleman, under the influence of the atmosphere once prevailing there, had collected a large number of books dealing with magic, magnetism, and the "dark" sciences. As times changed, bringing other interests, he had relegated the whole collection to an attic. The boy, discovering the volumes, devoured them, and, being a very impressionable child, he bore ever afterwards the traces of hermetic hallucination.

Henceforward the common experiences of life were for him transformed into mystic symbols, full of hidden meaning. While still adolescent, he chanced to catch a glimpse of a beautiful *châtelaine* and fancied himself in love with her.

Indiscreet biographers have shown us that she was only a common English adventuress who, after being the favorite of an *émigré* of royal blood, the duc de Bourbon, became Baronne de Feuchères. She received through the generosity of her old admirer the Château of Mortefontaine. For Gérard, however, she was not simply the passing preoccupation of a young man's fancy; she was the actual embodiment of the being whose reincarnation he was morbidly to pursue until his dying day. Later, in Paris, he imagined he had found "Her" again in the person of an actress, Jenny Colon; his mind, working more strongly than ever on an exalted, supra-terrestrial plane, very easily idealized a liaison that was most banal and short-lived.

When this liaison came to an end, Gérard de Nerval, in-stead of being rudely awakened by the shock, lapsed slowly into insanity. Insanity was not by any means a harrowing experience for him. His was not a case of mental disintegra-tion brought about by organic trouble, drugs, or disease. It was a purely psychic process, carrying his mind to spheres that human reason cannot frequent with impunity for any length of time. He felt within himself the blossoming of a new Ego, freed from the limitations of time and space, un-trammeled by the fetters of rational categories, capable of twisting, assembling, dissolving, and combining again all kinds of images and shapes, as though possessed of an un-limited power of spiritual re-creation. To him the whole world became a mirage, rich with the suggestive intensity of a vision, suffused with a thousand hues of enchanting fancy, light and delicate as the fabric of a dream. As he said him-self, this was indeed the overflowing of the dream-world into real life: "l'épanchement du songe dans la vie réelle" (3).

No wonder that when Gérard de Nerval had been nursed

(3) "Aurélia," *Le Rêve et la vie* (Paris: Michel Lévy, 1868), pt. I, chap. III, p. 6.

back to reason he almost regretted having to return to "real" existence. He remembered dimly the marvels of the hallucinatory world he had been led to explore; he found the normal, lucid world too sharply defined, too harsh and too crude. He set himself to cultivate an indefinite, intermediate state of mind, in which these two worlds would fuse and blend into one another. He succeeded only too well, living in a kind of waking dream, half way between the real and the unreal; although relatively sane for everyday purposes, he kept open the lines of communication with the mysterious forces that lie outside the domain of normal consciousness. Of course, such a condition could not be stable; he would oscillate first in one direction and then in another. Periodically his mind rose, as it were, on the crest of a powerful wave of mystic exaltation. Riding the wave, he lost all contact with reality and had to be kept among the insane. Then, falling back into the deep trough of the billows, he appeared merely as a correct and somewhat pedestrian writer of unsuccessful plays. But hovering as he did most of the time between these two extremes, he was capable during those privileged moments of producing pieces, such as *Sylvie*, *Aurélia*, and *Les Chimères*, which are generally regarded as among the most exquisite examples of imaginative writing that have ever graced French literature.

While to ordinary men the world of reality and the world of dreams are quite separate and distinct, and cannot be mingled without detriment to each other, to Gérard de Nerval there seemed to be between them a continuity and a mystic harmony. The works which were conceived by him in that aura, enriched with the glow of subliminal dreams, possess the most delicate and captivating beauty and exert the strangest, most potent appeal. They seem like a tracery of heraldic symbols, of graceful arabesques, a light efflorescence of free imagery and pure ideals. It would be idle to seek to find in them too precise a meaning; indeed, a literal explanation would spoil most of their charm. As Gérard de Nerval himself wrote: "ils . . . perdraient de leur charme à être expliqués, si la chose était possible" (4). Yet, standing as they do outside the petty censorship of common sense, they strike a note all their own, one which might come from another world, weird, bizarre, and moving. As if by magic, they open the door to a realm beyond that of sensible nature. "Supernaturaliste" (5) was the epithet by which Gérard de Nerval wanted to describe his revelations. Indeed, this word evokes adequately those fantastic and whimsical visions of half-forgotten things which hold such a strange fascination for us, arousing in our souls an irresistible nostalgic longing.

Victor Hugo, like many a man of his generation, felt a spontaneous curiosity concerning the mysterious forces lying behind the forms and appearances of everyday life. Then, having met with tragedy in his own domestic circle — the wrecking of his home by his wife's unfaithfulness, and the drowning of his daughter Léopoldine — he seems to have been impelled anxiously to seek a solution of the enigma of existence. Tirelessly he probed metaphysical hypotheses, esoteric revelations, myths and religious symbols. Alexandre Weill, a young Jew, initiated him into the arcanum of the old Hebraic Kabbala. For more than ten years he brooded over occult doctrines and mystic lore. Then came the shock of the *coup d'état* of Louis-Napoléon Bonaparte in 1851, which sent Hugo into exile. The anguish of sudden loneliness in the bleak and dismal climate of Jersey, the nerve-racking strain resulting from the practice of spiritism, in which he allowed himself to indulge, brought on for the distracted poet an amazing mental crisis.

(4) "A Alexandre Dumas," *Les Filles du feu* (Paris: Michel Lévy, 1868), p. 86.　　　　　　　　　　　　　　　　(5) *Ibid.*

Victor Hugo felt himself haunted by ghosts; at times the phantom apparition of a "Lady in White" would throw him into a terrified trance; occasionally at night he would awake in the grip of an unaccountable shuddering; he would hear mysterious voices, the voices of captive souls moaning for release. . . . He had the sensation of peering down into unfathomable depths beyond the experience of common mortals. Like a Prophet of old, he would attempt to penetrate the unknown and to reveal to men the awful mysteries of their destiny.

Here the doctors had to intervene. One of Hugo's brothers — Eugène — had already been stricken by insanity. One of his daughters — Adèle — was later to end in an asylum. He himself seems to have been at this time dangerously close to the great threatening shadow. He had to abandon spiritism, a move that eventually restored him to a state of comparative calm. Until his last day, however, Victor Hugo remained convinced that he had indeed been chosen from amongst men to communicate with the Great Beyond and even with God Himself.

Many a time he has evoked the perilous and irresistible fascination exerted by the great Unknown upon certain spirits, endowed like himself with the fateful gift of supernatural intuition. "Every man . . . is free to go or not to go upon that frightening promontory of thought from which one peers into darkness. If he goes not, he remains within ordinary life, within the domain of normal consciousness, of ordinary virtue, of ordinary faith or ordinary doubt. And rightly so. For internal peace, this is obviously the best. If he ventures upon those heights he is taken captive. The deep waves of the supernatural have appeared to him. No man can view that ocean with impunity. . . . He will not renounce that fatally alluring abyss, that sounding of the unexplored deep, that indifference to the earth and to life, that entry into the forbidden, that effort to feel the impalpable and to see the invisible. He comes back to it again and again, he leans and bends over it; he takes one step forward and then two; thus is achieved the penetration of the impenetrable, and thus is attained the complete release of infinite meditation" (6).

When so released from the bonds of our mediocre reality, Hugo feels that he truly shares in the obscure but tremendous pulsation of the whole Cosmos. In those moments of inspired rapture, instead of giving a precise and detailed account of objects and facts as they appear, he will offer a glimpse of indescribable creatures crawling indistinctly in gloomy depths, or display the hard, icy glare of an immaterial, boundless immensity, or call forth chaotic and tumultuous masses driven before some dark, furious, apocalyptic storm.

Such visions have, time and again, been held up to ridicule by rational and intelligent critics. The poet has been called stupid, and his imagery absurd. Indeed, these evocations have very little, if anything, to do with reason and intelligence. They simply conjure up, though with haunting intensity, the vision of some other world completely inaccessible except through the power of intuitive, mystic insight. Hugo seems to have been well aware of the discrepancy between the tenor of his visions and the more positive turn of mind of his contemporaries. He hardly ever unveiled his dreams except through the medium of allusions and metaphors, thus rendering them even more appalling and perplexing. The two main pieces in which he intended to convey the full import of his message, *La Fin de Satan* and *Dieu*, he decided were not to be published until many years after his death, since he was anxious to keep them in reserve until times were ripe.

Indeed, the second half of the nineteenth century was most

(6) Victor Hugo, "William Shakespeare," *Œuvres complètes* (Paris: Ed. Hetzel-Quantin, 1880–89), pt. I, chap. V, p. 141.

unfavorably disposed towards views of that kind. A period of comparative social stability and material comfort had set in with the establishment of the Second Empire. The first application on a large scale of scientific discoveries to practical life was then opening up a field of boundless expectation and hope; philosophers visualized man in the near future as in virtual control of all natural forces; scientific investigation seemed destined to reduce the unknown to within a small compass, making it almost negligible. There was no longer any widespread desire to escape from reality; realism was the creed and password of the contented and positive-minded new generation.

There were, however, a few discordant notes in this concert of materialistic confidence and satisfaction. The general self-complacency caused a few ill-adjusted, though outstandingly gifted, individuals to feel intensely their opposition to the prevailing spirit of the society in which they had to live, and threw them into extremes of revolt more daring and provoking than had ever been attempted by the Romanticists before them. Among these, Baudelaire, Rimbaud, and Lautréamont were to play a leading part in shaping the ideas of a newer generation.

Charles Baudelaire, offspring of an elderly man — his father was sixty-two at the time of his birth — had to bear the handicap of an exhausted, impoverished vitality from the very beginning of his life. Dissipation, disease, excesses of all sorts soon left him prematurely worn-out. Yet at the same time he displayed an intensely eager appetite for life, the source of which seems to have been a violent, almost morbid sensuality. His lack of vital energy prevented him from enjoying the pleasures which he craved; on the other hand, his ardent nature would not allow him to find peace in renunciation nor satisfaction in dreams. So he was tossed back and forth between desire and despair; he loathed life which had made him taste the ashes of frustration and failure; at the same time he could not help adoring life because of its promises of entrancing enjoyment and beauty. To use his own expression, "l'horreur de la vie et l'extase de la vie" (7) were the two poles between which he was condemned to swing incessantly, maddeningly. His first reaction was a sentiment of revolt, a mixture of anger and gloom — "mélancolie irritée" (8) — together with an irresistible impulse to run away from the torturing dilemma "n'importe où hors du monde" (9). But whither?

Then Baudelaire gradually came to believe that beyond the limits of this imperfect and disappointing world lay an invisible supernatural universe, which was his genuine spiritual home. On this earth he felt himself to be a soul "exilée dans l'imparfait" (10), tormented by "la soif insatiable de tout ce qui est au delà" (11) — an unquenchable thirst for that immaterial paradise of which he found within himself a compelling intuitive revelation.

Indeed, Baudelaire, sensuous being that he was, could not be content to lose himself in the abstract contemplation of a remote ideal. He needed one that could be encompassed; he wanted to make it his very own on this earth, and, as he himself said, "s'emparer immédiatement, sur cette terre même, d'un paradis révélé" (12). This, he thought, was by no means impossible. For him the common reality surrounding us did not possess a distinct, separate, autonomous existence; it was but the manifestation, the expression — or, as he says, the

(7) "Mon cœur mis à nu," *Journaux intimes* (Paris: G. Crès, 1920), XCV, p. 92.

(8) Baudelaire, *L'Art romantique* (Paris: Calmann-Lévy, 1899), pt. VIII, chap. III, p. 167.

(9) Baudelaire, *Petits Poèmes en prose* (Paris: Calmann-Lévy, 1900), XLVIII, p. 140.

(10) *L'Art romantique*, pt. VIII, chap. III, p. 167.

(11) *Ibid.*   (12) *Ibid.*

symbol — of the superior spiritual universe which alone constitutes the absolute reality. Complete understanding of the
meaning of life consists in being able to perceive the relations
between each element of our world and the various aspects
of the transcendent entity that lies above and beyond. In certain privileged moments of mystic ecstasy it is possible to apprehend these subtle affinities, to penetrate into the sublime,
and so enjoy its ineffable bliss.

Such attainment is of course by no means easy for man,
hampered as he is by the banality of the everyday scene which
prevents his soul from soaring into a more exalted sphere.
Yet Baudelaire has explored the ways of access to that higher
sphere. According to him, one and the same sublime form of
the supraterrestrial reality may be expressed in this world by
a series of different "symbols," say, for instance, by a given
shade of color, by a sentiment, and also by certain definite
sounds. Then between that particular color, that sentiment,
and those sounds — reflecting, symbolizing, as they do, the
same aspect of the invisible essence — there will be, as a matter of course, a perfect correspondence and harmony. Indeed,
it has been often noted that the tone of an aria, the tinge
of an emotion, the hues of a landscape, may present a subtle,
mysterious, and profound analogy. But if certain colors,
certain sounds, certain sentiments are — in their deep, intrinsic value — rigorously equivalent, it is obvious that any
one of them may replace any of the others without caus-
ing a disturbance or alteration in the general scheme of
things.

Now, in the common world in which we live, impressions
and sensations are constantly found linked together and following a certain regular sequence. Gradually that sequence
has come to appear immutable, inevitable, until it is generally assumed to be the only "logical" or "rational" order. In
fact, such is the force of habit that all the elements of our

earthly experience have become, as it were, welded together in that order and have hardened into a continuous crust, solid and opaque, completely concealing the higher spiritual universe.

The rôle of art is to open up again a view of that spiritual universe. This can be effected only by shattering to pieces the obnoxious layer of rational and conventional banalities. By so doing, the artist does not plan to destroy reality as we know it, but simply to dissociate its various elements, then, recombining them in an entirely different way, systematically to substitute one given aspect for another. This substitution is permissible — if it is done in agreement with the secret rhythm of universal harmonies. The principle to be followed in the process of rearranging the dislocated "symbols" must not be that of rational logic, which would inevitably impose upon the new construction its old, stiff, paralyzing cast; it must come from the individual inward intuition of the true artist, who alone can perceive the play of cosmic similarities, and who, through a permutation of interchangeable signs, may succeed in breaking the heavy constraint of customary associations without altering the deep meaning and the spiritual value of the whole. Thus the spirit, freed from the lazy suggestions of habit, soaring upon the revelation of the new, stimulating symbols, is at last capable of apprehending the sublime essence of the absolute.

So art, according to Baudelaire, does not consist in depicting or explaining accurately what can be seen around us. Art must try to conjure up what is *not* perceptible to ordinary eyes. It is almost second sight. The means it uses are not the means accepted by logic, which is nothing but the intellectual codification of the ordinary run of things; the ways by which the evocation of the invisible can be achieved must be extraordinary, supernatural — illegal, in the judgment of reason — very much like magic or witchcraft. What Baudelaire said about poetry applies to every manifestation of pure art: it is a case of "sorcellerie évocatoire" (13).

Whereas the mystic conceptions of Rousseau, Nerval, or Hugo merely constitute rather remote prefigurations of contemporary trends of thought, the theories of Baudelaire stand as a signpost at the very threshold of the present era. The idea of breaking up the world of appearances into fragments and rearranging these fragments according to a new order challenging by its novelty, springing only from the mind of the artist, who is striving to reveal a superior reality — that idea forms the very basis of all the most recent and astounding developments in the field of modern art.

Arthur Rimbaud, however, was to carry even farther his audacious investigations. Rimbaud was born in the ugly industrial town of Charleville, and was harshly brought up there by his narrow-minded, bigoted mother. Almost suffocated by the philistine atmosphere of this provincial, *petit bourgeois* environment, Rimbaud seems to have resented at an abnormally early age the oppressive, disheartening sordidness of modern life. Possessed of superabundant vitality, his wild, exuberant energy made the simple humdrum of conventional existence a perfect torture to him. In his adolescence the harum-scarum mischief that he perpetrated was but the outward manifestation of a profound and genuine distress: "Je suis celui qui souffre et qui s'est révolté" (14).

His ideas of revolt were not without a certain naïveté. With the uncompromising truculence of youth he simply wanted to destroy everything, proclaiming with brutal bravado: "Voici le temps des Assassins" (15). He lacked true

---

(13) *L'Art romantique*, pt. VIII, chap. III, p. 173.

(14) Rimbaud, "L'Homme juste," *Œuvres* (Paris: Mercure de France, 1912), p. 389.

(15) "Les Illuminations," *Œuvres*, p. 184.

scepticism, however. His iconoclastic furore was merely his way of rejecting the dull, drab picture of life offered him by society, and the plain, colorless features of the world of reason; for he was instinctively convinced of the existence of another world, more vivid and more intense, within which he longed to regale himself with orgiastic enthusiasm.

To reach that other world, thought Rimbaud, it was absolutely essential to pierce the outer shell of banal common sense by which its beauty is concealed from conventional minds. One had to discard ordinary standards of observation and reasoning, and in a trance of mystic rapture attain that visionary state wherein the unknown reveals itself to man in all its radiant splendor. "Je dis qu'il faut être VOYANT, se faire VOYANT" (16).

A visionary state cannot be achieved by one who is in a condition of complete mental equilibrium; the spirit must be wrenched from the grip of rational conceptions. The senses, which are the great means of communication with the ordinary world, must be put systematically out of their proper working order: "Le poète se fait voyant par un long, immense, raisonné dérèglement de tous les sens" (17). This is not to be effected by means of artificial devices but simply by forcing the senses into a paroxysm of action exceeding the limits of their normal working power. When the fiery intensity of "toutes les formes d'amour, de souffrance, de folie" (18), has caused a breakdown of our conventional receptive and interpretative mechanism, when the very excess of strain has filled our material nature with numbing "poisons" (19), then only is the mind liberated from all its shackles. Then, even though he may have become a physical

(16) "Lettre à Paul Demeny, 15 mai 1871," *Lettres de la vie littéraire d'Arthur Rimbaud* (Paris: Nouvelle Revue Française, 1931), p. 62.
(17) *Ibid.*
(18) *Ibid.*   (19) *Ibid.*

wreck, a criminal in the eyes of the world, a being accursed, man at last enters into supreme knowledge; he attains the unknown. "Il devient entre tous le grand malade, le grand criminel, le grand maudit — et le suprême savant! — car il arrive à l'INCONNU" (20).

Rimbaud, however, was of much too vital a nature to be able to view the "unknown" in a purely contemplative mood. His attitude has never been one of escape from life. "Changer la vie" (21) was his great message; he aspired to infuse into the hardened, inert forms round about us the vivifying fire that the "Unknown" conceals. Literary art, and especially poetry, appeared to him to be the most effective medium for the achievement of that aim. To him poetry is not an expression of feeling; it is a means of enlightenment — of "knowledge" in the highest sense of the word. Through it, common reality may be suffused with something of the higher essence. Like Prometheus, the Titan of old, who stole fire from Jupiter in order to animate the clay image of the first man, "le poète est vraiment Voleur de feu" (22). The poet will not describe objects, record emotions and facts, passively following their rhythm; he will actually create them by giving them the true spark of life. "La poésie ne rythmera plus l'action; elle sera en avant" (23).

The majority of Rimbaud's works, but particularly *Bateau ivre* and *Les Illuminations* are striking instances of that attempt to re-create the world through the medium of literary art. Very much like Baudelaire, whom he hails as "le premier voyant, roi des poètes, un vrai Dieu" (24), Rimbaud believes in the interplay of universal harmonies. With amazing bold-

(20) *Ibid.*
(21) "Une Saison en Enfer," *Œuvres*, p. 279.
(22) "Lettre à Paul Demeny, 15 mai 1871," *Lettres de la vie littéraire d'Arthur Rimbaud*, p. 64.
(23) *Ibid.*   (24) *Ibid.*, p. 66.

ness, yet with prodigious instinctive tact, he isolates and transposes the various aspects of our reality, rearranging them most independently and irregularly. Each element, detached from the surroundings in which we are accustomed to see it placed, instead of just belonging to a set of classified things, acquires a personality and a soul. By and by, the whole world seems to become queerly animated. Objects, colors, sentiments, begin to reel and dance before our eyes. We no longer see the staid and commonplace reality that we knew of yore but an entirely new universe, throbbing and pulsating, which soon swings into a Dionysiac saraband. Yet all our old impressions and sensations are still there, quite recognizable in their new guise, but now vibrant and glowing with a reflection of eternity. The miracle of Rimbaud's evocation is achieved by his method of warping reality sufficiently to disengage its elements from their customary setting and let them assume a life of their own — not so pronouncedly, however, as to constitute an absurd, caricature-like dream. His visionary universe retains a haunting kinship with the world of common experience, for it represents the world of common experience disturbingly blended with a hallucinatory vision of the supreme beyond. It is a new, fresh, and resplendent creation.

This creation, however, looks almost pale when compared with Lautréamont's lurid pictures. The personality of the Comte de Lautréamont himself has remained up to the present an almost complete mystery. We do know that his real name was Isidore Ducasse; that he was born in 1846; that he was the son of a French consular official in Montevideo; that he studied at the *lycées* of Tarbes and Pau; that he died in Paris at the age of twenty-four. This practically exhausts all that we know definitely about his brief and enigmatic existence. Lacking any dependable clue to his moral and psychological background, we face a most intriguing puzzle when confronted with a powerful and disturbing production of his, *Les Chants de Maldoror*. After having been neglected for a great many years, this work has recently been hailed by the younger generation as carrying an epoch-making, prophetic message.

Lautréamont appears to belong to the type of extreme or absolute *révolté*. While with Baudelaire and Rimbaud revolt was but a transitory stage, a means of clearing the way to a higher sphere of self-realization, with Lautréamont it seems to have been a real end in itself. His attacks are not confined to the domain of human morals, human society, or human reason; they are directed against even God Himself. God, as the first source of all things, is held responsible for the appalling atrocity that constitutes life on this earth. The spectacle of the gaping, raw wound which life inflicts on the unfortunate animated beings who inhabit the globe is held to be the just punishment of its original Cause and Creator. "J'ai reçu la vie comme une blessure. . . . Je veux que le Créateur en contemple, à chaque heure de son éternité, la crevasse béante. C'est le châtiment que je lui inflige" (25). Maldoror stands forth like a modern Prometheus, challenging and insulting the Supreme Deity, deliberately turning his own existence into a continuous, withering blasphemy.

First, he sets himself to disintegrate the world of God's creation by virulent and caustic sarcasm. All kinds of forms and shapes, principles and ideas, are made to appear impossibly preposterous. Maldoror systematically jumbles and confuses all normal connections and values; grave problems are treated as mere bubbles; trifles are investigated with methodical thoroughness. A feeling of utter absurdity slowly pervades a universe turned topsy-turvy. The concentrated

(25) Lautréamont, "Les Chants de Maldoror," *Œuvres complètes* (Paris: Ed. G. L. M., 1938), p. 130.

acid of the author's irony dissolves all the aspects of the world that we know into an inconsistent and odious nightmare.

But the most corrosive of all the means of destruction at his disposal is undoubtedly the existence of Evil itself. *Les Chants de Maldoror* constitutes a tremendous and amazing epic of Evil. Evil is here presented, without indictment, explanation, or excuse, simply as a stupendous fact dominating the whole creation. Malefic influences are shown creeping irresistibly everywhere; and Evil, developing and expanding monstrously, finally dwarfs everything else into insignificance, all but eclipsing the very spirit of God Himself.

The feeling of guilt, intoxicating as a powerful drug, causes Maldoror to experience a curious surge of exaltation, temporarily giving to an otherwise desperate and miserable existence a zest of lurid and violent intensity. Scenes of cruelty and lust, sadistic murders, torture of living bodies, profanation of corpses, are all evoked with a wealth of gory detail that creates a haunting impression of inescapable horror. The gripping fascination exerted by horror upon certain inferior but very deep-seated strata of common human nature is here brought to a climax, and the morbid appeal possessed by certain of Lautréamont's pictures goes far to disclose the unavowed and perhaps unsuspected elements lurking at the bottom of man's subconscious mind.

Lautréamont himself obviously did not draw these pictures with any cold-blooded consideration of their import and possible effects. He seems to have obeyed an impulse from within which bade him pour out a flood of images, without restraint or discrimination, from the innermost recesses of his soul. The continuous, though uneven flow of his sentences, in which the most unusual associations come together in overpowering abundance, precludes the idea that this is a deliberate combination of heterogeneous fragments

artificially pieced together. It is nothing more nor less than
the current of secret, turbid subconscious thought which is
allowed to come to the surface and escape through the free,
uncontrolled outlet of spontaneous verbal procreation.
Every metaphor brings forth an image which in turn begets
a comparison; so the poet watches — without trying to inter-
fere with — the amazing procession of strange things coming
from the depths of his own being, realizing that this automatic development can reveal a new world, truly momentous
and fundamental, which dialectical intelligence would certainly fail to approach.

The new world brought to light by the vision of Maldoror
is not without an internal logic of its own, but it is marked
by a prodigious efflorescence of weird forms with their roots
spreading down into the uncertain substratum of subliminal
dreams. We catch glimpses of ambiguous creatures, half-
human, half-plant, suggesting a monstrous submarine flora
stranded after the ebb of some preternatural tide; again,
swarming legions of polymorphic beings are shown crawling
on the face of some bald, arid immensity. . . . All that phantasmagoria, imbued with the elemental forces of fabulous
epochs, evokes the primal mysteries which must have haunted
the dreams of men from the very dawn of time. Even now it
arouses in us dormant memories, the remnants of an almost
vanished consciousness of potential cosmic forces whose display is for ever endowed with an enthralling, awe-inspiring
grandeur.

Alternating with the recurrent themes of inevitable male-
diction and universal suffering are the shrill notes of de-
mented, passionate frenzy, the chaotic torment of mutual
destruction, or the anguished appeals of a lone victim pursued
in the dark, shrieking with fear. But above it all sounds the
voice of fierce, exasperated human pride, constantly struck
down, yet indestructible, always rising again, always ready to

rebel and fight; then, joining in a tremendous chorus of de-
moniac fury, taking up the original motif of desperate revolt
against God.

Baudelaire, Rimbaud, Lautréamont, exceptional beings
that they were, in revolt against the general trend of their
generation, met with little or no success during their lifetime.
Of Baudelaire, it is true, Victor Hugo said that he had "in-
venté un frisson nouveau," but few seem to have perceived
at first the deeper meaning underlying the splendor of his
incomparable artistry and the audacity of his themes. Rimbaud was a complete failure in the literary circles of Paris;
his disappointment in this respect probably accounts largely
for his angrily casting off literature at the age of nineteen and
embarking on a course of mad adventures which were to end
only many years later with his death. As for Lautréamont,
his work went practically unnoticed; he himself passed from
the scene leaving hardly a trace in the recollections of his
contemporaries.

A few years afterwards, however, a violent reaction suddenly set in. Science had not, after all, fulfilled the extravagant promises which had been made in her name; it was
obvious that the kernel of every important problem would for
ever remain beyond the reach of her investigations. On the
other hand, common reality appeared in the long run as a
dull and unvaried routine; literary realism had turned into
a naturalistic notation of the most sordid aspects of human
life; the disasters of 1870 added a feeling of discouragement
and a sense of irremediable decadence. So once more the
desire to escape from the oppression of actual, material things
grew and spread; around 1880 it became the keynote of an
entirely new symphony of thought. The theories of Baudelaire concerning the liberating value of "symbols" were
accepted as the doctrine of the younger school, and "Symbol-

ism" then came officially into being. Soon it became the
prevailing literary fashion in France. But on being widely
adopted, almost vulgarized, the ideas of Baudelaire — and
soon also those of Rimbaud — inevitably lost their pungency
and vigor. A multitude of young poets saw in them countless
possibilities of lyrical development and forgot the deep, painful, anxious search for the Absolute that they originally
implied. From being a mystic conception of the universe,
Symbolism came to stand for an aesthetic utilization of delicate, subtle, but rather superficial literary *procédé*. Of all the
Symbolists, only one offered an original, profound, and last-
ing contribution. That was Stéphane Mallarmé.

Throughout his whole career Mallarmé was in the throes
of a harrowing internal conflict. He was endowed with a rich
and powerful mind, with a keen and subtle taste, which made
him supremely sensitive to the attraction of all things beautiful. Eagerly, almost greedily, he enjoyed the fresh, unique,
infinitely precious quality of each instant of time. The call
of the present moment, or, as he says,

> Le vierge, le vivace et le bel aujourd'hui (26)

would arouse in him an intense and passionate longing. Yet
at the same time, through some innate vital deficiency, the
gifts proffered to him by life seemed always to elude his grasp.
Notwithstanding his most brilliant intellectual capacities, he
never rose above the rank of a schoolteacher, and he spent
year after year in the drudgery of cramming English vocabulary and grammar into the heads of reluctant Parisian school
children. Lacking as he was in the aggressiveness that only a
rich, ardent vitality can give, he felt, with a cruel sense of
humiliating impotency, that he was doomed to yawn lan-
guidly through a life of mediocrity and failure.

(26) "Le vierge, le vivace et le bel aujourd'hui," *Poésies* (Paris: Nouvelle
   Revue Française, 1926), p. 124.

The result of that disharmony between impossible realization and inexhaustible desire was that an almost permanent mood of sadness and despondency settled upon Mallarmé,

Le poète impuissant qui maudit son génie (27),

and he would sometimes curse his very superiority, which prevented him from accepting with a degree of contentment the irremediable tameness of his lot. All his efforts at literary creation were but attempts to assuage the bitterness of this intimate discontent, born of the discrepancy between his glamorous dreams and the ineluctable disappointment of his miserable fate: "Il n'est point d'autre sujet, sachez le bien; l'antagonisme du rêve chez l'homme avec les fatalités de son existence départies par le malheur" (28).

By a process of half-spontaneous, half-studied transposition Mallarmé endeavored to recapture upon a higher plane, through the power of his mind, the brilliant, intense poetry which life had denied him in actuality. In compensation for his loss in the domain of reality, he was constantly striving to enter the realm of the Absolute, which for him meant simply a more or less abstract, immaterial conception of perfect, ideal beauty. Gradually he came to assume the attitude, which was not without a shade of affectation and pose, of being deliberately ignorant of what was going on in the world at large, in fact of everything that was not of the essence of the Absolute.

Mallarmé, however, was not altogether the dupe of his own scornful detachment from human affairs. Devoid of an ardent, personal, visionary mysticism, he must have regarded the substitution of a cold, theoretical Absolute for the warm, palpitating reality that was forever eluding him as an unsatisfactory and almost ironical barter. Indeed, we find him ad-

(27) "L'Azur," *Poésies*, p. 40.
(28) Mallarmé, *Divagations* (Paris: Fasquelle, 1897), p. 166.

mitting that the highest fulfillment of his ideal is, after all, only a makeshift or, in his own words, "ne remplace tout que faute de tout" (29) — hence its vague, indefinite, evanescent quality! It appears sublime and immaculately pure only by reason of its remoteness and perhaps, it might be added, of its unreality. Sometimes it seems almost like an inconsistent and shadowy dream which would slip from the grasp of even the most subtle imaginative intuition.

In order to seize hold of this Absolute, however, Mallarmé relied not upon intuition but mainly upon the hidden magic power of words. As a teacher of language, he must often have been led to ponder upon the deep intrinsic nature of words. He soon became aware that, outside of their value as signs of the various aspects of the reality that we know, words possess a character, an individuality, an entire existence of their own. They have their good qualities, their shortcomings, their affinities for certain other words, as well as their striking fundamental antipathies. It would be no mere metaphor to compare them with actual living organisms, with sentient, animated beings.

Yet it is obvious that the life of words does not belong to the world of coarse, material things wherein our own bodies reside, but is part of a higher spiritual realm far above and beyond this universe of ours. The secret virtue of a word depends hardly at all upon its objective meaning — that is, upon the thing to which it is supposed to refer; this virtue is derived for the most part from the word's sentimental connotation, the halo of psychic evocation surrounding its syllables, the power of mysterious, poetical suggestion radiating from its very essence.

Further, it sometimes happens that, when several words come into close juxtaposition, a sudden spark is struck, revealing in a flash of poetical illumination the supreme

(29) *Divagations,* p. 229.

beauty of the transcendent universe. This miracle of ideal transfiguration — which is the miracle of poetry itself — does not occur for reasons connected with the objective meaning conveyed by the association of these particular words. The most casual observation shows that the sense involved is of almost no importance: it may be superficial, it may be even commonplace; yet the vision of the ideal, of the Absolute, rises spontaneously and irresistibly from the very sound and connotation of the words themselves.

This miracle occurs, however, only in very rare instances. The majority of words have been used so often for practical purposes that they seem to have become worn out, to have gradually lost in the course of time all their power of lyrical evocation. And in certain habitual, idiomatic expressions the effect of long use has destroyed the load of potential revelation that each of the component words might secretly have concealed. Moreover, as language is primarily a system of convenient signs intended to indicate certain definite objects, it is only natural that the object called forth by the given sign-word should almost immediately drive the latter outside the field of the conscious mind. The word, once its practical modest ushering task is adequately performed, unobtrusively retires without being given a chance to display the bright, dazzling — though perhaps useless — aspects of its own individuality.

The methods followed by Mallarmé in order to restore to words their original force of ideal suggestion are manifold and complex. The best procedure, he suggests, would be to revive the spirit of the remote past, of a time when the free tribes of primitive man lived in a state of perpetual wonder and amazement because the world was to them still fresh, colorful, and young.

Donner un sens plus pur aux mots de la tribu (30)

(30) "Le Tombeau d'Edgar Poe," *Poésies*, p. 132.

would give back to the drab, stale vocabulary of modern days the youthful, vital spirit that it must once have possessed. . . . Also it is essential to break up the traditional grammatical associations between words, which, by their very banality, despoil the language of all power of suggestion. But Mallarmé wants to go even further: he wants to loosen, if not to sever completely, the links uniting vocables with the objects to which, by conventional long use, they correspond. Then words, freed from the tyranny of reality, released from the necessity of having to "mean" something definite, will encounter a thousand possibilities of self-realization. Of course, a conjunction of words gathered together without the imperious guidance of a clear-cut signification will be obscure, perhaps even occasionally unintelligible. But according to Mallarmé the loss will be only a small one, since the actual meaning of a sentence hardly ever aids — and very often hampers — the appearance of the ideal which verbal magic can evoke. Just as a spark is more easily seen in the darkness, so the poetical effulgence of words will be more vividly apparent in the midst of dialectic obscurity. The power of words to reveal the "other" world — the world of the ideal — will be more intensely perceived if the glare of obvious reality does not outshine their mystic brilliance.

The part of the poet consists, so thinks Mallarmé, in studying meticulously not the meaning but the secret properties of words. Then, with a full knowledge of their possible affinities and reactions, he will consciously combine them and let them achieve by themselves the work of revealing the infinite and the unknown. He will not try to express his own feelings or ideas. The poet's self-effacement, the exclusion of any dialectical interference, is indispensable in order to allow words their free action. "L'œuvre pure implique la disparition élocutoire du poète qui cède l'initiative aux mots" (31).

(31) *Divagations*, p. 246.

The result will be a series of words carefully selected for their magnetic value and disposed according to an elaborately definite scheme, but whose meaning is indefinite, in fact, almost indifferent, even purposely obscure. Yet, obscure and seemingly absurd as they are, they possess in themselves a strange capacity for suggesting the ideal, which enables them to penetrate the exalted realm of a poetical Absolute that observation or reason could never reach.

Concurrently with Symbolism, and to a large extent in sympathy with its aims and aspirations, there had developed in the field of painting the movement known as Impressionism, which was to influence profoundly the evolution of the public's understanding of the most advanced forms of literature and art. Among the complex theories which lie at the basis of Impressionism, two have been particularly important in shaping the modern point of view in this regard.

Before the advent of Impressionism, more often than not the various aspects of nature were represented by painters not as they appeared to a candid eye but as they might be interpreted by intelligent and conventional reasoning. For example, a distant forest, which the artist *knew* to be composed of green trees, was thought of as green and painted by him in green colors upon the canvas. Similarly, shadows had for so long been represented in pictures by more or less black tinges that no other possible color was ever conceived — or indeed was conceivable — by either connoisseur or artist. When the first Impressionists painted distant forests in purple and their shadows in blue, let us say, this was considered as a challenge both to reason and to reality. Yet the forests *were* purple; the shadows *were* blue; it had to be admitted that this *was* true; but the veil cast by interpretative intelligence over the aspects of nature had proved so deceptive that countless generations had been sincerely persuaded that forests and shadows always

were respectively green and black. When a progressive re-
education of vision took place among the public, it dawned
on many of the brighter spirits that the original data fur-
nished by our senses were probably all impregnated, unbe-
known to ourselves, with a thousand preconceived notions
that prevented us from grasping things in their essence. Not
a few were even ready to welcome any further attempt, however bold, to pierce and perhaps utterly destroy the screen that
reason and convention had placed between man and the real
nature of things.

The other aspect of Impressionism which was to revolutionize the standards of modern vision and art had its origin
in a purely technical discovery. For centuries painters had
striven in vain to render adequately the glitter of light in the
open air. Then all at once certain scientific researches on the
nature of luminous radiations led to the conclusion that, if a
given shade — of green, for instance — was to be obtained by
the blending, in definite proportions, of two other colors —
say, some blue and yellow — the mixture of these last two
colors on the painter's palette would result in a flat, dull, inert
tone, whereas their juxtaposition on the canvas side by side,
if seen from a distance, would produce a rich, enchanting,
vibrant hue. So the Impressionists began systematically to
decompose the complex colorings of nature into their original
elements and to apply these in their pure state, dotting the
surface of their paintings with a multitude of small, bright,
variegated patches.

The consequence was most startling and disconcerting. On
the one hand, this method undoubtedly made a revelation of
incomparable, dazzling, hitherto unexpressed beauty in the
play of light and color. On the other hand, the smooth, continuous surface of familiar objects now appeared, especially
if viewed at close range, to be parceled out in a series of small
colored units, all separate and independent of one another.

This breaking up of the external world into autonomous, un-related fragments was not accepted without reluctance by the general public. Yet it finally succeeded in imposing itself on the public by virtue of the wonderful achievements that the new process of painting had rendered possible in the domain of pure art.

At the same time the public, without suspecting it, was being gradually prepared for a much more fundamental and thoroughgoing dislocation of its universe. Impressionism was above all an aesthetic movement, with no philosophical pre-tensions and no ambition whatever to catch a glimpse of the "unknown." It served as a wedge, however, in splitting up the old, traditional, consistent vision of things. Following in the wake of Impressionism, daring, adventurous metaphysico-artistic speculation was to find the resistance of reasonable convention already broken. To shatter what had been left standing was to prove more of a noisy game than a difficult undertaking. But while the Impressionists had wrought de-struction only in order to offer a more attractive, more artistic representation of the world of appearances, their successors were to take advantage of the ruin in order to pry behind and beyond these appearances themselves.

So, as the nineteenth century was drawing to a close, the stage was set for a complete revision of the traditional, accepted values. The public no longer trusted implicitly the old historic conventions of vision. The principles which are the basis of present-day doctrines: the mystic search for a superior world, more truly real than the reality that we know; the systematic dislocation of the conventional order of things and the reconstruction of the universe on a new and arbitrary plan; the confidence in the power of subconscious thought by automatic development to reveal the domain of the Absolute; the belief that certain associations of words, independently of any logical meaning, possess a capacity of illumination far greater than that of intelligent thought — all these had been formulated by poets and prophets at strife with the general consensus of opinion of their time. For a long period, however, these inspired individuals struggled and labored in complete isolation, each one stressing, within the new conception of things then slowly taking shape, the special and particular aspect that corresponded with his own temperament and experience. During the first quarter of the twentieth century these scattered efforts were progressively brought together. They were to receive strong spiritual support and newly fortifying evidence from changing conditions of life, from psychological discoveries, from dramatic international events; finally, after violent fluctuations in doctrine, due to the very rapidity of their development and growth, they reached a climax in the strange and disturbing movement which goes by the name of Surrealism.

II. The Breakdown of the Old Conception of Reality

During the last decade of the nineteenth century and the opening years of the twentieth, a series of correlated discoveries in the field of pure science revolutionized the conception of the structure of the universe that had generally prevailed since about the time of the Renaissance.

The original cause of this complete change of outlook was a sudden great technical advance which opened undreamt-of possibilities of investigation and analysis, enabling scientists to dissociate certain aspects of reality that had been hitherto considered as forming an indivisible unity. Scientists succeeded in breaking up seemingly indestructible units and in exposing to view a multiplicity of complex, unsuspected forces underlying the apparent uniformity of natural phenomena. Mathematical physics and atomistic chemistry offer perhaps the most striking instances of the transformation then taking place in the most firmly established beliefs concerning the nature of material substances. Further, the revelations of experimental psychology in regard to the working of the subconscious mind, and even the practical applications of the cinema and the phonograph, contributed in no small measure to create the impression that every sentiment we entertain and every solid object we perceive is but a flimsy assemblage ready to collapse into fragments at the impact of some new discovery.

This disintegration of the world of our experience into minute particles brought about a thorough revision of the current ideas concerning the function and value of scientific knowledge. Up to then scientists had appeared to be progressively reducing the field of the unknown. Of course, it had been recognized latterly that there would always remain at the very core of things an important, impregnable domain of mystery. Yet that domain seemed to be limited in extent and even to be shrinking appreciably. Then the time-worn network of accepted hypotheses and general explanations gave way and broke under the strain; again and again it proved itself incapable of holding in its meshes the great bulk of new facts that were now constantly being brought to light. Finally and reluctantly it had to be in great part discarded. So man became conscious of the immensity of his ignorance and of the strange forces surrounding him, about which he knew next to nothing at all; the world was indeed infinitely more complex than had ever been imagined before. Thus science, instead of conveying as in former times a reassuring impression of conquering progress, now seemed disturbingly to magnify the widespread extent of mystery throughout the universe by revealing, all of a sudden, how enormous and profound were the unknown forces enveloping human life on all sides.

In past centuries, the mysterious, the fantastic, had had a realm of its own, but as a rule it was separate and distinct from the field of reality. Once in a while an inspired or adventurous man had tried to loosen the bonds of our material world in order to penetrate into that other, the immaterial realm of the spirit. But the "other" world had always seemed somehow problematic and remote. One could gain access to it only by crossing the threshold of mental aberration, as did Gérard de Nerval, or by being carried, like Baudelaire and Rimbaud, by some phase of mystic transport, or, like Mallarmé, by flying upon the wings of immaterial fancy. Now, however, a bewildering collection of incredible ideas were forcing their way into the very midst of the neat and tidy world which had formerly appeared so simple, so familiar, and so clear. The sanest, even, were obliged to admit that the unbelievable was true and that

the whole universe was filled with incomprehensible prod-
igies.

Then human intelligence, which the rationalistic Frenchman had so long trusted as the safest guide in the intricate
maze of puzzling reality, came to be regarded with suspicion
and even with contempt. After all, the logical pattern which
reason had drawn to represent the general order of things had
proved only too often to be erroneous and misleading; it even
appeared extremely doubtful whether the power of the normal human mind was equal to the task of grasping the deep,
fundamental relations which constitute the framework of the
universe.

In this state of general uncertainty a thinker appeared, the
meaning and influence of whose message can hardly be over-
estimated. This was Bergson, whose theories began to spread
throughout France and far beyond her borders. Themselves
issuing undoubtedly from the great anti-rationalistic current
which had its direct source in the altered spiritual circumstances prevailing at the close of the nineteenth century,
these theories powerfully reinforced that current by providing
a strong inspiration to those who, weary of the shallowness
of past concepts, were now seeking deeper channels of
thought. The views of Bergson must not be considered simply as the speculations of an isolated philosopher: they soon
became the *mot d'ordre* of a restless and dynamic younger
generation.

According to Bergson, intelligence is only an instrument
whose function is to interpret our surroundings in terms of
possible benefit or harm. Hence the necessity for the conscious mind to remain in permanent contact with the external
world. It is no wonder, then, that the data which form our
abstract ideas coincide with certain aspects of nature: these
data are culled from nature itself. It is not surprising that
the results of scientific investigation can be used for practical

purposes: science is merely a convenient set of recipes derived from the facts themselves. But to give practical information concerning the motley forms among which we live is not to delve deeply into their essential nature. Indeed, a thorough comprehension of the essence of things would, on account of their very inexhaustible richness, hamper intelligence in the fulfillment of its duty, which is to choose and to retain only those few elements that are of definite importance in determining our behavior. The other elements, however fundamental and rich they may be, must be rigorously discarded — or, rather, ignored — for they would be only a useless encumbrance to us. So, according to Bergson, the deep reality of things normally remains beyond the grasp of the clear conscious mind.

Yet we participate in that reality through the vital current of our subconscious existence. Instinct is the most cogent expression of that obscure harmony between our individual beings and the totality of the universe. But instinct can give only vague indications as to the nature of the substratum from which its roots proceed. Nevertheless we are not, thinks Bergson, altogether devoid of capacity for investigating what lies outside the field of rational logic. Intuition enables us to unite the mysterious throbbing forces of life with our own consciousness. Our roving intellectual perception detects the outstanding landmarks of our world, signals their presence, gives us clues to their worth and possible use, but is not concerned with their intrinsic nature. On the other hand, intuition, whose informative value in regard to our practical interests is almost negligible, allows us to sense the cosmic vibration and the rhythm of the universe.

By thus raising intuition to the privileged status of a mode of metaphysical insight, Bergson provided a ready-made justification for those who wished to go in search of the unknown along the path of irrational mysticism. At the same time his

Henri Rousseau: *Le Rêve* (1910)
A case of unsophisticated, spontaneous primitivism

analysis of the practical interpretative process of intelligence
ruined, in the eyes of his contemporaries, all that remained of
the prestige of reason as a means of obtaining knowledge of a
superior, transcendental kind.

So the generation that grew to manhood about 1900 realized
that the ground which their forbears had confidently trod
was now giving way beneath their own feet; reality was
everywhere breaking up into elusive, impalpable fragments.
Disbelief in the solidity of the world — formerly the subject
of paradoxical discussions on the part of philosophers, or
of wild conjectures by more or less unbalanced individuals
— became an actual issue, an urgent, crucial, and compelling
problem. The intellectual conceptions which for centuries
had been man's stay and support in hours of doubt and trial,
now suddenly collapsed, encumbering the path of progress
with their débris.

Then began in many eager young men an impatient desire
to clear away that wreckage, to tear down the tottering remnants of the ancient, useless, outmoded structure. This fever
of destruction was not the result of a deliberate program of
criticism, such as had occurred several times previously in the
course of French cultural development; it was the outcome
rather of an instinctive, spontaneous impulse to escape from
the conventional, the artificial, and to reach out for something truly authentic and genuine. Since intelligence had
betrayed the confidence placed in her, the desire was to return to a pre-intellectual state, to a primitivism akin to that
of the Negroes of Central Africa — a stage of development in
which intellect had not yet had a chance to draw an interpretative veil between the core of reality and man's sentient
being.

Shortly before the end of the nineteenth century a small
group of young men who were acutely aware of the prevailing
spiritual distress, though still very uncertain as to the goal to

be sought, began to voice their discontent, violently startling the general public out of its smug and deadening complacency. In the field of the plastic arts, as we shall see, the *Fauves* began roaring defiance at the established, sacred conventions of pictorial technique, and in the field of literature Alfred Jarry threw a bombshell that wrought havoc amidst the self-satisfied circles of traditional conformism.

Alfred Jarry was born in 1873 in the small town of Laval in Brittany. His father, a commercial traveler, at once insignificant and boastful, had absolutely no authority over his family. His mother — *née* Trernec'k de Coutouly — was a more picturesque character, in turn whimsically imaginative and violently obdurate, as some *Bretonnes* can be; she seems to have transmitted to her son many of the better as well as some of the less desirable features of her colorful personality.

At school young Jarry displayed brilliant intellectual gifts. He took first place in practically every subject; at an extraordinarily early age he had acquired a broad and solid culture, even, in certain fields, a truly astounding erudition. In particular, the knowledge of Greek was so deeply implanted in his mind that later on it frequently happened that he used unconsciously Hellenic turns of phrase in casual conversation with his friends in the cafés of Paris.

One of his teachers, however, failed to find favor in the eyes of this remarkable pupil; to that bizarre circumstance he owed the doubtful honor of having a not very flattering picture of himself preserved for posterity. Hébert, nicknamed "le Père Heb" by irreverent schoolboys, was teacher of physics at the *lycée* of Rennes, to which Alfred Jarry had gone to complete his course of studies. Uninspiring and vulgar, though personally honest, Hébert became a butt of jests and an object of derision to the whole school. A play, both heroic and grotesque, purporting to represent his al-

leged adventures — all entirely imaginary — was composed by
the schoolboys under the title of *Les Polonais*; a performance
was given, in the form of a puppet show, at the home of one
of Jarry's schoolmates. Nearly everyone in the school had
collaborated, and Jarry had thrown himself into the game
with all the violence of his passionate nature. So, through a
process of collective suggestion, for this young boy the unfortunate "Père Heb" became, and was henceforth to remain,
the embodiment of all that is evil and grotesque in this
world.

At the age of twenty Jarry went to Paris, officially in order
to prepare for the entrance examination to the famous Ecole
Normale Supérieure. In point of fact, he was already much
too independent and erratic to submit himself to the stern
intellectual discipline necessary for success in this most difficult test. He very soon drifted into the irregular and dis-
orderly life of Parisian literary Bohemia. His parents having
died, he fell heir to a sum of money which enabled him to
establish himself in an apartment on the Boulevard Saint-
Germain — and to become popular in the leading cafés of the
capital on account of his openhandedness and his almost
unlimited capacity for drinking. Before very long, however,
his modest fortune had dwindled and disappeared; and as he
had no other resources than his earnings from an occasional
article in a literary review, he sank rapidly to the lowest level
of Bohemian poverty.

Meanwhile his prestige was growing apace. His profound
and varied erudition, the ingenuity of his remarks, the very
exuberance of his language, and the eccentricity of his manners held spellbound an ever-increasing circle of youthful
and wondering admirers. In the course of time he found a
welcome in the house of Alfred Vallette, then director of the
Mercure de France, and so succeeded in gaining a foothold in
certain fashionable literary salons of the capital.

At first he was received with a mixture of curiosity and uneasiness; the invitations were continued, however, on account of his striking picturesqueness and his unusual brilliance. His short bow legs supported a squat figure with a powerful torso, usually covered by a close-fitting, dirty, striped sweater. His whole person presented a soiled and bedraggled appearance, even his toes only too often sticking out of his shoes, his pockets bulging with greasy tools or the threatening butt of a huge revolver. His very dark eyes, set in a pale, round face, had a fixed stare like that of a dangerous nocturnal bird. Almost constantly under the influence of alcohol — his favorite drink was absinthe, which he called *herbe sainte* — his moods oscillated between blackest despondency and flights of enchanting, iridescent dreams. This, however, rather enhanced his mysterious power of attraction. Tirelessly he would pour out with irrepressible volubility a continuous torrent of words, which were linked together not so much by logical sequence as by virtue of secret associative affinities. As he talked, with set face and short, spasmodic gestures, the sentences seemed to flow from his lips automatically in an endless stream, as though from some strange, superhuman machine. His desultory talk, somewhat reminiscent of the rambling style of Lautréamont, practically unhampered by the direction of control of conscious reasoning, seemed to spring spontaneously from a source much deeper than ordinary normal intelligence. The flow of his conversation, carrying along pell-mell fragments of weird poetry, biting sarcasm, brilliant sallies, and grotesque obscenities, would fill his listeners with mingled disgust, admiration, and awe.

About three years after his arrival in Paris, his growing reputation suddenly swelled to a climax of scandal and fame. Jarry had always kept by him a manuscript of *Les Polonais*, and the thought of the burlesque character of "Père Heb"

had haunted him continually. In 1896, taking the old sketch
of his schooldays as a foundation, he wrote the powerful
farce of *Ubu-Roi*. As far as he was concerned, this was much
less a manifestation of literary activity than a means of getting rid of the accumulation of festering thoughts which had
gathered around his first ignominious impressions of life.

The character of "Ubu" in Jarry's play is a hideous presentation of combined cupidity, cowardice, gluttony, lechery,
bourgeois respectability, philosophical wisdom, and sharp,
dangerous cunning. Endowed with inexhaustible grandilo-
quence and overflowing with primitive elemental force, his
enormous porcine figure bulking large on the stage, "Ubu"
possesses a monstrous vital intensity reminiscent of the powerful creations of Rabelais. He stands as a symbol of the lowest
human instincts, which, if given a free hand, might easily take
possession of our whole being and, as it is the case in *Ubu-Roi*,
fasten the tyranny of ignoble appetites upon our entire
personality. Generally these tendencies remain carefully
hidden within ourselves; nevertheless they do exist, and, by
bringing them forcibly to light, Jarry presents an image of
humiliating but compelling verity to the view of all who are
perspicacious and sincere. At the same time the play constitutes a bitter satire on the society in which we live. Just as
"Ubu" himself does, society conceals under a cloak of hypo-
critical righteousness the extremes of corruption, brutality,
and lust. With scathing directness, Jarry denounces the
mediocrity of our world, so stupidly blind to elevated sentiment and so stubbornly opposed to anything that might dis-
turb its coarse enjoyment of the most material pleasures.

Attacking simultaneously the smooth, conventional portrait of man's moral consciousness and the generally accepted
picture of what society is supposed to be, *Ubu-Roi* inevitably
aroused either violent resentment or wild enthusiasm. The
performance of the play, which took place on December 10,

1896, at the *Théâtre de l'Œuvre*, under the direction of Lugné-Poe, had the value and significance of a public manifesto. Important personages, upholding morality and order, solemn dignitaries, conservative critics — all the pillars of society — attended. Scattered among them, however, were numbers of long-haired artists and writers, the vanguard of a rebellious youth, all eager for the fray.

At the beginning Jarry himself, attired in an ill-fitting black suit much too large for him, made a short speech which nobody understood and then withdrew with a deep, jerky bow, like a puppet breaking in half. The very first word of the play — a word of intentionally aggressive crudeness — started a pandemonium of indignant protestations and wild applause. Whenever that word was repeated on the stage during the evening — and it was very often — a frantic uproar broke out afresh with renewed violence. In between these outbursts the spectators exclaimed and gesticulated in wild confusion, vociferously expressing their approval or their disgust. In the midst of this continuous rumbling din, *Ubu-Roi* rolled onwards with its tide of sarcasm and mire. . . .

The result of the performance was inconclusive; but the play itself made such a decided impression on contemporary opinion that it may be considered the first open break with the accepted standards of the past, the first public manifestation of the "modern" school.

As a consequence, Jarry skyrocketed to the position of a celebrity in Paris. He himself immediately received the nickname of "Père Ubu," and strangely enough very soon took on the characteristics of his fictitious creation. At first Jarry thought it a great jest to impersonate "Ubu," by way of indicting the ignominious things he so violently hated. In fun he adopted the attitude, the gestures, the mannerisms of "Ubu-Roi." Being a "king," he never referred to himself otherwise than by the royal "we." He cultivated a grandiose and obscure style of speech. Despite himself, he acted his part so perfectly, and so thoroughly, that he became quite absorbed in it. A most curious case of literary mimetism, Jarry fell a victim to his own imagination and gradually, in all but physique, turned into a veritable "Père Ubu" himself.

Meanwhile he had become a leading figure in the most advanced literary circles. His collaboration was eagerly sought by the modernist reviews of the day, which increased his influence even though it failed to make him prosperous. . . . He was now surrounded by a group of young admirers, among whom were Guillaume Apollinaire, André Salmon, Max Jacob, Pablo Picasso — that is to say, the future leaders of the Cubist movement that was to be, who were all subjugated by the power of his personality and captivated by the strange charm of his impossible and extravagant tales.

Success caused Jarry's personality to unfold and expand. Before everyone he affected an attitude of extreme courtesy, which he often varied with exhibitions of brutal insolence. On all occasions he displayed a ferocious sense of humor, indulging in wild, "ubuesque" jokes. At the same time there developed in him a queer, half-visionary strain. Mallarmé had strongly influenced his first publication: *Les Minutes de sable mémorial* (1894). Now, however, a definite hermetism began to insinuate itself into his works, blending curiously with an eroticism of the most sordid kind. *L'Amour en visites* (1898), *L'Amour absolu* (1900), *Ubu-Enchaîné* (1900), *Messaline* (1901), and *Le Surmâle* (1902) bear witness to the progressive reorientation that was taking place within him. Yet not one of these works had an influence in any way comparable to that exerted by the personality of Jarry himself.

In 1898 a number of his friends, among whom was Alfred Vallette, rented in Corbeil, near the river Marne, a country house which they called their "Phalanstère." Jarry decided to follow them. He took up his quarters near-by in an old stable which had formerly sheltered the mules used for towing the river barges. He existed there mainly on the product of his own fishing and also, it must be said, by ingeniously appropriating his neighbors' chickens. His lodgings exhibited the mixture of artistic refinement and filthy neglect typical of the man. With a few wild flowers in simple pottery vases, he was able to conjure up an atmosphere of fresh, rustic beauty; yet the floor was strewn with fragments of broken dishes and ancient fish-heads. . . . Sometimes he invited his friends from the "Phalanstère," or even from Paris, to epoch-making picnics. The fare was not of the best, but every subject under the sun was discussed with enthusiastic vehemence, and most of the guests usually drank until they could drink no more.

After the publication of *Messaline*, Jarry found himself with enough money to purchase a small plot of ground. There he had a little wooden cabin erected, to which he gave the name of "Tripode" *because* it stood upon *four* posts! The main advantage of this new abode was its proximity to an inn where he could obtain an abundant and varied supply of drinks — on credit. He was now living in a state of almost perpetual intoxication, subject to constant paroxysms. He always carried a revolver, and on the slightest pretext would shoot at objects around him with amazing accuracy. Sometimes he was seized with a frenzy of destruction, even killing the nightingales, "ces sales bêtes de rossignols qui Nous empêchaient de dormir!" (1)

Periodically he felt a longing for the literary cafés and the excitement of Paris, where he still kept a miserable, cheap lodging in the Rue Cassette. Then he would jump on his bicycle and ride there, completing the journey despite a blazing sun or a driving rain. Eventually he deserted the

(1) Quoted by Rachilde, *Alfred Jarry ou Le Surmâle de lettres* (Paris: B. Grasset, 1928), chap. VI, p. 135.

"Tripode" and Corbeil, and spent the better part of his days at the Bibliothèque Nationale, studying the history of the popes and making translations from modern Greek. . . . At the same time, perhaps under the influence of alcohol or of ether, in which he indulged freely, his life sank deeper into a half-hallucinatory world of dreams. He recorded his visions and fancies in *Gestes et opinions du Dr. Faustroll* (which was not published until after his death), and he talked interminably to his friends in a jumble of idealism and mockery about a new "science" of his own invention, "la Pataphysique," designed to explore the world of the unknown.

Then suddenly, in 1906, he became very ill, and collapsed; he had just enough strength left to go to his pious elder sister in Laval. One day his Parisian friends learned with astonishment that he was cured — and converted. Although nominally a Catholic, all his life he had delighted in being a scoffer and a blasphemer: it was not easy to imagine him as a meek communicant of the Church. . . . When he returned to the Rue Cassette in Paris, it was obvious that, in spite of the change which had come over him, he was rapidly nearing the end: his vitality had been drained and exhausted by all the excesses of his previous existence. A few more months dragged by in misery, until he was finally taken to a hospital, where he died on November 1, 1907, at the age of only thirty-four.

The circumstances of Jarry's death, adding a last dramatic touch to his wild career, only served to enhance the prestige he had enjoyed during his short and pathetic lifetime. He came to be regarded as the standard-bearer of a generation in revolt, a champion who had fallen in a lofty struggle. Jarry was pronounced a typical representative of a group of young men for whom the world, as it was generally accepted, had lost practically all interest and value. Undoubtedly influenced by the increasingly widespread impression that the universe, as revealed by our senses or by science, does not correspond to any true, profound reality, they had come to regard the play of appearances around them not merely as a comedy but even as a hoax. Roused to anger and contempt by the conviction that they were the victims of a grotesque farce, they dedicated themselves to demonstrating the terrifying insignificance and hopeless absurdity of every stage of human life.

Jarry had shown the way by his indictment of the principles which uphold both the sentiment of human dignity and society itself — the very framework of our existence. By insisting that they were essentially dismal compounds of the vilest, most despicable elements, he argued that it was absolutely impossible to use them as the foundation of any sound and solid structure. Everything that man had so far relied upon in this world must be destroyed and eternally swept away.

This work of destruction Jarry effected by means of a process not unlike that employed previously by Arthur Rimbaud. Jarry took the world as it appeared to him and contented himself with transposing and replacing a few details here and there. Nothing was profoundly altered in the general scheme of things; yet these few substitutions were sufficient to disrupt the illusory appearance of universal harmony. His peculiar humor, by unbalancing life at its center of gravity, imparted to reality a ludicrous drunken gait. Just as the grotesque deportment of an intoxicated man often reveals the true nature and fundamental inanity of an apparently imposing personage, the utter absurdity of the whole world was made so convincingly evident by Jarry's caricatural representation that it never again seemed possible to take it seriously.

The conceptions of Jarry were not exclusively negative, however. A subtle visionary strain is clearly perceptible throughout his spiritual evolution. First his admiration for

Mallarmé, then his love for hermetic formulae, and finally
his comico-mystic discovery of "la Pataphysique," marked
different stages in the progressive revelation of another world,
entirely different from the one wherein reigned the fleshy,
bloated "Ubu-Roi." In particular, among the lucubrations
of that curious character, Dr. Faustroll, appear strangely
illuminating statements. What, according to Jarry, was the
aim of "la Pataphysique"? It was to study the laws that
govern exceptions, and to explain "l'univers supplémentaire
à celui-ci. . . ." "It will describe," as he said, "a universe
which can, and perhaps ought to be, seen by us in place of
the traditional one" (2).

These glimpses into a superior world do not constitute by
any means the most important part of Jarry's message. In
the eyes of his contemporaries, Jarry represented, above all,
destruction and revolt. His name served as a rallying call for
young writers such as Guillaume Apollinaire, Max Jacob,
André Salmon, who wanted at any cost to get rid of the rub-
bish of an outmoded past, and who were seeking a truth of
their own. Most of these young writers, however, were to
reach their maturity and to make a name for themselves at a
somewhat later period.

For the time being, it was in the field of painting that the
first major conquests were achieved which marked in an unmistakable manner the beginning of the new era. Henceforward, very much as during the Romantic revolt, the artistic
and the literary movement were almost inextricably intertwined, the development of the one being always explained,
complemented, and illustrated by the progress and the variations of the other. So if, for the sake of clearness, their mani-

(2) Quoted by M. Raymond, *De Baudelaire au Surréalisme* (Paris:
R.-A. Corrêa, 1933), p. 259; cf. A. Jarry, *Gestes et opinions du Dr.
Faustroll, pataphysicien* (Paris: Fasquelle, 1911).

festations are examined separately here, it must be remembered that their constant interconnection in actual fact linked them in a compact spiritual unity.

As has been previously seen, Impressionism — mainly through its technical discoveries, but also through its rejection of a certain conventional mode of interpreting the aspects of the world — had prepared the way for the public's adoption of a new attitude towards the plastic arts. Impressionism, however, contained the germs of changes far more drastic and radical than had hitherto been imagined. The dispersion of the visual universe into a multiplicity of colored dots had deprived reputedly solid objects of much of their consistence, in fact, of the most obvious part of their reality. Correlatively, the personality and the emotions of the artist, no longer held in check by the obstacle of firm, resistant shapes, had thus found an unprecedentedly wide domain in which they had been free to expand. They had been kept within certain definite bounds, however, by the old, ingrained tradition that painting was essentially a graphic representation of external form.

Cézanne overstepped these bounds. He made his individual sentiments the law of the visible universe, and consequently declined to obey even the most imperative prescriptions of consecrated draftsmanship. For instance, if, when contemplating a scene, he was intensely conscious of the value of a mountain rising in the far distance — even though the laws of perspective told him that the outline of this mountain ought to occupy only a small space in the background of his picture — nothing could prevent him from putting it on his canvas as an enormous mass, towering above the surrounding landscape. This method of affective deformation of reality, when carried systematically into all phases of painting, engendered a complete disregard of actual proportions and forms, substituting for the old principle of the imitation of nature a new pictorial standard: the expression of the sentiments of the artist himself. Cézanne is the first great modern painter who deliberately refused to copy nature and definitely set out to reshape and reorganize all its elements according to the rhythm of his own sensibility.

Of course these ideas of Cézanne's would have had little opportunity of developing and growing had they not fallen on well-prepared and fertile ground. But Cézanne's daring innovations appeared at precisely the time when ancient reverence for objective reality was declining everywhere. Consequently, they were hailed with enthusiasm and adopted with glee by a numerous cohort of young and eager artists. At the Salon d'Automne of 1905, Matisse, Vlaminck, Braque, Derain, and a few others hurled their challenge in the face of an astonished and bewildered public, which, obscurely conscious of the fierce, savage impulse that made these youths leap up, as it were, and shake the bars of encaging tradition, immediately dubbed them "the wild beasts" — *les Fauves*.

Fauvisme constitutes a striking break in the evolution of painting in Europe and represents a complete departure from conceptions which had prevailed in art for over four centuries. Since the Renaissance, the essential purpose of painting had been to render on canvas the external appearance of things as they are revealed to us in space. The history of artistic theory up to our day had been marked by the progressive development of methods and rules — the most important being the laws of perspective — which enabled the artist to give a more and more adequate representation of the reality that constitutes our environment.

When, towards the end of the nineteenth century, this reality suddenly fell into discredit, the relations existing between the lines or volumes of its constituent parts, which had been considered of engrossing interest in the past, now seemed hardly worthy of any attention. A complete reversal of point of view took place: it was no longer the forms and aspects of nature but the soul of the artist himself, his aspirations, and his dreams, that were the all-important source of artistic inspiration.

Simultaneously, the actual process of painting, which had hitherto occupied a definitely subordinate position in regard to the reality it was supposed to represent, now, as reality faltered, acquired an intrinsic value of its own. A picture was not simply a more or less faithful, more or less original copy of a "model." A picture was henceforth considered as a complete creation, a self-contained, absolute entity.

Of course the artist still had to borrow elements from nature. Nevertheless, in order to impart meaning and value to his work he no longer had to rely upon a definite likeness and relation between the forms he painted and those existing in actuality. His most serious preoccupation was with combining shapes and colors in such a way that their association, through contrast or harmony, would produce a definite suggestive effect. So painting came to resemble, in some ways, a musical symphony. The interplay of shapes and colors, without strict and servile reference to any objective reality, but under the sway of the artist's own inspiration, turned out to be the fundamental principle of the new, "fauvist" pictorial art.

The *Fauves* did not fail to twist and stretch and warp the forms of reality according to their whims and fancies. In their pictures the most stable objects, as if intoxicated, lost their balance and began to stagger and reel. It is noteworthy, nevertheless, that even though their principles authorized them to dislocate reality to the fullest extent, actually their artistic presentations did not stray very far from the accepted pattern of things. The familiar aspects of our everyday world are quite recognizable, even if somewhat distorted, in the works of practically all these artists. Indeed, the *Fauves*, being one and all imbued with a rich artistic culture, could not help being influenced — perhaps unwittingly — by the prestige of the old masters, and so were prevented from starting entirely anew, after ostensibly making a complete break with the past. They did shake off the yoke of a number of inherited conventions; they destroyed the traditional fixity and rigidity of many a stale form. They did not go much further. Rich as their individual inspiration may have been, as a group they did not succeed in fostering a powerful new creative spirit.

It is in the works of an almost illiterate man, devoid of all cultural impediment, the famous *douanier* Rousseau, that we can best perceive the prefiguration of the tendencies then slowly coming into being. Rousseau was a discovery — one might almost say an invention — of Alfred Jarry himself. One day, when Jarry was visiting the Salon des Indépendants, he stopped before an amazing tropical landscape in which was depicted a tiger from whose mouth issued words painted on the canvas in large black capitals. A little gentleman, hovering around, approached Jarry, apparently anxious to know his opinion of the painting. Jarry, bent upon mystification as usual, treated him to a lyrical outburst in praise of the subject and the technique of this "work of art." The little gentleman then gave his name as Henri Rousseau, saying he was the painter of the picture, and adding, in all seriousness, an absurd and mirth-provoking commentary to explain his point of view. Jarry, thoroughly delighted at having discovered such a ludicrous character, decided to introduce him to his friends.

Henri Rousseau was a man of no education. He had formerly been a sergeant in the army and now held a job as collector of tolls at the gates of the city of Paris. He was immediately referred to, with comical emphasis, as *le douanier*

— the customs officer. With Jarry and Guillaume Apollinaire taking the lead, the whole of Parisian artistic and literary Bohemia launched jokingly into the most extravagant praise of his works, representing him as a great, misunderstood genius.

The joke was soon complicated by the fact that the works of Henri Rousseau were not altogether devoid of interest. In the midst of this oversophisticated milieu he was unique in possessing the simple mind and candid soul of the untaught, of an authentic *primitif*. His naïve compositions had the fresh, spontaneous quality of a child's dream. He was not related to the *Fauves*; he did not owe anything to Cézanne. Yet he possessed by instinct something they were all striving to attain: an inner sentiment that was unaffected and genuine. Of course, the mediocrity of his talent as a painter did not in any way justify the commotion artificially created around his name. Yet the fact that the "joke" could last, and that in the end even a Guillaume Apollinaire was almost able to believe in the superior value of Rousseau's bizarre paintings, casts a curious light on the direction the future was to take. The technical rendering of shapes and colors was being more and more discounted, and the spiritual content of the picture was coming to the fore. Objective reality having betrayed their trust, writers and artists set out to find another reality — one which could not be attained through the senses but was to be discovered, perhaps, in the obscure depths of human consciousness.

III. Cubism

On the slopes of Montmartre in the earlier years of the present century could be seen a huge, rambling, wooden structure extending along a narrow old street then known as the Rue Ravignan. This edifice was so unlike any ordinary building that it had been nicknamed humorously the "bateau-lavoir," for it did somehow remind one of those clumsy, lumbering, square-built boats which are to be seen moored along the banks of the Seine and to which poor housewives may go to do their washing in the more or less clean current of the river. In actuality this tenement bore a closer resemblance to a crowded rabbit warren, made of tiny studios, secondhand shops, dark corridors, and cheap rooms, where artists, poets, actors, seamstresses, gay ladies, and other picturesque, though somewhat irregular characters lived in happy, noisy, Bohemian familiarity. The "bateau-lavoir" of Montmartre was to become the cradle of the most modernistic tendencies in literature and art; for thither, or to its immediate vicinity, had drifted one by one such men as Pablo Picasso, Juan Gris, Georges Braque, Max Jacob, André Salmon, Pierre Reverdy, who were soon to be the recognized leaders of the Cubist movement in the years preceding the first World War.

The majority of these young artists and writers were not of ancient, sturdy, French stock. Feeling lonely and strange in the great, cosmopolitan city, uprooted from their respective natural surroundings and often struggling against material difficulties bordering on starvation and misery, they were perhaps more acutely conscious than anybody else of the profound and tragic crisis confronting their generation. Even though general conditions were on the whole fairly satisfactory in France during this period, all the members of this group, for individual and particular reasons, were reduced to circumstances which caused them to adopt a violent, aggressive attitude towards all forms of reality. In truth, reality offered them little but a distressing confusion of sordid, grotesque, and heartrending spectacles. Confidence in the intrinsic value of reality was already waning on every hand; yet, for those who were thriving and content, there was no urgent desire to throw off modes of life which, even if delusive, presented at least the great advantage of comfort. But the ill-starred inmates of the "bateau-lavoir" felt little compunction about taking the decisive, destructive step over which the more prosperous were still hesitating.

It must be added that many of them came of highly emotional and imaginative strains; Spaniards and Jews plainly predominated among them; so they did not feel themselves very strongly bound by the rationalistic categories which form such an essential part of the typically French mentality. In their case the rejection of reality and the transgressing of logical rules for the sake of a higher ideal did not imply the same spiritual disruption that would have occurred in the case of a more staid and balanced race. Once the way was opened up, the French hastened to follow in large numbers. Yet it must be noted that, though Cubism came into being on French soil and was later to grow and to develop through moral elements provided by French surroundings, the movement was first initiated by artists the great majority of whom were of foreign origin.

The most important of these artists was undoubtedly Pablo Picasso. Picasso was born in Malaga and spent his early youth in Barcelona. His father was a painter, and he himself from early childhood felt the irresistible urge towards an artistic vocation. While still very young, he went to Paris, which was considered the Mecca of all true artists, and joined the ranks of the Impressionists, who were then at the height — though nearing the end — of their influence and prestige.

Pablo Picasso: *Les Demoiselles d'Avignon* (1907)
An example of the influence of Negro art

Being unknown and miserably poor, Picasso drifted into circles where desperate immorality, wretchedness, and suffering were rampant. He then perceived tragic depths in life which the graceful, fluttering, superficial display of Impressionist painting utterly failed to convey. With impulsive violence, he rejected the brilliant but shallow effects that a skillful technique can produce and set out to discover some principle more fundamental and genuine.

In 1901 he made the acquaintance of Max Jacob, a young Jew who had come to Paris to seek his fortune — and so far had not attained it. Jacob also had seen certain aspects of existence which are ordinarily shunned by the official expounders of what man and society are supposed to be; yet he was lifted above the rank sordidness of his everyday life by the tenacious, latent mysticism typical of some of his race. Picasso and Max Jacob at once struck up an intimate friendship, and for a while even shared cheap and rather miserable rooms together. After a short visit to his native Spain, Picasso returned to Paris in 1903 and settled in the "bateau-lavoir" on the Rue Ravignan. Soon afterwards Max Jacob was easily persuaded to take lodgings on the same street.

In 1905, in a bar on the Rue d'Amsterdam, Picasso met the brilliant and whimsical Guillaume Apollinaire. At that time Apollinaire was associating mainly with the iconoclastic young writers who had adopted Jarry as a living symbol of their contempt for accepted realities and their intense, though still indefinite aspirations towards a new ideal. Jarry, however, was too undependable, too unsociable, and too unruly to serve as a leader and guide. Gradually, as Jarry's vitality ebbed away, Guillaume Apollinaire, on account of his vigorous personal qualities, emerged as the real, inspiring soul of the whole group.

The meeting of Picasso and Apollinaire, then the frequent visits of the latter to Montmartre and the Rue Ravignan, were of momentous import to the development of the newer literature and art. Apollinaire was followed by several of his friends, a few of them eventually settling in the "bateau-lavoir" itself. Thus was brought about the fusion of two distinct groups, which, though not without certain points of contact, had never worked in familiar, intimate collaboration. Cubism is the most direct and evident consequence of that collaboration. In the "bateau-lavoir," painters and poets found a common center where they could exchange views, build up their doctrines, and carry on without disturbance their most adventurous experimentations. The Cubist movement, therefore, has had almost as decisive a bearing on the evolution of modern literature as on the development of the plastic arts. Cubism has represented not only a change in pictorial technique but a fresh general conception of the world, a new trend of thought — in short, a philosophy. To the elaboration of this philosophy, the poets have contributed as much as the painters by adding their share of inspired enthusiasm and subtle inventive ingenuity.

The passionate discussions which marked the birth and growth of Cubism were not, it must be said, entirely confined within the rooms and studios of the Rue Ravignan. Very often they were carried on in the numerous cafés of the neighborhood; and many of the queerest theories of Cubism unmistakably betray the influence of the hazy, befuddled atmosphere wherein they were conceived. The most popular of these restaurants was undoubtedly "Le Lapin Agile." Its original sign bore the lurid appellation "Au Cabaret des Assassins," which was changed into "Le Lapin à Gill" when the whole house was bought by an artist named André Gill; then, through an easy play on words, it received its present name, under which it has attained international celebrity. There old "Père Frédé" extended to all artists both welcome and credit, occasionally accepting a picture to balance a long outstanding bill; there his wife, Berthe la Bourguignonne, was adept in preparing the most delicate and succulent dishes, all for two francs; there unbounded freedom, youthful exuberance, hearty conviviality reigned amidst laughter, music, and song.

In the Rue Ravignan circle, the painters at the beginning played the most important rôle. In the years just past, the *Fauves* had abruptly extinguished the vogue of Impressionism among the most modern artists; they were now slowly forcing their point of view upon a reluctant and diffident public. Yet, though the *Fauves* had introduced the idea of the lyrical, emotional distortion of visible shapes, they refrained from going very far in the practical application of their theories. So the feeling was growing, especially among the younger men, that a more radical departure from the traditional mode of vision must be put into effect if a more profound and authentic reality was ever to be brought to light.

The *douanier* Rousseau, who had been discovered several years before by Jarry, then became the mock hero of the whole Rue Ravignan group. In spite of a ridiculous technical clumsiness, there could be perceived in his works an element of priceless spontaneity which was absolutely free from any superimposed conventionalism. Rousseau's triumph reached its climax with a memorable banquet organized in his honor in 1908 within the famous "bateau-lavoir" itself. Elaborate and fanciful decorations were put up; numerous guests were invited and attended; long speeches were delivered; the wines proved abundant and varied; enthusiasm ran high; in short nothing was lacking — except the food itself, which Picasso had forgotten to order for the proper day. . . .

Yet, though Rousseau might be considered as a symptomatic phenomenon, he was in no sense a master and could not possibly be taken as a guide. Among the decisive factors which brought about a crystallization of the existing latent tendencies towards a new conception of art, it was perhaps the Negro influence which played the most curious and striking rôle. As early as 1902 little wooden statuettes, crudely carved by African natives, had been brought from the French colonies of the Ivory Coast and the Congo to Paris, where they aroused great interest. Then, about 1907, the fashion for Negro art all at once spread like wildfire throughout France. The reason for that wave of enthusiasm was not the sudden appreciation of a new type of "beauty," nor was it simply the manifestation of an ephemeral taste for a new form of exoticism. It was an element perceived in the work of the Negroes which had already conferred upon certain coarse creations of Jarry and upon the naïve images of the *douanier* an inexplicable power of appeal — that is, a direct suggestion of the most primitive instincts lying dormant at the bottom of our nature. The candid expression of genuine, though brutal, sensations and sentiments stirred man in a way that was beyond the power of a clever, sophisticated technique. So it became obvious that the hard crust of an age-old civilization, the thick layer of interpretative notions and traditions which intelligence had deposited upon all things, was the main obstacle to direct contact with the richest sources of human inspiration and emotion.

As they tried to discover how African Negroes were capable of conjuring up, through very simple, elementary forms, an atmosphere of intense spirituality, the artists of the Rue Ravignan were struck by the process of geometrical simplification which was exemplified in practically all of these imported carvings. They observed that details were either omitted entirely or indicated very roughly; only the essential features were retained, and they were marked by bold planes, bulbous masses, sharp notches, or violent projecting angles. Thanks to an almost complete elimination of accidental aspects of texture and to the placing of a vigorous emphasis — quite intuitively — on structural relations and proportions, the Negroes succeeded in suggesting with almost overpowering force a mysterious order, not thrust upon passive objects by an organizing intelligence but existing, as it were, at the very core of the things themselves.

From the same quarter, and at the same time, there came also the beginning of a new pictorial method that was to revolutionize the whole technique of modern art. Max Jacob had a brother who served for a number of years as an official in the French colonies of Senegal and the Sudan. One day, when on leave in Paris, he produced a portrait of himself which had been painted by a native artist in Dakar. The worthy Negro, very much impressed by the brass buttons glittering on the official's uniform, had been moved to paint them in the form of a semicircle around the head of his model.

This was the starting point of an animated controversy on the Rue Ravignan. The dislocation of the various components of reality and their redistribution in a different order had been advocated many a time in literature. Yet in the field of painting even the most daring artists had fought shy of reconstructing the visible world after the pattern of their own personal fancy. Then, in consideration of the Negro's picture of Max Jacob's brother, the idea was upheld by some of the young painters that, since they were admittedly in search of means to express forcibly what was truly essential in reality, the process of dissociation and recombination was legitimate and advisable. Through that process alone, it was claimed, could an artist accord a proper place and value — as he sensed them by intuition — to elements which, on account of their accidental localization, would otherwise be bereft of all pungency and significance.

After indulging in countless discussions, Braque, formerly one of the *Fauves* and now following the lead of Picasso, composed a series of pictures in an entirely new and disconcerting style. These pictures were first sent to the Salon d'Automne of 1908, later to be withdrawn and placed on exhibition in the private gallery of a dealer. Matisse, who had viewed the display with great curiosity and some misgivings, on meeting the art critic Louis Vauxcelles, tried to explain to him the odd technique used by Braque, saying that the paintings in question seemed to be made "avec des petits cubes." The name of "Cubists" was soon taken up by the general public as the designation of the young painters who were exponents of the new tendencies. This name was accepted by the painters themselves, in a defiant and challenging spirit.

Indeed, Cubism created a much greater commotion than had been previously aroused by Fauvism. Outside the immediate circle of the Rue Ravignan, however, it found little favor at first even with the vanguard artists. The *Fauves* were its bitterest opponents, since they suspected that the rival movement was simply an attempt to relegate their own audacities to a secondary position of meek and tame conventionalism. The climax came when a portrait of Guillaume Apollinaire by Jean Metzinger was exhibited in 1910. It was impossible to find on the canvas, streaked with harsh, crude, discordant tones, any resemblance to the familiar, rotund silhouette of Apollinaire himself. Nevertheless the picture had the force of a manifesto; for weeks friends and enemies raved or raged about its import, its implications, and its significance. Many must have been convinced that the new doctrine contained an important nucleus of truth, for numerous regular *Fauves*, and still more of the very young aritsts who were in search of a formula of their own, began, from that time on, to join the ranks of the Cubists in ever-increasing numbers.

The general public was still very reticent and puzzled.

Guillaume Apollinaire and his friends set out to champion
the cause of these new artistic ideas. A preface, written by
Apollinaire himself for the catalogue of a Cubist exhibition
which took place in Brussels in 1911, helped greatly to set
forth the Cubist problem in comparatively clear terms. Then,
in spite of much irony and laughter, Cubism became the rage
— very much as Negro art had been several years before —
partly, it must be said, because of its novelty, partly on account of a mysterious, bizarre, but undeniable charm that it
evidently possessed. The year 1913 marked the triumph and
apogee of Cubism in France. Cubist paintings were now
finding their way into private collections and even into certain
reputable public galleries; critics were violently taking sides
in the controversy regarding the new trend in art; Cubist
doctrines were reviewed, explained, and vehemently discussed everywhere.

The Cubist doctrines, it must be admitted, were on the
whole more than a little confusing. Among themselves the
exponents of these doctrines showed considerable divergencies of temperament and outlook. Moreover, as certain of the
most gifted Cubist painters were not in the least inclined to
metaphysical speculation, they were only too glad to have a
Guillaume Apollinaire or a Max Jacob refer to their work
with undoubtedly brilliant, though rather fantastic arguments. Apollinaire, especially, took an evident delight in
piling up indefatigably ingenious theories on top of crazy,
breath-taking paradoxes. So it was not always easy to know —
and perhaps Apollinaire himself did not know exactly — how
far his sincerity really went, how much he indulged his
mystifying humor, and to what extent he was himself carried
away, intoxicated by his own exaltation and eloquence.

At the bottom of the Cubist movement was an eager and
fervent desire to penetrate beneath the motley exterior of

material appearances and to grasp something of the fundamental substance of reality. After centuries of pointed but allegedly frivolous cleverness, poets and artists refused to play any longer with words and styles, with colors and shapes, merely for the pleasure of the mind or the amusement of the eye. They were now taking their mission seriously — as younger men will — and they confidently set out to discover and to reveal the mystic entity of nature.

Strangely enough, their mysticism was blended with a thoroughly mathematical conception of the world. This was to some extent the result of their admiration for the more or less geometrical technique of Negro carvings. Essentially, however, it must be considered as a remnant of the age-old reverence for the power of human reasoning. Of all the elements of rational thinking, mathematics is by far the most abstract, the most speculative, the most ethereal. It is by definition utterly free from entanglements and compromises with the materialism of life. Even though discursive logic were now discredited, the Cubists had little difficulty in persuading themselves that pure geometry reflected the basic architecture of the universe. An expert accountant, Princet by name, who lived in the "bateau-lavoir" on the Rue Ravignan, expounded to his friends, the painters, mathematical calculations to that end, which very few, if any, of them were capable of following, and which probably for this very reason impressed them all the more. Soon they were convinced that by systematic computation and clever combination of circles and angles, they would be able to attain the truer reality for which they were all longing. The rendering of this deep reality embodied in a given object was to be left no longer to the vague and uncertain suggestion of lights and shadows; it was to be brought out by the compelling figuration of pyramids, cubes, and cones, enclosing within the compass of their

Juan Gris: *Portrait of Picasso* (1912)
An effort to grasp the fundamental architecture of reality

mathematical properties what was truly essential in its profound being.

There was in Cubism, however, much more than merely
a reduction of volumes and masses to their geometrical framework. Following the advice of Baudelaire, and Rimbaud,
and encouraged by the precedent of Negro art, the Cubists
set out to dislocate the world of appearances, combining the
dissociated elements according to a new order. This had
the advantages — now implicitly recognized — of breaking up
the banal associations that rob every aspect of reality of its individual force and of disclosing a view of the transcendental
that each one of them may hold. The new order was not to
be determined logically, nor even mathematically, but solely
by intuition. It was assumed that the intrinsic value of
things and their proper reciprocal relationship were revealed,
through some mysterious inward enlightenment, to the poet
and to the artist alone.

Here arose a problem of capital importance to modern
literature and art. Even if the new order be legitimate, nay
essential, in the mind's eye of the writer or the painter himself, that order is by no means so evident to the general public,
normally lacking in that power of mystic insight with which
artists are supposed to be endowed. Thus a picture may be
perfectly clear to the one who has composed it consciously
and yet may present to the layman an insoluble, disconcerting
riddle. Under certain circumstances, however, the layman
may perhaps be able to sense by intuition the existence of the
magic universe in which the artist moves freely, but which is
irrevocably closed to all others. This partial revelation is
reserved for those who have something of the poet in them,
and who need only to be startled out of their usual lethargy
in order to have their eyes opened to the splendor of the
infinite.

This difficulty did not deter the Cubists from the pursuit

of their aim. Whoever undertakes to tread certain paths to which the vulgar have no access must give up all hope of being followed by the crowd; and obviously the domain of the ideal cannot be thrown open indiscriminately to one and all. But is it not enough that some at least are enabled to catch a glimpse of the forbidden realm from which otherwise they would be for ever excluded? The Cubist paintings, bright with the effulgence of a world beyond our common knowledge, were able — so at least thought their creators — to arouse an enraptured response in the souls of the privileged few who held within themselves a spark of the sublime. So the devotees of the new art, heedless of vulgar misunderstanding, went on painting as though with eyes fixed on a particular object, yet, through that model, gazing upon the infinite itself. As Guillaume Apollinaire said: "L'art des peintres nouveaux prend l'univers infini comme idéal" (1).

The principle of systematic dissociation of the elements of the universe, while helping to reveal the deep, mysterious essence of things, also provided the Cubist painters with a practical means of rendering them in their absolute totality. Artists in the past had been compelled by convention to confine themselves within the focal limits of perspective. For instance, an artist of the old school who took a vase as a model had to leave completely out of his picture, say, a handle, if that handle were outside his field of vision from the particular viewpoint he had happened to select. Similarly he was obliged to represent the opening of the vase as an oval, because the laws of perspective ordained that that opening, when seen from a certain angle, had an oblong and flattened shape. Now the neglected handle was certainly an integral part of the vase as a whole, and the opening was in fact circular and not oval at all. Any artist really anxious to give more than

(1) Guillaume Apollinaire, *Il y a . . .* (Paris: A. Messein, 1925), pp. 140–141.

an ephemeral and superficial view of reality would balk at
the necessity of such arbitrary and incongruous omissions.
The Cubist painter felt free to turn his model around, to
examine and study it from every possible angle; then he
would account for *all* the main features, grouping side by
side on his canvas the various elements that his intuition had
recognized as really essential, regardless of their accidental
position in space but in accordance with a truer arrangement determined by his own deeper instinct.

The simultaneous juxtaposition in the same picture of
aspects which can only be perceived successively in time was
not altogether an innovation in the history of painting. During the Middle Ages it was not unusual to behold, all in one
composition, illustrating, for instance, the life of a saint, first
perhaps the spectacle of the saint undergoing picturesque
maceration in solitude, then the scene of his trial before a
wicked judge, and then the gruesome display of his martyr-
dom; he might even sometimes be shown performing a few
edifying miracles after his death. . . . Far from being dis-
turbed by this bringing together of widely distant occurrences, our candid ancestors felt that they could apprehend
the spirit of sainthood much better in this way than if intelligence had sliced their pious sentiment into a succession of
disconnected pictures. Indeed each scene acquired its full
force and significance only in conjunction with and in relation to all the others. Each picture, considered separately,
could at best be only a more or less skillfully wrought image;
when all of them were seen at a glance they had the value of
a composite symbol, evoking mystically a lofty religious ideal.

This spirit of idealism, which came to the *Primitifs* spontaneously and without effort, the Cubists strove consciously
and laboriously to re-create. They were fully aware of the
intervening rationalistic evolution that would have to be
eradicated. They realized the extent of the inevitable sacri-

fice: they were prepared to reject all the intellectual and technical advances achieved in the field of painting since the Renaissance. As rationalistic methods had only led ultimately to the parceling out of the world into stale and spiritless fragments, their discard was not a very high price to pay in order to recapture a sense of the totality of the universe and to resume close contact with a sublime spiritual entity.

A few characteristics of reality, such as color, line, and mass, had, it is true, been rendered by the old traditional art with commendable accuracy. The Cubists scorned these as the coarse, obvious, hackneyed properties of nature; they preferred to devote themselves entirely to the evocation of nature's most elusive and ineffable attributes. So, in painting a vase, they would pay scant attention to formal outline but concentrate their efforts on the suggestion of iridescent transparency. When trying to express the charm of a woman, they sought to capture not the exact shade of her hair but rather its undulating quality; not the rich and firm substance of her contour but the graceful sweep of her alluring suppleness. In their view, the essentials of our world consisted of rare subtleties, hardly perceptible to our senses, unanalyzable by intelligence, almost evanescent and nebulous.

Most of the earlier painters had simply overlooked these impalpable elements, which they were powerless to grasp and to analyze. That is why seemingly accurate representations of objective models so often appear to us lifeless and dull. The Cubists never attempted to give an accurate representation of any object whatsoever; but by means of equivalents and analogies they endeavored to impart a spiritual vibration suggestive of the most intimate and secret characteristics of nature. So when they contended, before a nonplused or derisive public, that their incomprehensible pictures were truer to reality than those of more conventional artists, they were in a way undoubtedly right; but they referred to a reality different from that which we apprehend through our senses, a reality that can be perceived only by intuitive vision and which therefore always appears to the common people as chimerical and fabulous.

Becoming more and more preoccupied with the expression of abstract qualities, the Cubists derived increasing satisfaction from the force of spiritual energy involved in that expression. After all, the intrinsic form of a vase and even the charm of a particular woman do not hold as a rule an overpowering and universal interest. But the magic flash that lights up the communication of their essence may arouse in some cases a curious exaltation of brief but miraculous intensity. It was soon found out that any too precise reference either to the form of the vase or to the person of the woman weighed down the spirit and all but paralyzed the faculty for uplifting enthusiasm. The main thing was evidently a mysterious current passing directly from the artist into the soul of the sympathetic onlooker. Thus it appeared that the value of a work of art depended much less upon the subject treated than on the potential magnetism issuing from the individuality of its creator. So Cubism, which at first represented a passionate and sincere quest for the profound essence of things, progressively discovered that whatever the artist could grasp of that essence was of little worth compared to the absolutely priceless outpouring of the spirit from the deepest recesses of man's fundamental vitality.

This seemingly unimportant shifting of accentuation in the relative scale of their interests was to have the most ominous consequences for the Cubists. They came to consider their art very much in the nature of an incantation whose strength lay in its power of enchantment, regardless of its original signification. The geometrical figures which had been at first worshiped because they were said to express the very architecture of the world were now enjoyed not for any spiritual meaning that might accrue to them but for themselves alone.

They were not, however, appreciated for their ornamental value, for the Cubists of this period vehemently repudiated any interest whatever in decorative art. The Cubist attitude towards forms was not unlike that of Mallarmé towards words. For Mallarmé, words had a power independent of their general acceptation, and that power came from the poetical radiation emanating from their syllables. In a similar manner, the Cubists considered volume and shape much less as functions of the object they were supposed to stand for than from the point of view of their innate power of mystic suggestion. More and more unmindful of the too remote and elusive soul of the universe, fascinated by the entrancing experience of the transfer of psychic revelation, their art tended gradually towards a pictorial lyricism, devoid of any precise significance, yet capable of stirring up intense feeling in those who could attune themselves to their bizarre mode of personal expression.

The result was that Cubism, which had been originally constructed upon a mathematical, or pseudo-mathematical, basis, came closely to resemble music, whose strains may signify nothing definite and yet move us to the depths. Guillaume Apollinaire clearly indicated this unexpected turn which the Cubist theories had taken when he said: "We are drifting towards an entirely new art which will stand in relation to painting, as hitherto regarded, just as music stands in relation to literature" (2).

The evolution of Cubism from a mathematical computation to something like a musical mood was not accepted by all the artists to the same extent, nor was it followed at the same pace. When after a few years the most revolutionizing conclusions had been reached by the boldest of them, many

(2) *Il y a . . .* , p. 135.

others, not sharing their views altogether, felt the necessity of asserting their own personal standpoint. Cubism then branched out into several subdivisions; it has even become customary of late to distinguish between scientific Cubism, orphic Cubism, physical Cubism, and instinctive Cubism.

Scientific Cubism to the last remained faithful to the original tendency of the movement, trying systematically to reduce the whole of nature to mathematical relations and proportions. The most arresting of its theories is the contention that the great masters of the past were, so to speak, and of course unwittingly, Cubists. The scientific Cubists set themselves to "decompose" the best-known masterpieces of Leonardo da Vinci, Raphael, Michelangelo, and others into geometrical figures, conclusively demonstrating that practically all these paintings could indeed be divided into regular sets of triangles, spheres, spirals, and pyramids. They pretended — perhaps not without reason — that a great deal of the charm of these celebrated works comes from the unconscious perception by our eyes of delicately balanced, yet mathematically perfect relations between their elements.

Orphic Cubism tended towards a much more elevated, mystic, and ambitious cult. According to the old Greek legend, Orpheus enchanted all that came within sound of his lyre — men, animals, plants, even stones. Orphic Cubists refused to recognize the conventional division of the universe into separate units and assumed that they could draw the whole psychic content of the world into an ecstatic communion of universal consciousness.

Physical Cubism, in spite of its misleading name, went a step further in the way of idealism and sought to do away entirely with the elements of common reality that the other Cubists still consented to borrow from nature. In their ardent desire to communicate with the spirit alone, and to be unencumbered by material implications of any sort, the physical Cubists were ready to create out of their own minds even the *physical* objects to which a painter must of necessity have recourse as a basis for his message. While the work of other Cubist painters still retained fragments of natural shapes, combined, it is true, according to the imagination of the artists themselves, these rabid idealists attempted to draw forms and figures derived from the depths of their consciousness — thus paving the way for the daring attempts of more recent artists.

As the Cubist theories had been elaborated mainly by clever and subtle poets, many young painters who were entirely lacking in metaphysical training failed to understand the purport of the doctrines of the school. Yet certain of them produced authentic Cubist pictures. It was disconcerting, if not humiliating, for the pure theorists to observe that some of the best Cubist pictures — those with the highest power of mystic suggestion — came from these ignorant artists. Fortunately, since Bergson had rehabilitated instinct, assigning that formerly despised faculty its place as a means of transcendental insight, it was possible, without any disparaging implication, to designate their work by the honorable title of "instinctive Cubism."

This fourfold division provides a convenient, though rather artificial method of classifying the various trends in the Cubist doctrines. In point of fact, the fundamental divergencies in the outlook of the Cubist painters seem to have sprung from more deeply rooted differences of temperament and character. These divergencies were not very noticeable at the beginning of the movement, when all the young artists fought shoulder to shoulder for the right to express their common ideal after their own fashion. However, as each painter attempted to define his own personal conception of that ideal and tried as far as possible to attain its complete fulfillment, it became obvious that the original background of the various individuals was the cause of their considerable differences in outlook.

Among the Cubists there was a large proportion of artists of foreign birth, and Spaniards such as Pablo Picasso and Juan Gris, owing to their personal ascendency, soon assumed a distinct position of leadership. On the other hand, the French, who constituted numerically the most important fraction within the whole group, from the very start brought forward and imposed upon the movement certain definitely French ways of considering both reality and art. The result was that two separate currents developed and ran side by side, sometimes mingling with one another, it is true, and by no means strictly confined within sharply drawn lines of national distinctiveness, yet certainly at variance spiritually, and even markedly dissimilar in their artistic technique.

The French, perhaps on account of their atavistic reverence for reason and reality, generally showed themselves reluctant to give up altogether the world of external appearances and its time-honored intellectual framework. They insisted more urgently than their foreign associates upon the geometrical basis of the Cubist theories. It seemed to them that, through the mathematical proportions of their figures, they were saving something at least of the forms of reality and the mental categories habitual to man. Their paintings represented a compromise between the ideal they carried deep in their souls and the shapes which they saw with their own eyes, and which they were loath to exclude from the field of their spiritual vision.

In consequence, their technique, bearing the mark of an uncertain, intermediate position between two antagonistic concepts, was often hazy, indistinct, and characterized by light, soft tones and blurred outlines. Roger de La Fresnaye, André Lhote, Jean Metzinger, Marie Laurencin, and Le Fauconnier were the best known representatives of that particular tendency in Cubism. To most of them, Cubism has represented only one phase in the development of their respective careers; indeed, even while strongly emphasizing the value of geometrical relations in painting, they never found in them enough substance to satisfy their inborn craving for consistency and solidity, nor sufficient inward fulfillment to justify the utter disregard of the testimony of our senses. So after a conscientious and sincere attempt at assimilation, they were among the first to look beyond Cubism for a more satisfactory means of expressing their aspirations and desires.

The Spaniards were not impeded by any such inveterate scruples. The latent but intense mysticism of their race inclined them, on the contrary, to consider Cubism essentially as a means of passionate interpretation of a sublime idea. They accepted geometrical forms as the foundation of the new art, but they looked upon these as a kind of springboard from which they could bound upwards and reach an even higher spiritual plane. Insensibly they deflected Cubism from its original purpose — the precise investigation of a fundamental reality — and turned it into an endeavor to soar indefinitely towards supreme, immaterial spheres. Picasso and Juan Gris were followed in this direction by the Polish painter Marcoussis, and also by certain French artists such as Georges Braque and Albert Gleizes, who were apparently fascinated by the attraction of the dizzy heights which they all dreamed of ascending.

Their technique, in contrast to that of the preceding group, was violent and incisive, their colors harsh and crude, their outlines always clear-cut and sharp. Indeed their pictures did not represent the meeting point of an inward vision and an external world: they expressed purely and simply the ideal of the artist's soul, without the interference or intrusion of outside objects and shapes. Their work represented Cubism

Pablo Picasso: *Portrait Arrangement with the Words "J'aime Eva"* (1910)
Evolution of Cubism towards the rendering of abstract qualities

in its purest form, and under their progressively increasing influence, Cubism became even more ethereal and abstract. Finally it lost every trace of the substance it had hitherto secretly retained, and, on being thus emptied of all material content, it dwindled to a sublimated, dreamlike conception of fantastic forms devoid of any solid earthly signification.

After reaching this sublimated stage, Cubism began to wane and rapidly lost its influence as a school. It has been said sometimes that the end of Cubism was caused by the first World War. The war undoubtedly brought about moral and material changes that disorganized and disintegrated the particular environment in which Cubism had developed and flourished. But the aspirations which had given birth to the movement were not by any means destroyed. If anything, they were fortified and intensified by the new trend of events; in fact, after a temporary eclipse, they were soon to reappear with added strength and very much increased prestige.

That Cubism itself passed so quickly from the scene was mainly because the solutions it had propounded were found to be inadequate for its general purpose. The hastily adopted pictorial process, which consisted in reducing the whole universe to its geometrical skeleton, proved to be the greatest weakness of a school whose scope went far beyond the limits of a particular technical mode of painting. As a matter of fact, all the mathematical theories put forward by the Cubists turned out to be quite unsound on actual application. The Cubist painters had no profound or solid mathematical knowledge; they never strove for mathematical precision and accuracy. It has not been difficult to demonstrate that their pretended geometrical framework of the world was nought but an accumulation of more or less regular forms, imposed one upon the other without fundamental justification. No sincere man could delude himself very long into believing that he could thus capture the "essence of the universe."

Indeed the most sincerely and deeply convinced among the Cubists did not care to dwell rigorously upon the value of their method; they were inclined to emphasize rather what was in their view the true aim of the school, the search for an absolute. Becoming less and less able to adapt their technique to their aspirations, they drifted insensibly into an increasingly abstract and mystic conception of their art. Thus was brought about a curious dissociation between the technical practice of the artist and his original, inspiring thought.

The geometrical forms on which the Cubists had at first founded their hopes and which had appealed so forcibly to the imagination of the public continued to exhibit an existence of their own. As the Cubists had accurately perceived — though they may have exaggerated the bearing of their discovery — these forms contained in themselves something of the profound substance of terrestrial things. Even when no longer endowed with the wealth of meaning that the early Cubists had wanted them to express, they retained a certain charm and appeal, bound up, as it were, in their very being. That intrinsic charm, completely independent of any mystic conception of the universe, found a practical application at the hands of certain artists for purely ornamental purposes. Two painters, Fernand Léger and Robert Delaunay, are mainly responsible for this evolution of Cubism towards decorative art. It was through their initiative and example that, from the time of the first World War, but especially during the post-war period, figurations of square blocks, bare surfaces, pyramids, spheres, and truncated cones invaded the domains of the designer of furniture, the interior decorator, and the commercial artist. The sharp, angular, plain lines, typical of "modernistic" art, are a direct heritage of the Cubist technique. Indeed, when this new fashion attained its climax about the year 1925, true Cubism was already dead. Its vestiges were at that time — and are still to a certain extent today — objects of practical utilization on the part of clever craftsmen. Its ideal spirit had departed.

The essence of Cubism — or rather its most mystic elements — helped to nourish the newer theories that sprang up in France after the first World War. These elements were absorbed into younger and more vigorous systems; they became part of the complex metaphysico-artistic movement flourishing in our days under the name of Surrealism.

In correlation with the Cubist trend in painting and almost on a parallel with it, a literary movement developed in France which has been designated by the same name, and which indeed reflects the same fundamental tendencies. It must be noted, however, that the artistic doctrines were elaborated first; though the writers inspired many of the painters' theories, all their own poetical ideas were evolved from direct contact with the inspiration provided by the plastic arts. Literary Cubism corresponded to a second stage in the evolution of modernistic thought, and it developed in an environment somewhat different from that of the original artistic Cubism.

Cubist art had been cradled in Montmartre. But in the course of time many painters, as official recognition and financial success came to them, left the "bateau-lavoir" and moved to better and more comfortable residences. Also, Montmartre was becoming more conspicuously the haunt of the Parisian *apaches*. Artists and poets, despite their fondness for excitement and for the picturesque, were inclined to draw the line at too frequent revolver shots in their neighborhood. One by one they shifted their establishments to other quarters of Paris.

For the sudden vogue of Montparnasse, succeeding Montmartre, Guillaume Apollinaire was mainly responsible. Alfred Jarry, it is true, had already established his headquarters there in days gone by. Apollinaire always felt more at home in this cosmopolitan environment than anywhere else in the capital. As early as 1909 he began to prevail on some of his Montmartre friends to join him on the left bank of the Seine; by 1912 Montparnasse had become the most important center of Parisian literary Bohemia. Montmartre still continued to exercise its attraction for some time to come, especially upon artists, while Montparnasse was favored chiefly by novelists and poets. Montparnasse, it must be admitted, lacked the striking picturesqueness of Montmartre; further, the group that congregated at the café of "Les Deux Magots" never presented the same familiar unity as the one which had gathered at the "Lapin Agile." Yet even though a few writers, Max Jacob among them, remained faithful to old Montmartre, Montparnasse became definitely the rallying point of the cohort of vanguard poets whose acknowledged leader was Guillaume Apollinaire.

Wilhelm Apollinaris de Kostrowitzki was born in Rome, August 26, 1880. His birth certificate bore only the name of his mother. . . . She was a small but spirited lady, probably the daughter of a Polish general. She had acquired a degree of fame in certain cosmopolitan circles in Europe for her mysterious demeanor, her indisputable charm, and her broad-minded unconventionality. It was rumored that she counted among her intimate friends even prelates of the Roman Church. Many years later, when the Cubist painters made portraits of her son, they seldom failed to include among the paraphernalia intended to represent the "original essence" of their model a bishop's miter and crosier.

Madame de Kostrowitzki moved from Rome to the French Riviera. Here she brought up her young son in an atmosphere of refinement, elegance, and opulent luxury, though perhaps not of over-strict morals. The indulgence and even laxity prevailing in Guillaume's early environment may to some extent account for some of the typical traits in his character, such as an easygoing, good-natured friendliness and a marked taste for the open and unrestrained enjoyment of material pleasures. They may also perhaps explain his utter lack of respect for rules and self-imposed discipline.

He received his first schooling in a Catholic institution, the Collège Saint-Charles, situated in the little city of Monaco. He did not prove to be in any way a remarkable pupil, except for his indulgence in boyish pranks, jests, and jokes, for which he displayed a more than average aptitude. In this field he had a constant and faithful confederate in René Dupuy, who was to become his lifelong friend. Under the pen name of René Dalize, Dupuy was to later prove very helpful to him as a literary collaborator. The rebelliousness of these two mischievous youngsters was not a painful revolt against harsh treatment and oppression, for the régime of the school was of the mildest, but was merely the spontaneous manifestation of a natural exuberance of spirit which, since it was left unchecked, frequently overflowed with uncontrollable vehemence.

In the intervals between the pieces of devilry they perpetrated together, the two boys, perhaps by way of compensation, experienced moods of intense religious fervor. Guillaume Apollinaire has himself recounted how at these times he would leave his bed stealthily during the night and spend hours praying in the school chapel. From these days on, the imprint of deep religious emotion was for ever stamped upon his soul. In truth the course of his life was not regulated by a strict observance of the ritual practices of the Church, nor was his moral behavior always determined by virtuous obedience to the Ten Commandments; but a ferment of spiritual exaltation was always at work within him, concealed from public view, yet secretly potent and active.

Guillaume Apollinaire's education proceeded, still on the Riviera, until he completed his studies at the well-organized and efficiently conducted Collège de Cannes. He seems then to have passed beyond the stage of irrepressible boyhood and to have applied himself at last very seriously to his work. Thus he gained a solid classical culture, which formed the basis of the extraordinary erudition which he was later on to acquire. It is not unimportant that his first initiation into the realm of literature and art should have taken place amid scenes of unsurpassed beauty on the glorious Mediterranean shores. The luminous splendor of the landscape undoubtedly helped him to grasp the marvels of the ancient civilizations of Rome and Greece. Throughout his life he nourished a secret longing for an ideal that was gone, but for which he entertained a feeling of profound reverence, and whose spirit he finally almost hoped to retrieve.

While still an adolescent, Guillaume Apollinaire left both school and home to go and seek his fortune in the world. The exact reasons for his early departure are still unknown. His mother may have suffered some financial reverses; she also may have thought that he was old enough to fend for himself — and indeed she never subsequently displayed very much interest in the troubles or achievements of her son; perhaps, too, the young man felt an irresistible impulse to go, urged on by a natural restlessness and an inborn love of freedom and adventure. At any rate, after divers wanderings, stopping on his way, for instance, in the city of Lyons, he arrived in Paris in 1898.

He was then a slender youth of eighteen. The contradictory aspects of his appearance reflected the conflicting tendencies which were at variance within himself. His reddish hair, his full lips, his heavy jaw, his rich, overflowing vitality bore witness to a sensuous material nature. His light, dreamy eyes, his unfailing courtesy, the sweet *gentillesse* of his manners, and his almost feminine charm bespoke an idealistic turn which seemed foreign to the common world of everyday trivialities.

Guillaume Apollinaire soon drifted into Parisian literary Bohemia, enjoying the independent, amusing, picturesque, hand-to-mouth existence which was the lot of many impecunious but merry young writers and artists. He gravitated towards the circle surrounding Alfred Jarry, then at the height of his influence and prestige. Jarry's truculence and daring roused the admiration of the timid newcomer, who secretly dreamed of emulating his actions, who indeed adopted some of his mannerisms and accepted for himself many of the paradoxical and iconoclastic ideas of the arch fantast.

Though Paris became — and was to remain — Apollinaire's headquarters, an ungovernable wanderlust drove him soon to undertake long travels throughout Europe. In August 1901 he left France to accept a position as a tutor to the only daughter of the Viscountess von Hölterhoff-Milhau, whose residence was at Neu Glück, near Honnef, in Germany. Apollinaire stayed there one whole year. His duties however were not too exacting, and he often obtained leave to take very extended trips, generally with very little money in his pocket and most of the time on foot, just for the sake of excitement and change. In this way he visited the greatest part of the Rheinland, the Black Forest, and even Bohemia, meeting, to his great delight, with picturesque companions and entertaining adventures. He has related how once, in Prague, he had nothing to eat for two days, except a Camembert cheese. Further, he also went to Belgium and Holland. This contact with the northern regions of Europe seems to have revealed to Guillaume Apollinaire a romantic aspect of reality that his Mediterranean and classical education had consistently suppressed or ignored. The taste for the mysterious and the fantastic — to which the strong Slavic element in his nature must have predisposed him — seems to have been liberated, as it were, within his conscious mind. From that time on, the dualism of his character, which combined the traits of an inveterate mystic and dreamer with those of a frolicsome, life-loving epicure, came clearly and definitely to the fore. The influence of his classical culture receded into the background, remaining obscure, though still vigorous and alive.

When Apollinaire came back to Paris after a few years of intermittent ramblings, his personality had matured and expanded, and he had no difficulty in asserting himself strongly within the circle in which he had been accepted formerly as a bashful beginner. In 1903 the young men who were still surrounding Jarry founded a literary review called *Le Festin d'Esope*. Guillaume Apollinaire by universal consent was made the *directeur* of the magazine, while André Salmon was appointed *secrétaire de rédaction*. For the nine months which constituted the life span of *Le Festin d'Esope*, Apollinaire presided over its destinies with a characteristic mixture of buffoonery and suave dignity.

Meanwhile he had somehow to make a living. At first, a position as a bank clerk provided him with indispensable bread and butter; then the opportune bankruptcy of his firm released him from the drudgery of office work, and he threw himself into journalism. The then well-known newspaper *La Démocratie sociale* entrusted him with a regular column in which he had to report how France was judged by foreign countries. In this task he derived much help from his own imagination when positive knowledge was lacking. He also contributed articles to several other daily papers, whenever his energy ran high or his funds ran low.

To these precarious resources he had soon to add systematic "ghost writing." He would undertake almost any kind of work for which a publisher would give a profitable return. The Bibliothèque Nationale then became the center of his activities. There he compiled tirelessly notes either on the most risqué and frivolous subjects or on the most ponderous and abstruse problems, depending upon his editor's orders. Once he even wrote a complete doctor's thesis on certain phases of the French Revolution for a particularly lazy and apparently wealthy professor. Thus Apollinaire acquired an amazing knowledge of an immense variety of facts. His erudition, however, did not cover a continuous, definite field of study but was scattered over a multitude of disconnected questions, after the manner of a patchwork. This undoubtedly predisposed him to understand the point of view of the Cubist painters, to whom reality appeared as a set of isolated pieces each of which may be of engrossing interest but whose order in relation to one another is not immutably fixed and therefore can be altered almost at will.

Even with the foregoing restriction, it would be a mistake to imagine Apollinaire as a conscientious savant, spending the best part of his time in research work. Whenever it was possible, he had recourse simply to scissors and paste as a means of collecting the necessary information, and after he had established some sort of reputation in this type of work, he himself made use of the labor of other "ghosts." The most helpful of his "secretaries" was his old schoolmate, René Dalize, who after many adventures as an officer in the French navy had become a writer, and who, being none too prosperous, was very glad to earn easy money under the name of his more enterprising and successful comrade. Some of Apollinaire's writings, such as *La Rome des Borgia* and *La Fin de Babylone*, owe a great deal to the pen of the modest Dalize.

The life of Guillaume Apollinaire took a new turn when in 1905 he met Picasso and his *bande*. So far he had been nothing but a Bohemian. Although he was perhaps more popular and dynamic than some of the others, his true originality had not yet had a chance to appear. His association with painters provided him a unique opportunity for developing the potential creative power that was in him. In the field of literature, the example of the great poets of the past which, owing to his classical schooling, he could not but deeply admire, cramped and paralyzed his own originality; almost in spite of himself his thought was inclined to flow in the accustomed, traditional channels. In the field of painting, with which he was far less familiar, he did not feel to any such degree the obsession of old established models. As a consequence, in the domain of plastic art he was much more free to destroy without any consciousness of sacrilege and to create entirely anew without any feeling of ridiculous presumptuousness. Conversely, many painters, from their very appreciation of their art, experienced the same reluctance towards upsetting certain rules of painting as Guillaume Apollinaire himself did at the idea of transgressing certain rules of poetry. It is probable that these artists would not have gone very far in their technical innovations had they not received encouragement and justification for their audacities from a master-mind endowed with intense personal attractiveness and recognized superiority of intelligence.

For that reason, the part played by Apollinaire in the formation of Cubism and consequently in the whole movement of "modernistic" art can hardly be overrated. Being much more cultivated and brilliant than the painters with whom he associated, he could give them the decisive support of his ingenious interpretations and his philosophical training. He explained not only to the public but even to the painters themselves the goal towards which they were almost unconsciously tending — thus, as it were, revealing Cubism to the Cubists. At the same time, in the midst of impassioned controversies, he was taking full cognizance of his own potentialities and aspirations. Without Apollinaire, Cubism would have soon expired; without Cubism, Apollinaire would probably never have been able to develop his inward personality to the full.

When Guillaume Apollinaire made himself known as the outstanding figure in Cubism, his physical appearance was very different from that of the smiling and acquiescent youth who had come to Paris from the Riviera a few years before. He had acquired a remarkable *embonpoint*; his broad chest and his still more extensive waistline invested him with an impressive dignity, offset, however, by his plump, pink, and perspiring countenance, always beaming with good nature and gaiety. One of his chief interests in life seems to have been the art of eating. He ate tremendously, and if a friend came to his table when he had just finished his repast he was always ready, in order to keep him company, to start all over again. His expert culinary knowledge was not limited to French dishes but extended to outlandish food such as grace the Bulgarian or Arabic cuisine; and he liked them all except — for some unknown reason — those produced by English methods of cooking.

Next to the pleasure of the table, Apollinaire's greatest delight was in conversation. In contrast with his imposing avoirdupois, the piping sound of his voice, which had remained high-pitched, at first seemed strange and disconcerting. Yet no one could withstand the fascination of his words, as he gave vent to a crescendo of pointed and clever observations, erudite remarks, daring anecdotes, profound views, humorous sallies, and brilliant paradoxes, while underneath it all, as if on muted strings, ran the poetical modulation of a subdued melancholy or the fantastic coloratura of an inexhaustible imagination. His elocution recalled certain of Jarry's affected mannerisms of speech; for instance, the latter's "ubuesque" emphasis on insignificant details, and his penchant for truculent expressions and crude words. He also shared Jarry's taste for monumental practical jokes and even his contempt for sartorial elegance: he would go about for days wearing a frayed shirt and the same doubtful collar, his pockets bulging with tobacco, papers, and books.

The secret of his influence was less in the entertaining and stimulating power of his conversation than in a certain quality of soul, perceptible underneath the thick outward shell of his material sensuousness. While enjoying lustily and even greedily the good things of this earth, he never was in any way their slave, for inwardly he paid allegiance to an intrinsically pure dominion — the magic realm of dreams. His internal world held none of the eerie and dismal hallucinations of a Lautréamont, for instance. His reverie was elegiac, tender, and elevated. Even amidst the crudities of real life he could always evoke a thousand graceful and animated figures gliding and dancing in a dim, mysterious light, delicately tinged with a magic poetical radiance.

Once he thought he had found the living embodiment of his ideal in Marie Laurencin, vivacious, mischievous, enigmatic yet friendly, sophisticated and candidly naïve by turns, but always supremely alluring, with her tall, slender figure and her rich golden-brown hair. She became his "Muse," and for her in return he opened the door to the enchanting world of dreams. They were happy at first, but it did not last, and the poor poet was torn with anguish and despair. Many years later, during the war, when he saw the earth of France torn open by the trenches, he was reminded of his past love and remarked: "L'amour a retourné ma vie comme on retourne la terre dans la zone des armées" (3).

So far, beyond his journalistic tasks and paid compilations, he had never succeeded in persuading the publishers to accept

(3) Guillaume Apollinaire, "A l'Italie," *Calligrammes* (Paris: Nouvelle Revue Française, 1925), p. 164.

an original manuscript of his own. In 1909 the critic Paul Léautaud, dazzled by the personal magnetism and brilliance of the man, arranged to have a selection of his poems printed in the *Mercure de France*. Recognition was universal and instantaneous. Shortly afterwards (1910) he published, again with very marked success, a collection of short stories, *L'Hérésiarque et Cie*, drawn from episodes dating from the period of his first travels in Europe. All these works, though bearing the definite stamp of Apollinaire's original genius, owe very little, if anything, to Cubism. Some of them possess great charm, but they do not constitute in any way an innovation, being often reminiscent of the Romantic or of the Symbolist tradition. Apparently the poet was too firmly anchored in literary tradition to be able to apply to poetry or prose the radical changes which he did not hesitate to advocate in painting.

In 1911 an unexpected adventure tore him away from his moorings. On August 21 of that year the famous "Mona Lisa" was stolen from the Louvre. At once newspaper headlines all over the world magnified this unaccountable incident till it became an international sensation. On September 7 Guillaume Apollinaire was arrested and thrown into jail.

Apollinaire, who had never been very discriminate in his choice of friends, had associated for several years with a Belgian adventurer of the name of Géry. He had used the latter frequently as "secretary"; he had even given him shelter in his house on occasions of particular stress. Now Géry had been guilty of stealing ancient statuettes from the Louvre in the past, and detectives were on his track. Hastily running down their clues in the midst of the general excitement, the police jumped at the conclusion that Guillaume Apollinaire was the leader of an organized gang of thieves.

The poet was placed in a cell at La Santé; there he was designated by a number and no longer by his name; his fingerprints were taken; a judge grilled him mercilessly for several days; he was confronted with his supposed confederates, among whom was Picasso; in short, he was treated like a dangerous criminal.

Meanwhile his friends had started a campaign in his favor; they had no difficulty in showing how preposterous the accusation was. After six days he was given his freedom again.

On the unanimous testimony of his contemporaries, it is evident that the shock of this humiliating experience left a very deep and permanent mark on its victim. Although he affected to laugh and joke about the whole adventure, the instinctive terror that had struck him when he found himself in jail had actually destroyed the better part of his merry carelessness and self-assurance. Nor was he allowed to forget this unpleasant and distressing affair. A few years passed before the "Mona Lisa" was recovered and replaced in the Louvre; meanwhile Apollinaire was the subject of sly digs, even of open sarcasms on the part of dignified officials, conservative writers, and academic artists whom he had himself formerly attacked with the shafts of his irony. Very soon a profound change became noticeable in the embittered man's general outlook on life.

This change did not actually coincide with the enunciation of a new set of ideas by Apollinaire. Even in 1911 he had held very definite opinions, considered highly revolutionary, but these were limited to the theory of painting. When, however, his sudden imprisonment gave him the impression that his whole world was crumbling beneath him, he lost completely the instinctive reverence which had been to him a mental safeguard for certain forms of thought. This was not a conscious revolt against certain aspects of society, but the natural extension to the whole of existence of a philosophy which, as far as he was concerned, had been hitherto confined by circumstance to a certain department of art. From then on,

Apollinaire was to speak and write indefatigably on the
subject of "l'Esprit nouveau." But the public was not mis-
taken when it christened the new genre "littérature cubiste."
It was indeed the spirit of Cubism, now with his help spreading to poetry and the novel.

At the beginning of 1912 a few of Apollinaire's most faithful friends, including René Dalize, André Billy, and André
Salmon, who were aware of the alteration in his outlook,
founded with his assistance and mainly for his benefit a literary review which they called *Les Soirées de Paris*. Guillaume
Apollinaire wanted forthwith to start his crusade on behalf
of "l'Esprit nouveau." But this project raised difficulties and
created misgivings. His friends tried their utmost to protect
him against unfair attacks and to restore his self-confidence;
but certain of them, especially René Dalize, had little sympathy for the moral tendencies represented by Cubism.
Thereupon, for a very modest sum, Guillaume Apollinaire
bought out their interests in the review and pursued its publication on his own account until 1914, devoting all his energy
to the diffusion of the new doctrine. In 1913 he published a
volume of verse under the title *Alcools*, offering striking
examples of the new poetical technique — obscure, disjointed,
jerky, after the manner of the most angular and dislocated
Cubist paintings.

When the first World War broke out, Guillaume Apollinaire, who was not a French citizen, could have remained
quite safely a noncombatant. With characteristically generous
idealism, he at once took steps to become naturalized and then
enlisted in a regiment of artillery. In 1915 he was sent to the
front. For him the war was not a depressing and doleful
experience. He enjoyed the spiritual exaltation inspired by
constant danger, the proximity of death, and a thousand
weird and exciting adventures. Moreover, he could now see
all the outworn conventions, which he had himself but lately

discarded, collapsing one by one; and in this universal break-down of traditional values he found an inspiriting confirmation of his own views and of his fondest hopes. He went on writing, mostly poetry when he was in the trenches, novels when he was on leave. As is only human, he liked his absences from the front to be as long as possible. Once he applied for permission to go as far as Oran, in Algeria, because the time of the long journey was added to the regular number of days of leave to which he was entitled. . . . Anxious to become an officer, he succeeded in getting assigned to the infantry with the rank of second lieutenant. Then, on March 17, 1916, as he was reading the *Mercure de France* in the front line, a German shell, bursting at a distance, wounded him severely in the head.

For many weary months he was transported from hospital to hospital, undergoing operation after operation, till he was finally put on his feet again. With his head still wrapped in white bandages, he experienced in the Paris of 1917 the darkest moments of the long war, the French morale at its lowest ebb, evidently the end of a world; but he could also perceive, as though through a vision, the dawn of a new era glowing dimly in a hopeful, distant future.

It was under these circumstances that the conception of "Surrealism" came to him. The word *surréaliste* was used for the first time in connection with a play which he wrote during his convalescence, and which was performed on June 24, 1917, under the title *Les Mamelles de Tirésias — drame surréaliste.* Apollinaire did not imply in the word *surréaliste* all the complex notions which have since accrued to that term. Yet there cannot be any doubt but that he caught more than a glimpse of what was to be the eventual development of his own initiative. *Les Mamelles de Tirésias* was composed mainly of grotesque and farcical scenes after the manner of Jarry; but behind a rather crude caricature of our present-day existence it involved the mystic appeal of a supreme Verity.

Meanwhile Apollinaire's health, which had been seriously impaired by his wound, was showing alarming signs of breaking down altogether. He had been working very hard preparing his war poems for publication, under the title *Calligrammes,* and also completing his new novel, *La Femme assise.* Moreover, he was attached to the Board of Censors, and had the delicate and strenuous task of expurgating all untoward or indiscreet allusions from the text of the small vanguard literary reviews. He who had always been so kind and cheerful was now becoming irritable and nervous. In girth he had never been slight, but now he grew enormous. In an attempt to settle down and lead a more wholesome, well-regulated existence, he married on May 2, 1918, a young lady, Jacqueline by name, whom he had previously celebrated in his verses as "La Jolie Rousse." Tragically, at the beginning of November 1918, he fell a victim to the prevailing epidemic of influenza and succumbed on the ninth of that month. Among other manuscripts he left an essay which was published by the *Mercure de France* on the first of December, 1918, with a title which at once epitomizes and symbolizes the portent of his message, *L'Esprit nouveau et les poètes.*

In this spiritual testament of his, Guillaume Apollinaire emphasized what he considered to be the essential calling of the poet: "exalter la vie sous quelque forme qu'elle se présente" (4). Instead of being content to look at life from a particular and well-chosen angle, instead of selecting — as so many had done before him — only a few "things of beauty" to celebrate in his verses, he, like the Cubist painters, was moved by the imperious desire to hold within his embrace *all*

(4) "L'Esprit nouveau et les poètes," *Le Mercure de France,* December 1, 1918, p. 385.

things in their totality. Even the lowest, the crudest, the most banal, the most despised aspects of everyday existence, even the most hideous and repulsive actions committed in the war, were not to be excluded but joyously welcomed in their entirety. For they all contain a magic kernel of essential poetry which the vulgar may not perceive but which inspired men like Apollinaire himself can express with compelling power. The secret of his charm is his gift for discerning in the most humble forms of human experience an element of intense spirituality.

This, of course, cannot be achieved through careful, rational analysis, nor through cold-blooded dissection of the external aspects of the world. It can be realized only in a state of lyrical enthusiasm, when the soul of man enters into communion with the spirit of the whole Cosmos and the two vibrate together in perfect harmony. In order to rise to this exalted state, man has to leave behind discursive intelligence, which distinguishes and isolates him from the rest of creation. Then at last he can come into contact with the primitive, elemental forces that are the source of all superior, transcendental energy. A poet in the grip of such an intoxicating transport cannot be expected to draw a regular and undeviating image of all forms of reality.

Je suis ivre d'avoir bu tout l'univers (5),

says Guillaume Apollinaire appropriately. Precisely because in the process the rigid and too well-proportioned lines of our own world lose their imperative necessity, another world, richer and truer, blossoms within the soul of the artist or the poet.

When the poet reaches this ecstatic stage, he rises well above all human limitations. Like the Cubist painter, the

(5) Guillaume Apollinaire, "Vendémiaire," *Alcools* (Paris: Nouvelle Revue Française, 1932), p. 169.

Cubist poet brings us the revelation of another world, seen through the intuitive power of the mind and lying beyond the reach of the "normal" man. A few normal men may perhaps be initiated indirectly and may eventually catch a reflection of the "vision splendid" that illumines the spirit of an Apollinaire. To the majority, however, this vision will always remain inaccessible. Like the prophets of old, the modern poet will encounter incredulity and contempt. Yet he will remain confident in his mission, because he knows that he proclaims a world that is superhuman and, though challenging belief, supremely real and true. "C'est pourquoi," says Apollinaire, "vous trouverez trace de prophétie dans la plupart des ouvrages conçus d'après l'esprit nouveau" (6).

This absolute self-confidence of Guillaume Apollinaire's can be easily understood in view of his early religious experience. Brought up as a Catholic, he retained to the end his strong and implicit faith and never appeared in the rôle of a creature tormented with doubt and anxiously searching for hidden truth. It must be admitted that, in spite of not infrequent allusions to Catholic dogmas, the works of Apollinaire can hardly be considered as belonging to the domain of religious literature. Yet they all imply the conviction on the part of the author that he does possess the truth. His investigations were directed towards the discovery not so much of the authentic nature of that truth as of a process that would enable man to clear away the obstacles which stand embarrassingly in the path of the questing human mind.

Guillaume Apollinaire found that in France the first, the most insidious, perhaps the most formidable obstacle to any frank and sincere search for truth was the superstitious reverence for good taste. Many a Frenchman who goes clear

(6) "L'Esprit nouveau et les poètes," *Le Mercure de France*, December 1, 1918, p. 392.

over the hurdles of rationalism and common sense would balk at the prospect of infringing upon the unwritten laws of good taste. So Apollinaire declared war on "le bon goût." By that term he meant the set of conventions and prejudices, particularly developed in the old civilizations, that forbid the direct and unpolished expression of spontaneous and instinctive feelings. He openly revolted against the unjustifiable suppressions that conventions always imply. In order to give vent to his feelings in this regard, he bought in a Paris department store a cheap and horrible — but monumental — inkstand in gilt metal; this he displayed on all possible occasions as a material symbol of his utter contempt for the taboos which every "well-bred" man is supposed to observe meekly and submissively.

Similarly he fought against all the technical artifices and *procédés* which have done so much to smother inspiration and to sever literature from the domain of human emotion. That is why he very early in his career rejected all the rules of prosody, all the hitherto accepted methods of exposition, and claimed for himself unbounded freedom, the right to try his own hand and to express himself absolutely as he pleased. There was in his attitude something of the venturesome boldness of the gambler contemptuous of plodding, mediocre, and cheerless effort, ready to risk total loss or a fortune simply on the throw of the dice. In this way, he felt that writing was no longer a tedious task but a glorious enterprise with unlimited possibilities ahead — a vital, hopeful thrust into the future.

Yet it would be wrong to imagine Guillaume Apollinaire as a contemner of the past. In his essay, *L'Esprit nouveau*, he has explained at full length what he would like to retain of the contradictory qualities of both the Classicists and the Romanticists. As he himself wrote in a personal letter to a friend a few months before his death: "I only wanted to add new domains to arts and letters in general without in any way failing to appreciate the merits of the true masterpieces either of the past or of the present" (7). Further, commenting upon a very crude word which he had used in *L'Antitradizione futurista* in reference to a number of recognized glories of literature and art, he declared that this word "did not apply to the works of the ancient masters but to their names when set up as a barrier to the new generation" (8).

So, in spite of all his revolutionary outbursts, one sees him constantly impeded by his reverence for the spiritual ties linking him to traditional culture, which he feels loath to sever. He himself gave voice to the crying need for a hero capable of making us forget the immensities of memories among which our spirits exhaust themselves in endless wanderings. According to him, such a hero would be as much a benefactor to mankind as Christopher Columbus. If only man could drop the load of tradition that weighs so heavily on his soul! Not merely to lay aside that burden temporarily, but to lose it for ever! Then man would be free to go and find something new, something real, at last.

> Qui donc saura nous faire oublier telle ou telle partie du monde
> Où est le Christophe Colomb à qui on devra l'oubli d'un continent
> Perdre
> Mais perdre vraiment
> Pour laisser place à la trouvaille (9).

These last three lines appealed to the new, restless generation as an adequate formula for its innermost longings. They very soon became a slogan, and in the years following the first World War many there were who set their hearts on the

(7) Quoted by H. Fabureau, *Guillaume Apollinaire* (Paris: Nouvelle Revue Critique, 1932), p. 47.

(8) *Ibid.*

(9) "Toujours," *Calligrammes*, p. 111.

absolute, integral fulfillment of the program which these words implied. As for Guillaume Apollinaire himself, he was perpetually hovering between two irreconcilable domains. He was too strongly attached to the culture of the past to cut himself adrift entirely and launch blindly into the unknown; yet, though still belonging to our world, he opened up vast prospects in the other. Undoubtedly a great deal of his captivating charm is derived from the odd blending of these two opposed views of the universe.

Even if Apollinaire could not bring himself to destroy the commonly accepted construction of our cultivated mind, he succeeded in dissolving most of the intellectual "cement" that normally holds each and all of its elements in their proper setting. With large parts of the outer structure argued away, a view was to be had of the ordinarily impenetrable recesses. Further, throughout the whole edifice, partial dislocations set the various components of the ensemble at a queer angle, bringing about the weirdest and most startling effects, simply by inverting their normal customary order. In actual fact the fundamental aspects of reality were not in any way altered or damaged. Yet they were rearranged, very much after the fashion of the Cubist paintings, not in their ordinary positions and according to accepted rules of perspective but in absolutely new, unexpected, and most disconcerting places. As a result, each aspect depicted was more strongly, more forcibly individualized; yet at the same time it was set free to float in a vague, uncertain, hallucinatory atmosphere.

The suggestion of that illusory atmosphere was achieved by Apollinaire almost exclusively through the sheer power of words. He possessed the inborn gift of calling forth, by the juxtaposition of the most simple, unassuming vocables, spiritual entities beyond the grasp of our senses. Profoundly sensitive to the mysterious affinities between words, he was

Fernand Léger: *Composition No. 7* (1925)
Cubism becomes purely decorative

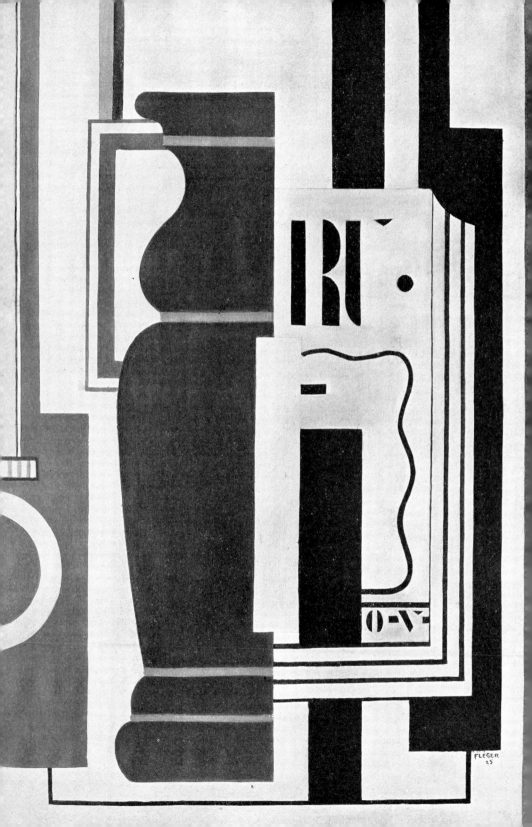

able by their association to evoke the most extraordinarily delicate shades of feeling. There is to his words a miraculous ring that a Mallarmé might have envied. Nevertheless these associations of words were not, as in the case of Mallarmé, the result of conscious, systematic effort. They came in the course of the rhythmic development of the sentences as these unfolded themselves spontaneously. His sentences may not have any strict, definite signification; often they do not seem designed to give any clear statement of a particular idea or fact; they unroll and spread by virtue of an internal force, being engendered, as it were, automatically, as they slowly but irresistibly progress and grow.

The origin of that internal force of verbal procreation is evidently within the depths of the poet's mind itself. Hence the exquisite quality and the penetrating charm of the current of thoughts issuing from this source. This current bears along intact marvelous "flowers" of spirituality which the mill of intellectual reasoning would undoubtedly have bruised or even crushed. Their unique fragrance arouses in us a nostalgic longing because they originate in the innermost recesses of the human soul; or, according to Apollinaire, because they are impregnated with the supreme spiritual essence that permeates the whole universe.

In order to start this magic flow of words and thoughts, Guillaume Apollinaire did not have recourse to strenuous and patient effort. He simply sat at his desk and let his pen run over the paper, allowing the sentences to form freely, independently, even incoherently. At first little but absurdities or platitudes were phrased. By and by, however, as the inward lyrical impulse gathered strength, the sentences would gradually fit together, correlate themselves, and finally expand into a continuous and regular development. Apollinaire felt then as if certain forces within himself, different and independent from his normal consciousness, were at last being allowed to display their potentialities. It seemed as if new beings in the mind of the poet were at work fashioning with surprising dexterity and ease a universe more glamorous and more real than that of the shoddy, mechanical forms which our intellectual reasoning and our senses are for ever attempting to impose upon our vision of things.

> Je sentais en moi des êtres neufs pleins de dextérité
> Bâtir et aussi agencer un univers nouveau (10).

Apollinaire, however, did not trust the spontaneous verbal development of his subconscious mind to the extent of giving to the public the crude and unpolished product of his automatic divagations. He never entirely lost control of his reveries; he always took care to direct the flux of images surging up from the depths of his personality into predefined and well-marked channels. Moreover, he obviously touched up and corrected his first drafts, using the resources of a thoroughly conscious intelligence in order to make his sketches into consummate works of art. This process is typically illustrative of Guillaume Apollinaire's literary position: though inclined, on principle, to give free rein to the instinctive mystic forces lying within him, he always felt reluctant to go to the very extremities implied by his own premises, and he would unobtrusively reintroduce an element of organizing intelligence in order to elaborate the data of his subconscious Ego. His works thus gained undeniably in external, artistic beauty; but to the more uncompromising poets, who were to come later, it seemed that he had stopped short of the full realization of his program. They assumed the duty of pursuing further the course that he had daringly initiated.

Intellectual elaboration is such an obvious element in Guillaume Apollinaire's work that it is possible to detect in

(10) "La Petite Auto," *Calligrammes*, p. 68.

his style a certain number of habitual methods which he uses
with the definite intention of obtaining a particular effect.
These methods differ considerably from the ordinary literary
rules, yet they are evidence of a perfectly conscious technique
on his part.

Apollinaire's most striking trait is perhaps his intent to
astonish the reader almost at any cost. Since he was admittedly bent upon discovering "something new," and as something new invariably arouses a feeling of surprise, he naturally
came to identify novelty with surprise, overlooking the fact
that the degree of surprise is not by any means in direct relation to the degree of novelty. So, not without a certain
superficiality, he declared: "Le nouveau est tout dans la
surprise. C'est ce qu'il y a en lui de plus neuf, de plus
vivant" (11).

His favorite means of provoking surprise was through
mystification. He liked to indulge in all sorts of jests, from
subtle pleasantry to grotesque hoax, all calculated first to lead
the trusting reader astray, then to startle him suddenly with
the truth. Although these jests are at first sight reminiscent
of those practised by Jarry, they are as a rule inspired by a
somewhat different spirit. Jarry was consistently sardonic
and bent on destruction. Apollinaire's laughter, on the contrary, almost always sounds a cheerful note; it seems as if he
were jostling good-naturedly a rather slow-witted but well-
liked companion, pushing him off the beaten track in order
to show him the joys of adventure and discovery.

The most extreme examples of combined surprise and
mystification are offered in his "poèmes-conversations." If
Apollinaire had contracted to turn in manuscript on a given
day, and inspiration was definitely lagging, he would sit at a
table, preferably in a café, and put down, one after another,

(11) "L'Esprit nouveau et les poètes," *Le Mercure de France*, December 1,
1918, p. 391.

fragments of sentences spoken by his friends or overheard from strangers. These bits of conversation had absolutely no connection with each other, though certain zealous readers and a few over-shrewd critics worked hard to find an intelligible meaning in them, and sometimes succeeded in persuading themselves that they had discovered satisfactory clues. . . . As a matter of fact, these "poèmes-conversations" are not altogether devoid of charm. They can best be compared to those old kaleidoscopes in which loose fragments of many-colored glass, seen through a small tube against a brilliant light, produced curious and fantastic patterns by their unexpected and ever-changing combinations. Similarly, the sentences strung together by Apollinaire may not have any definite counterpart in the world of reality, but they stimulate our imagination and enable us to visualize a new and motley supernatural creation.

With a poem by Apollinaire as with a kaleidoscope, the first impression obtained is often one of baffled disappointment: all the normal relations between known forms seem to have been hopelessly shuffled and jumbled. For instance, in an ordinary piece of French poetry or prose, the articulations between phrases and their respective interdependence are strongly marked by punctuation. In most of his later poems Apollinaire did away with all punctuation. It has been said that this innovation was suggested to him by the example of certain liturgic songs of the Catholic Church which are uniformly psalmodized, regardless of grammatical construction. Though this explanation is only hypothetical, it is indicative of the lofty reaches of Apollinaire's verse; like a religious hymn, his poetry strives to create an elevating sentiment, tending upwards towards the sublime. This can be achieved only if the spirit is liberated from petty details and if an enveloping mystic atmosphere pervades and lifts up the soul of man.

The impression of such an atmosphere Apollinaire tried to create by means of a singular typographical technique. He attempted it especially in the collection of poems which — for that very reason — he called *Calligrammes*. There, instead of having the verses printed in straight lines suggestive of uniformity and regularity, he tried to have them arranged to suit the sentiment they were supposed to express. For example, in order to convey the impression of rain, he made the letters look as if they had dripped on the page, vertically, one by one (12). Again, giving way to his own mystifying humor, he had the words of his poem *La Petite Auto* printed in such a way as to represent a little automobile, complete with wheels and chauffeur (13).

But such extremes of extravaganza are not frequent in Apollinaire's works. His earlier productions, especially those collected in *Alcools* are, as a rule, quite intelligible, not differing too aggressively from the pattern of poetry in vogue in France at that time. In his later pieces, however, as the examples from the *Calligrammes* show, he definitely forsakes the traditional forms and upholds vehemently a newer technique proceeding from his new outlook on life and art.

In spite of certain variations in his technique, there are permanent traits related to the temperament of the man himself which give to his poetry a distinctive character. The most engaging, perhaps, is an elegiac sensibility which enables him to infuse into such age-old themes as the passing of the years, the glamor of woman, the deception of love, the harmony of nature, the stimulating virtue of war, a deeply moving and thoroughly personal appeal. The delicate tracery of his figurative symbols seems to hold in its web an iridescent mist of melancholy and hope, whilst, from time to time, the pangs of deep, secret suffering are revealed in brief flashes of

(12) "Il pleut," *Calligrammes*, p. 64.
(13) "La Petite Auto," *Calligrammes*, p. 69.

intense lyrical emotion. In contrast to this almost sentimental strain, there is in Guillaume Apollinaire's nature a vigorous, ardent, even violent sensuousness, expressing itself in powerful suggestions of the most material kind. These concrete aspects stand out vividly, almost hauntingly, before us and constitute a firm and solid counterpart to the poet's elusive spiritual divagations. Adding to the complexity of the whole, Apollinaire's reminiscent erudition often recalls by indirect and learned allusions the twisted and bizarre characteristics of the Alexandrian school of Greek literature. This composite mixture of heterogeneous elements faithfully reflects the unsettled outlook of a man typically representative of a transition period. Yet such was his gift of lyric creation that, in spite of numerous blemishes, many of his poems will undoubtedly remain as an enduring testimony to his lofty spirit.

In his short stories and in his novels, Guillaume Apollinaire was not so successful by far. Yet he displayed in them perhaps even more strongly than in his verse the new tendencies which were making their way in the field of modern thought and literature. His best short stories are contained in *L'Hérésiarque et Cie*, and he left three fairly important novels: *L'Enchanteur pourrissant*, *Le Poète assassiné*, and *La Femme assise*. He had also begun a novel on the subject of *Les Mormons*, but he never finished that work, though he included several fragments of it in *La Femme assise*.

In all these writings, the dislocation of the forms of reality — a process which was typical of the Cubist technique — is carried almost to excess. The narrative is broken up arbitrarily into short or long passages, arranged in direct sequence but with almost no ascertainable connection between them, interrupted by digressions, personal reflections, or unexpected anecdotes. All statements are made abruptly, without any preparation or transition, in a manner suggestive of the angles and bare surfaces to be found in the paintings of the same period. The plot — in so far as a plot is discernible at all — proceeds spasmodically in an atmosphere of unbridled fancy and odd supernatural occurrence, carrying the reader into a half-real, half-imaginary world where the objects are solid enough, although their setting has none of the compelling stability that our senses find in normal circumstances. Everything there seems to wobble. . . .

Is this the "superior" world of which Apollinaire had promised us a glimpse? Perhaps so, since a deep religiosity permeates this extraordinary realm — not a general religiosity, but a definite obsession with the Catholic dogmas of transsubstantiation and papal infallibility, together with an incongruous display of curiosity concerning certain aspects of Mormonism. Alongside these spiritual tonalities are sounded somewhat too frequently the harsh and discordant notes of cruelty and sex. Strange outbursts of sadism call up disturbingly the truly infernal abysses existing in human consciousness. Doubtless we thus become aware of the penetrating excursions of the author beneath the smooth surface of conventional sentiments, and of his sincere attempts to grasp something more essential than what our ordinary literature has to offer. Yet on the whole the discoveries made by Apollinaire in this respect are contradictory, incomplete, inadequate; and the final result is decidedly disappointing.

One of the causes for such insufficiency is that Guillaume Apollinaire rarely took the time or the trouble to bring his works to a point of perfection. But the reason for this was not always hurry or carelessness. He was fully aware that at that early stage in the evolution of the new art it was impossible for him to achieve a final masterpiece: he could only gather material for generations to come. He realized that the few elements of truth which he could disengage from underneath the heavy layer of conventionality were very simple and modest indeed. He did not feel disheartened, however, hoping that in the future great results would come from these insignificant beginnings. As he wrote in *L'Esprit nouveau*: "Ce sont des matériaux qu'amasse le poète, qu'amasse l'esprit nouveau et ces matériaux formeront un fond de vérité dont la simplicité, la modestie ne doit pas rebuter, car les conséquences, les résultats peuvent être de grandes, de bien grandes choses" (14).

For the future, he visualized the birth of a new conception of life and art of equal value and beauty with the conception for which since his schooldays he had retained a profound respect and admiration, the art of ancient Greece. But the Moderns, he held, should not try to ape the Greeks. In their own way, they should pursue their own truth, their own "realism," which should not be a vulgar account of the external features of things, such as was attempted by the literary school which had appropriated for its own use the title of Realist, but an earnest endeavor to reach a higher reality, with all its unexplored wonders. If that goal could ever be attained, contemporary poets, thought Apollinaire, would not have fought and striven in vain; "Leurs recherches seront utiles; elles constitueront les bases d'un nouveau réalisme qui ne sera peut-être pas inférieur à celui si poétique et si savant de la Grèce antique" (15).

With a strange mixture of humility and pride, Apollinaire has revealed his ambitious transcendental dreams and confessed his errors and mistakes, pleading for all those who, like himself, ever go forward as pioneers of the absolute and the infinite.

(14) "L'Esprit nouveau et les poètes," *Le Mercure de France*, December 1, 1918, p. 390.
(15) *Ibid.*

Nous ne sommes pas vos ennemis
Nous voulons vous donner de vastes et d'étranges domaines
Où le mystère en fleurs s'offre à qui veut le cueillir
Il y a là des feux nouveaux des couleurs jamais vues
Mille phantasmes impondérables
Auxquels il faut donner de la réalité

. . . .

Pitié pour nous qui combattons toujours aux frontières
De l'illimité et de l'avenir
Pitié pour nos erreurs pitié pour nos péchés (16).

Next to Guillaume Apollinaire, the most important of the Cubist writers is undoubtedly Max Jacob. Although Jacob possessed neither the personal magnetism nor the philosophical aptitude of the leader of the school, he attracted nearly as much attention from the general public on account of his exalted mysticism, which in his case was curiously blended with a thoroughly simian extravagance.

Max Jacob came of a modest but thriving Jewish family living in Quimper, a small town in Brittany. His father did a good business in a small clothing and antique shop, while upstairs romped and frolicked a swarm of noisy and unruly children. In this lively and on the whole normal environment, young Max Jacob, born on July 11, 1876, was profoundly unhappy. Of course he received his share of teasing from his brothers and sisters and perhaps somewhat more than his share of punishment from his mother, who was not a miracle of calm forbearance. The neurotic child dramatized these incidents into imaginary tortures. Three times he attempted to commit suicide. It is, indeed, not always easy to discern in Max Jacob's behavior how much is sincere and how much mere acting; yet his whole attitude during his childhood seems to indicate that he was suffering acutely — though without apparent cause — and that, in his despair, he

(16) "La Jolie Rousse," *Calligrammes*, p. 220.

was often seized by a frenzy of destruction which he even sometimes turned against himself.

One of the main reasons for the boy's unbalanced outlook seems to have been the utter lack of any form of spiritual idealism in his education. His parents had given up the practice of the Hebraic religion altogether, living themselves and bringing up their children as atheists. Probably without being himself aware of it, Max Jacob must have craved an inspiration which he did not find at home. He did not find that inspiration at school either. There, in spite of his application and his cleverness, he did not distinguish himself particularly among his schoolmates. For a while, he took refuge in a chimeric world of his own creation, the elements of which were drawn from the works of Edgar Allan Poe, from the fantastic tales of E. T. A. Hoffman, and also, it must be said, from the unexpurgated text of the *Arabian Nights*. But this was only a temporary escape from his besetting difficulties.

When at the age of eighteen he had to make definite plans for his future, he decided to go to Paris to enter the Ecole Coloniale, where the regular French colonial administrators are trained. Max Jacob was attracted much less by the prospect of an administrative career than by the glamor of remote and mysterious lands beyond the seas which he would color with all the magnificent hues of a vivid imagination. He was still enveloped in a haze of exotic contemplation when he was brutally awakened by the necessity of doing his military service. He found the crudeness of the barracks most unpleasant and even painful; but after six weeks, much to his own relief and that of his instructors, he was declared unfit for service on account of general debility and allowed to return home.

Back in Quimper again, the inevitable crisis was precipitated. The young man obviously indulged in vague but irrepressible aspirations which could not be satisfied within the framework of a well-regulated practical existence. These aspirations were now struggling for an outlet in one direction or another. Within his home, Max Jacob brought all his family to the verge of hysterical exasperation by hammering out the symphonies of Beethoven on the piano with merciless enthusiasm. At the same time he went into ecstasies over the beauty of the Breton landscape and announced that his vocation was to be a painter, much to the dismay of his father, who could see no tangible profit in art. Finally Max ran away from home, after surreptitiously purloining from a drawer a few francs that his thrifty mother had saved.

Back in Paris, his first step was to hand in his formal resignation to the director of the Ecole Coloniale. Then followed years of trial and misery, which were all the more distressing for him because he had no guide to follow in the quest of his own soul. At first he attempted to join a well-known school of painting, but his shabby and puny appearance brought on him such scornful remarks on the part of masters and students alike — one of them even asking him if he had come to sell pencils or shoe-laces — that he withdrew immediately, overcome with humiliation and bitterness. For a while he managed to eke out a living as a piano accompanist to an Italian actress attempting to become a grand opera singer. But even that resource came to an end.

Upon the advice of a practical-minded acquaintance, he set himself up as an art critic. At once he met with unqualified success. For several months Max Jacob went about importantly, interviewing painters and visiting galleries, with a black frock coat, a monocle and a top hat. Then suddenly and impulsively he threw off this bluff and sham, and, caring little for recognition and reward, resumed his quest for that truth which alone could satisfy his innate sincerity.

Still painting and writing at random without master or

method, though always in dead earnest, he went through a gamut of bizarre jobs in the course of a few years, being in turn cabinetmaker, lawyer's clerk, shop assistant, secretary to a rich philanthropist, tutor, and at last — as he himself puts it — nursemaid. There would have been an element of tragedy in these circumstances had not Jacob — perhaps as a kind of defense reaction — hastened to turn all his misadventures into droll and absurd comedies. It was in the midst of this erratic and disjointed existence that he had his first and only serious love affair. A certain Madame Pfeipfer, who was nineteen and gay, cast a benevolent eye upon the eager and ardent young man. Their liaison abounded in comical episodes, as the lover, who was anything but physically impressive, assumed the character of a redoubtable bandit in order to terrify the jealous but timorous husband and his friends. After a few months, however, he and his ladylove parted company without heartbreak, for Max Jacob was yearning for something higher than a banal sentimental attachment.

His friendship with Picasso, which has already been referred to, helped him greatly towards a realization of his latent potentialities. At the beginning of their acquaintance, in 1901, it was Max Jacob who gave comfort and assistance to the struggling Spaniard, even sharing his extremely modest lodging with him for a while. Gradually, however, it fell to Picasso, who was by far the stronger of the two, to encourage his oversensitive companion in his many hours of despondency and gloom. Picasso seems to have been the first to perceive the true originality of his friend's mind, and he repeated to him constantly: "Tu es le seul poète de l'époque" (17).

Subsequently Picasso went on a visit to Spain. When he came back to Paris in 1904, he found Max Jacob completely

(17) Robert Guiette, "Vie de Max Jacob," *La Nouvelle Revue Française,* July 1, 1934, p. 14.

discouraged by his failure to accomplish anything worth while. All else having disappointed him, he was striving pathetically to attain at least a modicum of worldly respectability. Indignantly Picasso exclaimed, "Qu'est-ce que c'est que cette existence? . . . Vis comme les poètes!" (18) — and Max Jacob's life forthwith took a new turn.

That same year Picasso had established himself in the "bateau-lavoir," No. 13 Rue Ravignan. Max Jacob followed him to the same street, renting a room close by at No. 7. There Jacob passed the truly heroic period of his life. He soon met and appreciated Guillaume Apollinaire; André Salmon came to be one of his most intimate friends. But above all he found in Cubism an echo of his own fervent inward longings. He contributed personally to the formation of the Cubist theories, and his room in time became the center of motley gatherings where the spirit of Montmartre found perhaps its most definite and striking expression.

This room — Max Jacob's only room — opening on to an inner court as narrow and as deep as a well, was so dark that an oil lamp had to be kept burning even in the middle of the day. It was at once sordid and yet curiously tidy. Placed neatly side by side on a shelf were an old chipped cup, a washing basin, and an empty sardine can in which he used to fry eggs. There were no window curtains, but the layer of dirt on the window-pane was thick enough to ensure complete privacy. The confined air held the effluvia of petroleum, frankincense, and stale tobacco — also of the ether in which Max Jacob found comfort and inspiration. On the walls were scribbled esoteric formulae and fantastic drawings, for Jacob, in his search for an unknown Absolute, had become an adept in occultism. Further he became thoroughly versed in phrenology, astrology, palmistry, and even cartomancy. Many

(18) *Ibid.*, August 1, 1934, p. 250.

came to consult him, for he was always ready to interrupt his own work in order to tell the fortune of anyone who called, whether a friend in trouble, a superstitious artist, or simply a gossip of the neighborhood.

Every Monday evening he held regular receptions which the Cubist Bohemians attended in large numbers. Then Max Jacob was seen at his best, reciting poetry or showing his latest pictures, always nervous and fidgety, but elaborately courteous and supremely entertaining. His lean frame was clad in bizarre clothes from the family shop in Quimper, but the attention of his guests was soon concentrated on his eager face, with its long curved nose, bluish cheeks, and piercing eyes beneath an expanse of shiny bald pate. He could talk endlessly on almost any question, stringing together amazing collections of words with inexhaustible volubility. His comic verve was prodigious. He jumped from one subject to another, finding a ludicrous side to the most banal anecdotes and in the commonest occurrences a pretext for his sarcasm. He made fun of everything and everybody, including himself; the only one he respected was Picasso, his friend. Gesticulating, now with the effrontery of a monkey, now with the burlesque of a clown, he kept his audience constantly amused and laughing.

Nevertheless there was clearly perceptible in the man a profoundly honest and earnest quality, in a way almost ascetic and monachal. Though by no means a puritan, he gave little attention to women. Constantly, however, he opened his heart to children and to all those who were in distress or suffering. Whenever he was able to earn a little money — by selling one of his water-colors, for instance — the greater part of it went in discreet almsgiving to people more miserable than himself. His caustic remarks and ludicrous grimaces probably constituted only an instinctive protest both against a world which denied him the fulfillment of his aspirations and against himself; for he was still yearning sincerely for something infinite, yet he fell extremely far short of his own lofty ideal. His curiosity about occult sciences, his weakness for ether, his enthusiasm for Cubism were but indirect means of attaining to the realm which was beyond the reach of his reason or his senses.

Suddenly the long-hoped-for illumination came. On the evening of September 22, 1909, as Max Jacob was returning from the Bibliothèque Nationale to his room on the Rue Ravignan, there appeared to him what he took to be an entrancing supernatural vision of the Deity Himself. He has recorded this overwhelming experience in burning terms of ecstatic exaltation: "Ma chair est tombée par terre! j'ai été déshabillé par la foudre! Oh! impérissable seconde! oh! vérité! vérité! larmes de la vérité! joie de la vérité! inoubliable vérité! Le Corps Céleste est sur le mur de la pauvre chambre!" (19) The day after, still wild with excitement, he rushed to a church asking to be baptized at once. A jovial priest, suspecting one of his usual antics, laughed at what he thought to be merely a jest, and, self-consciously, the little Jewish convert withdrew.

He then embarked on a most extraordinary mode of existence. Neither ether nor occultism nor Cubism was abandoned, but they became absorbed, integrated, as it were, within the compass of his Christian mystic revelation. Under the influence of ether, he felt he could converse with angels. The practice of spiritism, he was sure, brought him into communion with the blessed souls of the departed. Cubism for him was but a means of evoking graphically a supreme religious ideal. Soon he fell to prophesying. He went regularly to the Church of the Sacred Heart in Montmartre, praying aloud night and day; much to the dismay of his friends,

(19) Max Jacob, "La Révélation," *La Défense de Tartufe* (Paris: Société Littéraire de France, 1919), p. 31.

he often experienced, even in public, spectacular outbursts of tearful ecstasy.

Max Jacob's sincere mysticism did not, however, eliminate the grotesque clowning which had been for so many years a part of his personality. His character was now set, and even a change in spiritual outlook could not modify its essential nature. Certain of his declarations contain a strange mixture of a profound Christian religiosity with a curious emtionalism and cunning. In explaining how he could extract from God forgiveness of his sins, he said: "If I have sinned horribly on a certain day, then on the following day . . . I choke, I sob, I cry, I beat my face, my breast, my limbs, my hands; I bleed, I make the sign of the cross with my blood, with my tears. In the end God is taken in" (20). He carried his proselytism enthusiastically into the most unexpected situations and places. Once in a cabaret in Montmartre he undertook to convert a lady of light virtue — until her "protector," a huge fierce-looking Negro, stepped in and, seizing Max Jacob's thumbs, broke them both with a sudden jerk.

In spite of such misadventures Max Jacob now experienced, with a feeling of complete inward fulfillment of his aspirations, the urgent desire to communicate his message more effectively. As early as 1904 he had written two long tales for children, *Le Roi Kaboul et le marmiton Gauvin* and *Le Géant du soleil*, which had attracted the attention of a few connoisseurs. But it was only after his mystic illumination that his career as a writer really began. A Jewish picture dealer, Kahnweiler by name, about to start a publishing enterprise in addition to his art gallery, asked Max Jacob to submit the manuscript of a book. Max Jacob gave him *Saint Matorel* (1909). *Saint Matorel* traced the life of an imaginary saint bearing a striking similarity to the person

(20) Quoted by H. Fabureau, *Max Jacob* (Paris: Nouvelle Revue Critique, 1935), p. 40.

of the author himself. This was soon afterwards followed by *Les Œuvres mystiques et burlesques de Frère Matorel* (1911), in which were collected most of the poems written by Jacob in preceding years. Finally came a play, *Le Siège de Jérusalem, grande tentation céleste de Saint Matorel* (1912). About this time he also composed a series of poems, allegedly translations of old Breton folk songs; these appeared under the title of *La Côte* (1913).

These productions brought to Max Jacob wide recognition — and prosperity. He did not leave Montmartre, however, nor his room on the Rue Ravignan, nor did he change immediately his eccentric ways of living. His odd manners contributed almost as much as his talent to make him popular and welcome in the fashionable salons of the capital. Once more he went about with his top hat, being now the qualified and official representative of Cubist literature in society. Meanwhile Montmartre was slowly losing its old appeal, and Max Jacob, who had not so long ago written on the walls of his room the motto "Ne jamais aller à Montparnasse," was now to be seen from time to time at the "Deux Magots." . . .

The World War at first made but little impression on Max Jacob, still lost in his mystic rapture. On December 17, 1914, he had a second vision similar to that of 1909; on February 18, 1915, he succeeded at long last in receiving baptism, having Pablo Picasso himself for a godfather! He then wrote, in the most typical Cubist idiom, a collection of autobiographical poems, *Le Cornet à dés* (1917), and he gave an account of his religious experiences in *La Défense de Tartufe, extases, remords, visions, prières, poèmes et méditations d'un Juif converti* (1919).

The post-war period placed Max Jacob in an awkward and equivocal situation. He had left the Rue Ravignan, which was now completely deserted by artists, and very soon he had to abandon Montmartre altogether, as it was swamped by foreign tourists. He had become, especially since the death of Guillaume Apollinaire, one of the recognized and best-qualified exponents of advanced literary doctrines in France. As he had found his "Truth," however, he could not be in complete harmony with a bewildered new generation still groping for a personal conception of life. Yet the new generation was taking full advantage of the ground won previously by the Cubists and was progressing along very similar lines; moreover, Max Jacob could not but feel sincerely sympathetic towards efforts which were identical in spirit with what his own had been just a few years before. So there was more than one connecting link between them, after all; for a while the influence of the new-fangled "Dadaism" was clearly noticeable in certain of his works, such as *Le Cinématoma* (1920) and *Le Laboratoire central* (1921).

Nevertheless, Max Jacob must have realized that he was no longer in the van of the forward-marching host. Secretly he wanted to withdraw from a world that was outdistancing him at an ever-increasing pace. In 1921, after an automobile accident which resulted in his spending several weeks in a hospital, he decided to retire and meditate in peace. He repaired to the small village of Saint-Benoît-sur-Loire, not far from Orléans, and stayed there for seven years, taking up his abode first at the parsonage and later with the custodian of an old deserted monastery dating back to the time of the Merovingian kings. When his friends from Paris came occasionally to visit him, he took special pleasure in guiding them through the gardens and the monastic cells, always carrying with him an enormous, jingling bunch of keys. When alone, he spent much of his time in devout meditation, the rest in painting water-colors or in writing indefatigably. There he composed numerous works: his poetical testament, *Art poétique* (1922); long novels like *Le Terrain Bouchaballe* (1923) and *Filibuth ou la montre en or* (1923); edifying pamphlets such as

L'Homme de chair et l'homme reflet (1924); and also poems,
perhaps less edifying, such as *Visions infernales* (1924).

Gradually, however, he seems to have tired of this solitary,
monachal retreat, and in 1928 he returned to Paris. He is
still living there, apparently content, though to some extent
forgotten. He goes nearly every day to Montmartre, but now
only to pray at the Basilica of the Sacred Heart (21).

The works of Max Jacob do not present the same consistency and harmonious development as those of Guillaume
Apollinaire. This is probably due chiefly to the fundamental
instability of the former, who for many years was a true "wan-
dering Jew" with an undefined ideal, in quest of a goal which
he could not himself determine, dabbling in everything,
leaving his mark everywhere, exploring alternately the most
grandiose and the most grotesque aspects of existence, often
weary and despondent, yet sustained in his search by an in-
vincible pertinacity. In his case, however, obstinacy was not
synonymous with patience. Dejected on account of his repeated failures to attain his goal, neurotic and unbalanced,
he curiously combined a persistent enthusiasm for the sublime
with a concentrated fury against a disappointing reality.

In this blending of idealism and subversive madness —
which is by no means exceptional among those of his race —
the desire for destruction was at first sight the most evident
feature. It was probably reinforced by the inward dissatisfaction prevailing among certain groups of young men at that
period; it was in perfect alignment with the program of the
Cubists, who wanted to make a clean sweep of the past. The
corrosive irony of Max Jacob was directed not only against a
few outmoded forms of culture but against the whole world,
including himself. In particular he seems to have set himself
to revile and destroy everything that was noble and respected

(21) It has been reported that Max Jacob has lately gone back to his
retreat of Saint-Benoît-sur-Loire.

in man; personally assuming the rôle of universal buffoon, he played the part with an alarming naturalness.

He ridiculed indiscriminately all the concepts and sentiments for which every normal Frenchman entertains an avowed or a secret reverence. The stateliness of classical antiquity, the moral standards of mediaeval chivalry, the prestige of towering literary reputations, the emotion of love, the imperious categories of rational thinking, all served indifferently as targets for his incessant sarcasms. The process he employed most frequently in order to bring discredit on the various forms of reality was that of systematic parody. By mimicking in a ludicrous manner the most respected features of our world, he made it impossible for one to take seriously the original models of his grotesque imitations. At the basis of his caricatural displays was a most distressing postulate, namely, that the world as it appears to us is just as absurd as the preposterous representations offered by Max Jacob. It was therefore unnecessary to try to distinguish the former from the latter, and they might well be relegated together to the domain of absolute inanity.

This was achieved to a great extent by means of an incoherent verbalism. Max Jacob, like many "modern" authors, delights in letting a continuous flow of sentences run unrestrainedly from the depths of his consciousness. Yet while other poets hope in the free association of words to find gems of super-rational beauty, Max Jacob's aim in marshaling his words is avowedly destructive. He does not cultivate spiritual consonances but rejoices in discords and clashes. He likes to bring together words which have no mutual affinities; for instance, he might combine an expression applying particularly to an old Greek legend with a technical term connected with ultramodern machinery. The incompatibility of the emotional connotations attached to such different words at first causes a feeling of unpleasant surprise; then the antago-

nistic energies contained in the individual words begin to
militate against each other until they grate and grind together, leaving in the end an impression of fundamental
disharmony and universal incongruity.

Yet there is nothing either woeful or obnoxious in Max
Jacob's verbalism. He reminds us of a clown in a circus,
cutting capers and turning somersaults, performing tricks
and prancing about, arousing laughter by his assumed clumsiness and his elaborately stupid mimicry of the most sensible
actions of men. His extraordinary combinations of words
often resemble nothing so much as acrobatic stunts, entertaining on account of the virtuosity they imply, and at the
same time intended to convey devastating allusions to all
accepted and respected forms of literature and art. Thus his
keen and penetrating humor tore to pieces the glittering and
elegant frills which Romanticism and Symbolism had artificially draped around modern poetry. So Max Jacob has
assisted perhaps more than any of our contemporaries in
ridding the French sentence of all its superfluous literary
ornaments and in reducing it to a plain, angular bareness
reminiscent of the most aggressive Cubist paintings. Further-
more, his verbal eccentricity struck at intellectual reasoning
itself. Only too often, indeed, does the compelling authority
of discursive logic rest upon formal links between cleverly
worded propositions. By ruining on principle the power of
carefully arrayed words, Max Jacob assailed the organizing
force that is behind them, thus bringing about a widespread
collapse of our accepted system of reasoning, whose façade
seems very impressive but whose foundation is more often
than not completely illusory.

But once the field of human experience has been cleared
of all rational construction, what remains but a choice between the supernatural and mere nonsense? Both the supernatural and the nonsensical abound in Max Jacob's works,

often inextricably mixed. Few modern French poets have had a more intense perception of the place of mystery in our lives. While most writers try to grasp the comprehensible relationship linking one aspect of the world with another, he is mainly concerned with the strangeness, the inexplicableness of the universe. Like many of the Cubist painters, he is inclined to neglect the outstanding characteristics of things and to attach himself to the elusive, ineffable, evanescent qualities which appear to him the really essential.

Towards these essential, though impalpable, qualities, he always displays a marked reverence. He does not allow himself consciously to distort them for the sake of a particular literary effect. He does simplify them — again after the manner of the Cubist painters — stripping them of what he considers accessory and adventitious, but earnestly attempting to show them in their integral character without artificial adjustment of any sort. So we frequently find in his works fragments of intense and precise realism, always presented soberly, squarely, abruptly. Yet since their usual rational supports have been withdrawn, these blocks of reality seem to float on the surface of a misty, translucent expanse, spreading indefinitely into the unknown.

Thus it comes about that many of Max Jacob's productions bear a striking analogy to the visions that arise within us during the hours of sleep. In fact, Max Jacob is one of the first French writers to have made use deliberately of the material provided by dreams. Recent psychological discoveries in the field of the subconscious have emphasized the informative value of dream phenomena; but these theories were not yet known when Max Jacob started to write, and it was intuition alone which led him to ascribe a peculiar significance to such manifestations.

He, however, did not try to interpret dreams in terms of human activities or interests. He recognized their eminent importance in themselves, and he was content to let them reveal their justification in their own intrinsic worth. In the same way, most of his writings constitute self-justified and independent entities, in no way obligated to give an account of external circumstance. They form in themselves a self-sufficient creation, being their own end and their own justification. The idea of the self-supporting, autonomous work of art was very common among Cubist painters. So Max Jacob came to compose poems without any relation to external reality, without any subject, without any signification whatever — "pure" poems. In these phantasmagorical creations it is impossible to discern any intention or meaning; at best one may distinguish in them weird forms, instinct with a monstrous life, passing and melting into one another like misshapen figures in a feverish nightmare.

Of course, there was no question of encaging such monsters within the regular limits of any given type of poetry. All normal rules as to rhyme, rhythm, or the number of syllables to a line had to be discarded. Apart from their general "poetical" tone, the better part of the poems written by Max Jacob look very much like prose. He himself gave them the name of "poèmes en prose." This was not altogether a new invention on his part. During the Romantic period, Aloysius Bertrand, with similar extra-rational intentions, had introduced short writings of an analogous tenor. Later Baudelaire and Rimbaud had composed similar pieces. But, apparently because literary evolution was not then far enough advanced, the new *genre* had met at first with more curiosity than approval. Max Jacob, on the contrary, was immediately copied by countless followers, and the "poème en prose" attained so much success that it became the essential literary mold into which the Surrealists, a few years later, poured the most typical of their productions.

So the rôle played by Max Jacob in the development of

contemporary French literature can now be accurately perceived and defined. His personal literary achievements are
not in themselves of exceptional worth or importance, owing
perhaps to the equivocal character of the man himself, buffoon
and prophet rolled into one. Yet similar contrasts were
noticeable in many young men of the same period. The
Cubists relied mainly upon mystification as a means of breaking the shackles of the past, but at the same time they were
consumed with the desire to attain an absolute ideal. If they
failed to reach their overambitious goal, they were nevertheless, as Guillaume Apollinaire had already discerned, preparing the way for the future. In that work of preparation, Max
Jacob, who identified himself so completely with the Cubist
generation, has undoubtedly played both a decisive and an
outstanding part.

The other Cubist writers are less important by far than
Guillaume Apollinaire and Max Jacob. Two of them, however, André Salmon and Pierre Reverdy, deserve more than
a cursory reference. Their works have a distinctly representative value, illustrating opposite though complementary aspects of the Cubist doctrine. They display the richness and
complexity of a movement which admitted within the general Cubist style all sorts of modalities and variations, rang-
ing from the reduction of our world into solid blocks of
essential qualities to the other extreme of the mystic evocation of an ethereal and metaphysical atmosphere. Of these
two complementary tendencies the former was clearly embodied in literature by André Salmon, while Pierre Reverdy
spontaneously inclined towards the latter.

André Salmon, born in Paris on October 4, 1881, was a
young and sensitive adolescent when Symbolism reached the
height of its prestige. He was very strongly influenced by the
best poets of that school. He was less interested in the literary

procédés by which some of the Symbolists achieved pretty but superficial "masterpieces" than impressed by the earnest longing for an ideal absolute evinced by a poet like Mallarmé. He likewise felt the urge to penetrate beyond the dull mediocrity of everyday existence. He had already spent several years in Russia as a young boy; at the age of eighteen he had the opportunity of joining the staff of the French embassy in St. Petersburg, and he eagerly seized this chance for travel and adventure. When he returned to Paris in 1902, he was, on account of this long association with Slav mentality, more uncertain in his aspirations, more dissatisfied, and more perplexed than ever. He joined the circle of Jarry's admirers and became very well acquainted with Guillaume Apollinaire. He took a leading part, along with the latter, in the publication of the ephemeral *Festin d'Esope,* and he seems to have shared fully in the restlessness of Parisian literary Bohemia.

Yet there was something in his personality which clearly distinguished him from the other Bohemians. Though he was not by any means well off, a certain strain of common sense always prevented him from sinking into the down-at-heel poverty in which so many of his friends wallowed unconcernedly. He had the faculty of looking facts squarely in the face, and he always managed somehow to earn a decent, normal living. He was made "Secrétaire de Rédaction" of *Vers et Prose,* a literary review with Symbolist affinities. After 1907 his contributions to various newspapers were so steady and regular that he soon came to be regarded as a full-fledged journalist.

Nevertheless, due consideration on his part for material things did not imply a philistine indifference towards the ideal which the Symbolists had enabled him to glimpse in his youth. When he was introduced, through Apollinaire, to the group of painters of the Rue Ravignan, he found the atmosphere there so congenial that he moved into the "bateau-lavoir" itself. Yet, even though he at once struck up a warm friendship with Max Jacob, he always remained a little apart from the boisterous troupe of artists and poets then crowding the studios and garrets of old Montmartre. Tall, slender, smartly dressed, reserved in manner, almost timid and rather pale, he did not attract attention by an overflowing vitality like Guillaume Apollinaire or by a constant nervous agitation like Max Jacob. Though remaining in the background he nevertheless played with determination a part of no mean order. His subtle and penetrating intelligence helped greatly in the elucidation of Cubist theories; his connections with the newspaper world enabled him to present to a large public the aspirations and convictions of his friends, which were also his own. In the capacity of art critic, he contributed most effectively to the diffusion of Cubism, and he soon qualified as a Cubist poet. His poems, collected in *Féeries, Le Calumet,* and *Le Livre et la Bouteille* — the last-mentioned not being published till after the War — bear witness to his sincere and wholehearted adherence to what Apollinaire called "L'Esprit nouveau."

Yet André Salmon was by no means lost in speculation and dreams. Facts were always of paramount importance to him. When the first World War broke out, though he had been declared physically unfit, he decided not to miss the tremendous experience offered at the front. Dressed in plain civilian clothes, he managed somehow to worm his way up to the very fighting lines in Artois. There he met with a Dr. H. Saunier — well known as the author of either gruesome or farcical plays, written especially for the Grand Guignol — who, humorously appreciating the situation, had André Salmon accepted at once for active service. After remaining in the trenches for about ten months, Salmon was invalided home in 1916. Subsequently the Russian Revolution started, and Salmon, bubbling over with curiosity, succeeded in reaching Petrograd. There, during the Kerensky period, he saw the complete breakdown of the old order he had known, the gradual, irresistible spreading of chaos.

When he returned to France, he found a changed society, seething with incomprehensible ferment. His rôle in the development of Cubism, as well as his more recent verses on the Russian upheaval, published under the title of *Prikaz*, gave him for a while a place of leadership among the young Dadaists. But, very much like Max Jacob, he was loath to approve of audacities associated with a state of mind which was not that of his own generation. So he broke with the Dadaists and turned insensibly towards a more conservative point of view.

He had successfully resumed his profession of journalist. In the field of literature properly speaking, he gave up poetry to concentrate chiefly on short stories and novels. *La Négresse du Sacré-Cœur, L'Entrepreneur d'illuminations, C'est une belle fille,* and *Archives du Club des Onze* mark the main stages of a progressive evolution towards a realism that recalls sometimes the manner of Balzac. Cubism, of course, has left a strong imprint upon André Salmon's technique, as exemplified by his jerky, dislocated presentation of facts and also by his suggestion of an invisible reality. Yet Salmon's personal conception of Cubism was such that it made the transition to a less revolutionary type of writing comparatively easy, and at the same time did not seriously impair his fundamental originality.

Like all Cubists, André Salmon left the safe and quiet realm of rational thinking and traditional literature in order to launch into an adventurous exploration of the unknown. The title and the tenor of his book *Le Livre et la Bouteille* are symbolical of his attitude in this respect. "Le livre" represents organized reasoning, discursive logic, staid and methodical investigation of a well-regulated and tame reality. "La bouteille" stands for the intoxicating pursuit of a forever elusive mystery, and a Dionysiac rapture in the midst of fantastic happenings. In choosing between Book and Bottle — like Hercules between Vice and Virtue — André Salmon decided on the Bottle.

The Bottle, however, did not becloud his very keen sense of proportion. Very much after the fashion of the Cubist painters, who, in their desire to reach the essential, reduced the motley spectacle of the universe to a framework of geometrical figures, André Salmon applied himself to the isolation and forceful presentation of certain topical facts. He did not try with the help of his subconscious imagination to wrap them in the vaporous atmosphere of a supersensible Absolute. The facts themselves were raised by him to the eminent dignity of the Absolute. Salmon is content to do away with all the rational covering in which traditional thought used to encase them neatly and tidily. He presents the facts pell-mell, as they come, in their original disorder. This disorder, reminiscent of the chaotic Cubist paintings, does not in any way detract from the intrinsic value of the facts but, on the contrary, enhances their power.

For André Salmon, brute facts are not soulless. From them emanates a spontaneous poetry, a thousand times more enthralling than any embellishment that our imagination could possibly confer on them. By accepting them as they are, without esthetic improvement or intellectual interpretation, simply as ever-renewed miracles produced by a mysterious and marvelous cosmic energy, Salmon can see an apocalyptic light radiating from their essence.

A psychological explanation of Salmon's mystic cult of facts is perhaps provided by the very circumstances of his life. He has been for a long time actively engaged in journalism; he has the reporter's respect for definite, arresting events, caring very little for their implications or their significance.

It has been said that he made poetry out of newspaper reporting. Without denying the influence of a lifelong calling upon his outlook on reality, one may still suggest that, had he not possessed an instinctive regard for facts, he probably would not have achieved any success as a journalist. Yet it must be noticed that André Salmon is not interested indiscriminately in any kind of fact. He is definitely attracted by strange, tragic, scandalous, and violent deeds — that is to say, by precisely those happenings which a newspaperman collects with special predilection to make sensational news items in his hurriedly written columns.

The poetry emanating from such events has little if anything in common with the poetry of the old masters. Neither charm nor harmony, neither the description of nature nor the expression of tender sentiment, can find a place in Salmon's brutal portrayal of modern restlessness. A suggestion of morbid instability pervades the whole atmosphere; the deep gloom which is shown to be settling over all things is lit only by an occasional lightning flash of hallucinatory pain. This turbid calling forth of a world in the throes of formidable change does not present the attractive hues of an old-fashioned idyll, but it has the merit of expressing with haunting intensity the actual feverish spirit of our time.

Pierre Reverdy is not identified to any comparable degree with the present period. He was born in Narbonne on September 13, 1889, of a very old family, claiming to date back to the time of the Roman conquest of Gaul. His father was a plain businessman, but there were among his forebears countless painters and sculptors, many of whom specialized in religious art. At a very early age Pierre Reverdy showed a dreamy, unpractical disposition; at school — he attended the *lycées* of Toulouse and Narbonne — he was considered a dunce. When he announced to his family that he intended to become a writer, however, he received enthusiastic approval and support. His father had always bemoaned the waste of his own literary capacities, which had been smothered by the dullness of provincial life; he promised his son unlimited help if he wanted to go to Paris to try his hand at journalism.

At the end of 1910 Pierre Reverdy arrived in the capital to begin his literary career. He first approached the small vanguard reviews, which were more accessible to a young beginner than the sacrosanct conservative magazines. Cubism being then the rage, Reverdy must have felt a strong curiosity regarding the much-talked-of new theories. Moreover, by ancestral tradition he was keenly interested in art and familiar with the ways and manners of artists. Very soon he became personally acquainted with all the leading painters of the young Cubist group.

After one year in Paris the death of his father left him practically dependent on his own efforts. Then began for him years of bitter struggle. He was physically delicate, of a sensitive nature, filled at once with eagerness and with natural melancholy, endowed with a rich inward spirituality, poorly equipped for the rough and tumble of a trying existence. As an introvert, he lacked the cheerful aggressiveness which makes a successful journalist, and he was too refined to bear with happy-go-lucky indifference the trials and hardships of Bohemian poverty. He went to reside in the "bateau-lavoir," partly for reasons of economy, partly because it had become in a manner the fashion among poets and artists. The great vogue of Montmartre, it is true, was already on the wane; yet he found there in the company of the Cubists, and especially in a close friendship with Juan Gris, that spark of idealism which was now his only *raison d'être*. This Bohemian phase of his life — of which many poets retain wistful and pleasurable memories — left him with recollections full of despondency and sadness.

Isolated from others on account of his own introspective nature, he suffered through his loneliness and yet at the same time had a morbid desire for solitude. Soon he adopted the habit of going all by himself to a farm in the country, there to indulge unrestrainedly in his dreams. Discomfited by the harshness of a trying material life for which he was ill-adapted, he lived almost exclusively in the world of his own imagination, borrowing from external reality only an indispensable minimum of fragmentary shapes. This attitude was in full agreement with the most abstract of the Cubist doctrines and also in close harmony with his need for a perfect sublimation of his own frustrated desires. He retained only a few aspects of the disappointing world, culled mostly from the spectacle of nature, rarely from the sentiments of men, but all released from the tyrannical oppression of their habitual environment and now moving freely in an aura of poetical mysticism. His works, *Poèmes en prose, La Lucarne ovale, Les Ardoises du toit,* and *La Guitare endormie,* all offer striking evidence of Reverdy's escape from an uncongenial mode of life into a universe of his own creation.

After the turmoil of the war of 1914–18 and the complete disruption of his circle of former friends, Reverdy felt more than ever alone. In a way, it is true, he was perhaps morally closer than any of the other Cubists to the new group of the Surrealists. His utter disregard for the reality surrounding him and his intuitive perception of a higher spiritual world rendered him for a while extremely popular with the most forward representatives of the younger generation. When he collected a number of his former poems under the title *Epaves du Ciel,* the publication was hailed by them with the most flattering enthusiasm.

Nevertheless Pierre Reverdy did not join the ranks of the Surrealists. The main reason for his abstention was that, like Max Jacob, he had found in religious mysticism the fulfillment of his long-sought ideal. He belonged to a Catholic family, though for many years he had not conformed to the practices of the Church. When he returned formally to the fold, he found his very faith a deterrent to any further spiritual search and an obstacle also to the vindication of man's inferior, subconscious cravings. Again, very much like Max Jacob, realizing that the ties binding him to the modern world were growing weaker every day, in 1926 he decided at last to retire. A friend had induced him to come to the celebrated Benedictine Abbey of Solesmes. After a while he established himself permanently in the village near-by, spending his days in praying, reading, or working in his garden. From time to time he published short collections of delicate poems, such as *Ecumes de la mer, Grande Nature, Sources du vent, Pierres blanches, Risques et périls*. He also summed up his ideas on art in *Le Gant de crin*. Yet even though his literary works remain as definite and outstanding landmarks in the development of contemporary French literature, his normal personality seems to lose itself more and more in a state of sublime, supraterrestrial contemplation.

Throughout his life, Reverdy has had his eyes fixed on a supreme ideal. This ideal has been for a long time vague and indistinct. There never was in it anything even remotely intellectual: he did not feel the need of discovering with his mind the answer to the great enigma. It possessed nothing forcefully vital either: he did not experience the urge to obtain a stronger grip on things than that vouchsafed to us by our merely human senses. His aspiration was more akin to a longing for pure ecstasy. Cubism offered him not so much a ready-made solution to his indefinite problem as a program and guide for his anxious and sincere search.

While André Salmon, for instance, saw in Cubism mainly a system enabling him to determine the fundamental architecture of objects and of facts, Pierre Reverdy was especially influenced by the particular trend, within Cubism, which emphasized the value of the spiritual atmosphere in which objects and facts are steeped. Indeed, for him, objects and facts are often merely accessories whose surface here and there catches reflections of a transcendental cosmic effulgence. So he devoted himself to a subtle notation of the impalpable qualities of the universe revealing themselves in the most elemental spectacles of nature. For him the stars glittering against a dark velvet sky, the limitless expanse of the ocean, or the silent epic of the crimson-stained clouds under the setting sun are authentic fragments of a sublime, heavenly entity or, as he himself calls them in his suggestive title, genuine *Epaves du Ciel*. Taking up a position opposed to the journalistic standpoint of such a one as André Salmon, for example, for whom the essentials of our experience are contained in more or less sensational happenings, Reverdy declared: "Il ne s'agit plus d'émouvoir par l'exposé plus ou moins pathétique d'un fait-divers, mais aussi largement, aussi purement que le peuvent faire, le soir, un ciel tout crépitant d'étoiles, la mer calme, grandiose, tragique, ou un grand drame muet joué par les nuages sous le soleil" (22).

But if the essentials of our world are reduced to such elusive impressions and shades, one cannot help feeling that its very existence is thereby rendered alarmingly doubtful and problematic. Are not all physical appearances but vain images indiscreetly thrust upon our senses by some gigantic imposture? Is there in the external forms of our experience any true, solid reality? Pierre Reverdy is obviously sure of the existence of another, a much more inspiring reality — the reality we find in our inner consciousness. There lies a prodigiously rich and varied universe, wherein we should let ourselves sink and be absorbed completely.

The Surrealists, after reaching similar conclusions, delib-

(22) Pierre Reverdy, *Le Gant de crin* (Paris: Plon, 1926), p. 41.

erately renounced the world of our reason and our senses, hoping thus to enter unhampered into the realm of the inward infinite. Pierre Reverdy did not dare to go that far, and he remained, as it were, astride the two domains. He has not had the courage to reject external appearances entirely; yet he has always felt that the domain of the absolute was his real spiritual home. He himself has explained the ambiguity of his situation in the following terms: "The poet is in a difficult and often dangerous position, at the intersection of two planes having a cruelly sharp edge: the plane of dreams and the plane of reality. A prisoner of appearances, cramped in the narrow confines of this world — which is, moreover, a purely imaginary one — with which the common run of people are content, the poet clears the obstacle it constitutes in order to reach the absolute and the real; there his spirit moves freely" (23).

In order to attain this Absolute, Pierre Reverdy resorts largely to introspection. His introspection, however, is not analytical and methodical. It is more like a kind of second sight through which the poet can explore a mysterious region of the soul where only a few distinct psychic islands emerge above the stream of subliminal thought. But Pierre Reverdy is too much impregnated with religious ideas to accept indiscriminately, as the Surrealists do, everything that is carried on the obscure current of the subconscious. He turns his eyes away from all that is repulsive and dismal, so much so that hardly anything is left for him to behold, and in the end he finds himself in the center of a veritable vacuum. "Le monde s'efface" — this phrase recurs again and again as a *leit-motif* in Reverdy's poems, expressing his perfect spirituality and at the same time his unbearable loneliness.

For Reverdy is not an abstract metaphysical spirit but a warm and tenderhearted man, intensely sensitive to pain and

(23) *Le Gant de crin*, p. 15.

to love. Love was the origin of his quest, and now he comes back empty-handed. He suffers through his solitude; yet he is in no way either blasé or downcast. He is still burning with a pure flame, but that flame has not found on earth an object worthy of its ardor. His love consumes itself in the rarefied atmosphere of exalted moral heights where no ordinary human being can establish a permanent abode.

It is customary to include Jean Cocteau among the Cubist poets, for during a brief period of his life he produced works in accordance with the Cubist technique. But at the beginning of his career Cocteau passed with such rapidity from one school to another, being always at the forefront of the most recent literary fashion, that many people at that time came to question the depth of his feelings and even the sincerity of his reactions. It was often said then that Cocteau wanted above all to be up-to-date. He was always seen experimenting with whatever *genre* might be the last vogue of the day; he used to change his point of view so frequently that it was next to impossible to follow the line of his spiritual evolution. Subsequently, it is true, Cocteau reached a thoroughly personal philosophy of life and displayed, especially in his theater, indisputable evidence of complete artistic originality. Yet his deeper conceptions did not manifest themselves very clearly from the start, and, whatever effect the various schools through which he passed may have had upon his development, he obviously attained his full maturity only after he had moved beyond the somewhat limited orbit of their influence.

During his early period, one could perceive in Cocteau, beside a few traits typical of the atmosphere prevailing in the Cubist environment, certain more individual features indicating that Cubism was for him hardly more than a transitory stage. Thus Cocteau showed himself to be a fervent admirer of Picasso, and, like many young men of his generation, he was anxious — intermittently — to cut all ties that link us with a banal and mediocre reality. In his Cubist works he often appears to be longing to ascend into a higher sphere; many of his poems seem about to rise heavenwards like glittering, iridescent soap bubbles. But these pretty things do not go very far. Now and then a suggestion of the Unknown can be faintly discerned among their rapidly changing shades. Sensations are noted which portend something different from the casual occurrences of our visible world. Yet these light signs very soon fade away or are lost amidst the intricate pattern of clever arabesques which the poet's nimble intelligence delights in tracing around the most serious as well as the most frivolous themes.

During the few years immediately preceding the first World War, a new artistic and literary movement known as Futurism aroused marked curiosity. This movement was closely related in spirit to Cubism; but while Cubism was born of technical experiments made by enterprising painters, which only later received their theoretical justification, Futurism was elaborated as a theory before being applied systematically by its exponents to the plastic arts and in some degree to literature.

Cubism had started in France; Futurism had its beginnings in Italy. A few Italian artists, among whom were Marinetti, Severini, and Boccioni, launched a vigorous campaign against traditionalism. They set up, in opposition to the old standards of classical beauty, a new mystic ideal, together with an original conception of the modern world. In 1912 five of these Italian artists held an exhibition of their paintings in Paris. Their influence, however, was almost negligible until Guillaume Apollinaire, keenly interested in all things Italian, and recognizing in their doctrine unmistakable evidence of "L'Esprit nouveau," decided to espouse their cause. He

Gino Severini: *Train Blindé en Action* (1915)
Futurism attempts to give the impression of mechanical power and speed

wrote a manifesto entitled *L'Antitradizione futurista* which was published in Milan in 1913. He strove with his genial enthusiasm to have Futurism accepted by the French public on a par with Cubism.

Futurism and Cubism, both of which issued from the same moral source, had many aspirations in common. Like the Cubists, the Futurists revolted against the shoddy and conventional representation of the world that we are trained to consider as the sole existing reality. They proclaimed the necessity of destroying the generally accepted pattern of things established by our reason. They wanted to dissociate its elements and to rearrange them in such a way as to let men perceive the truer, deeper reality lying beyond the banal shapes surrounding us. They refused to allow intelligence to regulate the plan of reconstruction; they trusted to intuition to discern the essential element that was to be retained and to determine the most effective manner by which its fundamental quality could be demonstrated.

The startling originality of the Futurists, however, proceeded from their conception of the "essential." For them the essential of our world did not reside, as so many have believed, at the very core of Nature. In their view, the most striking feature of our time, representing probably the most fundamental aspect of man's destiny on earth, is the almost total mastery achieved by mankind over Nature. Formerly the elemental display of the forces of Nature sufficed to inspire poets with inexhaustible admiration and wonder. How much more wonderful to see these very forces at the beck and call of our needs and whims, utterly subjugated, reduced to the rôle of obedient slaves! Nature's former supremacy over man has practically ceased to exist. On all sides natural energies have been tamed, harnessed, and made to work at our bidding. Only in the most remote corners of our planet is it possible to find fairly extensive tracts of wilderness corresponding to the state of virgin Nature. The word "Nature," as we understand it, no longer corresponds to the experience and conception of our primitive ancestors. Practically everywhere modern man has obliterated the original facies of the *natural* world.

So by an unexpected inversion of traditional values, Nature has almost ceased to be real, and the man-made, the artificial, has become the great reality. In order to act in conformity with the spirit of our age, we should, say the Futurists, take an active and definite stand *against* Nature: thus we would hasten its complete disintegration and ensure the rapid triumph of artificiality. It is the still unassimilated fragments of untamed Nature, remaining like foreign bodies within the complex and delicate organism of modern civilization, that are mainly responsible for the disharmonies and difficulties of the present day. When absolutely everything on earth has become artificial, man will be able to plan and adjust to a nicety all the details of human life on the surface of our planet. This ideal will not be realized till some time in the fairly distant future. When that day arrives, should we not be fully prepared for it? That is why the upholders of this audacious theory took unto themselves the name "Futurists."

In their view, the best way to work for the future is to break down the prejudices so effectively protecting what is left of Nature, and to glorify the great instrument of man's domination over the material world: modern industry. Henceforth the weird beauty of factories, dockyards, and railroads, the hustle and bustle of human activity under the blinding glare of electric lamps or under the thick clouds of smoke belching from tall, slender chimneys, the mysterious intricacies of pistons, driving rods, and cogwheels, will constitute the background for a tremendous epic of a new kind whose protagonists are machinism and speed.

The creative throb of machinery and the swift impulse

of motion cannot be adequately suggested by an exact and
meticulous representation of inert material. The dynamism
of our modern world can be conjured up only by means as
artificial as the qualities they have to express. Availing
themselves of the Cubist method of dislocation and arbitrary
re-creation, the Futurists performed in this respect amazing
feats of evocative figuration. If, for example, they wished to
convey in their paintings the impression of extremely rapid
movement, as in the case of horses or dogs running, they
unhesitatingly assigned to each animal a score of legs in
various successive positions but painted on the canvas side
by side. They also purposely eliminated all artistic prepara-
tions and transitions, bringing into brutal contact elements
normally situated at vast distances from one another and
imparting to objects and facts by this paradoxical juxtaposition an unnatural, nay, an almost supernatural character.

This apotheosis of speed and this raising of the artificial
to the rank of Absolute have been conjoined, it must be
said, with a prophetic tone sometimes bordering on hysteria,
the particular contribution of the Futurists to the theories
of the modernistic school. The special note they sounded
has brought a response from contemporaries. Yet Futurism
has not succeeded in implanting itself vigorously in France.
No French writer or artist has ever accepted its doctrines in
their totality. But the ideas which were put into circula-
tion by Marinetti and his friends undoubtedly exerted a
marked influence upon several outstanding French novelists,
especially upon Paul Morand and Blaise Cendrars.

Neither of these two authors can be considered as, properly speaking, Futurist. Nevertheless both of them have
shown a distinct predilection for those traits of our modern
life which had been emphasized as essential by the Futurist
school. Paul Morand, particularly in his early works, has
adopted a typically syncopated style; he has been for many

years an enthusiastic worshipper of speed; even now he is still perhaps the most inspiring exponent of the poetical beauty of the modern world. Blaise Cendrars has sketched an epic of the most brutal, artificial, and mechanical aspects of human activity, in which he visualizes the tragic basis of contemporary European and American civilizations. It must be understood, however, that Cendrars and more especially Morand possess a more humane depth to their personalities than has been displayed by any of the members of the Futurist group. In point of fact, while Futurism has enriched the flow of the modernistic tendencies with a number of interesting concepts, its current has not remained individualized or distinct. Futurism may be considered as a derivation of Cubism. In the course of time it came to join the main stream again, bringing along fragments of new thought which soon became indistinguishable in the whirling mass of tumultuous modern theories.

The general public often confuses Futurism and Cubism, and indeed these two movements represent kindred efforts to attain, through very similar methods, the same superior reality. Both Cubism and Futurism aspired to a sincere mystic idealism. Repudiating discursive logic and discarding the testimony of the senses, the Cubists attempted to penetrate directly into a sublime region to which reason and the senses have no access. In their eagerness to discover a direct way to reach that closed domain, they persuaded themselves that the key was to be found in geometrical abstractions. But their notion of mathematics was inadequate and fanciful. So instead of grasping, as they had hoped, a truly abstract perfection, they found that they were moving vaguely among insubstantial shadows and that their efforts generally ended in pure, formal emptiness. Cubist painters and poets alike oscillated between dry schematism and disappointing immateriality. The Futurists fared no better, alternating between a rough figuration of machinism and a theoretical concept of speed. The spiritual atmosphere that unquestionably pervades certain of the modernistic creations may have been released by the disintegration of our visible rational universe, but it seems also frequently to appear simply in direct response to the personal psychic powers of the artist or the poet himself. And, as the price to be paid for a fugitive and doubtful glimpse of "another world," there lies at our feet the wreckage of the world in which we have to live.

This world of ours, it is true, especially since the beginning of the twentieth century, has sunk into more and more profound discredit. Yet many people have wondered, not without reason, whether the substitute offered by the Cubists and the Futurists really is of greater worth. The number of sceptics finally increased to such an extent that Cubism had to be pronounced a failure, though not a total one. From an artistic or literary standpoint the results obtained were undoubtedly disappointing, but the spirit which had animated the search was supremely valuable. For the first time in the history of modern French thought, after the isolated and disconnected attempts of Gérard de Nerval, Victor Hugo, Baudelaire, Rimbaud, Lautréamont, Mallarmé, and a few others, a regularly organized group of young men, refusing to be content with a banal, superficial view of things, had made a collective effort to reach the soul of the universe. It is true that they often mingled sincerity with disconcerting mystification, that they were overconfident and hasty. In their ambition to attain the Absolute immediately, they launched into bold and extravagant conjectures that submerged the fragments of truth which they actually discovered. Once their worst lucubrations were swept away, however, these fragments of truth remained, and the example of their genuine enthusiasm for a truer reality was left for the benefit of the succeeding generation.

IV. Dada

The short-lived but notorious movement known as Dadaism, which interrupted the regular evolution of modernistic literature, was a direct consequence of the first World War. For the men who reached their twentieth year between 1914 and 1918, the war was more than a tragic experience; it definitely warped their entire outlook upon life. Arriving at the age when every young man takes stock of what existence has offered him so far, tries to find his bearings and to map his course into the future, the war generation discovered only ruin and despair. With the uncompromising spirit of generalization natural to youth, these victims of circumstance systematized their distress and in all sincerity pictured the world as an abode of unmitigated gloom.

Actually, there was at that time no dearth of moral and physiological causes to substantiate this attitude. The lack of adequate nourishment for young growing organisms, the nervous strain due to long-distance bombardments and to frequent air raids, above all the tension prevailing in a country threatened with total destruction, tended to create in all sensitive minds a grave and permanent neurotic state. What with the wave of war profiteering, with the plight of French and Belgian refugees, and with gross immorality now rampant everywhere, French society presented a sorry spectacle indeed. Those who were at the front could find in their own sacrifice or in the comradeship of the trenches an element of uplifting idealism. But for those still too young to take part in the struggle and for those who, being disabled, had to spend endless months in the hospitals behind the lines, demoralization seemed universal and complete. Thus a feeling of profound disgust and a haunting obsession with death preyed upon these unfortunates, leading in the years to come, as in the generation which followed the Napoleonic wars, to a long trail of suicides.

Indeed, almost everything that gives life its meaning and purpose had fallen suddenly into the utmost disrepute. Religion had become subservient to nationalism; practically everywhere the churches were heard to preach both hatred and slaughter; science was obviously responsible for the most horrible features of contemporary warfare; art and literature had also been enlisted in the conflict and had been turned into instruments of propaganda. This was the outcome of centuries of efforts towards civilization! The prospects for the future were still more bleak and discouraging. . . . Amidst the general bankruptcy of all respected values, nothing seemed deserving of salvage. Before such an accumulation of moral ruin men felt the irresistible urge to clear the ground of all the dismal wreckage that remained and to sweep all the spiritual and intellectual refuse into final oblivion. This destructive impulse was not prompted by the conscious hope of building anew on a better plan: nobody dreamt of reconstruction at that stage. The mad desire prevalent among young men of the war and post-war period to get rid of everything indiscriminately was only a spontaneous reaction to the state of our civilization, prompted by anger, disgust, and despair.

Yet, even if suicide was the logical conclusion of these mental shambles, very few, on the whole, cared to pursue their ideas to such an extremity. In order to remain alive, men had to adapt themselves somehow to an unprecedented moral and material confusion. The spectacle offered by the modern world was too atrocious to be accepted with equanimity and calm. It was bearable only when regarded as a vain and empty phantasmagoria. Swayed by the instinct of self-protection and self-defense — and not at all by frivolity, which was inconceivable in the midst of the cruel circumstances of that day — they came to consider the whole of life as a jest. There was, of course, nothing gay and diverting in their conception of this "jest," but they found in ironical and contemptuous bravado a measure of courage with which to face their disastrous destiny.

Their grotesque humor was reminiscent of the grimaces of Jarry, and it was impregnated with the same secret rage against an unbearable reality. But Jarry had struck his "ubuesque" attitude in the midst of a comparatively sound environment and at a time when sensible thinking still appeared to many as a rock of unshakeable solidity. So, by contrast, his actions had seemed stupid, and, after all, were not his followers only a mere handful? The war generation, on the contrary, developed in a disjointed and chaotic universe. All basis for "reasonable" judgment seemed to have vanished irretrievably, and the whole world appeared to have been struck with hopeless insanity. Any irrational statement which a few years before would have been branded preposterous and mad was now considered simply as an expression of the general spirit of the time.

Yet the World War was not alone responsible for the growth of the bewildering notions which flourished with such abundance during that period. Many wars had been fought by France before without bringing about any comparable disruption of human mental categories. In the particular case of the 1914–18 conflict, the younger men found in the doctrines put forward by the generation that had immediately preceded them a nucleus around which they crystallized their own disastrous experiences. Even though they rejected practically all the Cubist and Futurist constructive principles, they were, for the negative part of their views, the direct successors and heirs of Cubism. The Cubists had for many years deliberately discounted the importance of external reality; they had used humor as an instrument of methodical destruction. The existence of such a school enabled dissatisfied individuals to turn their bitterness into a coherent system. Without the precedent of Cubism, the woes and sufferings of the World War period undoubtedly would have found some confused modality of expression, probably without general bearing; but encouraged by the audacities of its predecessors, the war generation dared to launch into a furious destructive movement which was soon to acquire a cyclonic force and leave nothing in its wake but devastation and ruin.

Shortly after the outbreak of the war, it became evident to the members of the old Cubist group that a more radical departure from traditionalism than the one they had themselves attempted would soon be inevitable. The direction in which the impending change would take place was still indefinite and vague. But, obviously, men like Guillaume Apollinaire, Max Jacob, Jean Cocteau, and Pierre Reverdy either precipitated their own inward evolution or went anxiously in search of further spiritual domains to explore. As a mark of the increasing restlessness among vanguard literary groups, two new magazines, *Sic* and *Nord-Sud*, were founded during the most critical moments of the war, with the object of testing eventual possibilities of reorientation and discovery.

Sic, first published in January 1916, represented essentially the prolongation of the Futurist trend of thought. Pierre-Albert Birot, Guillaume Apollinaire, and Gino Severini were the most important contributors to the review. Their program was aptly summarized by the title they had chosen: *Sic* — which is the Latin equivalent of "Yes." The group gathering under the aegis of *Sic* said "Yes" to every aspect of life. This optimistic, affirmative attitude was conjoined with the belief that man cannot go on living without continually changing and moving. Worship of movement had been one of the main tenets of the Futurists' doctrine. Movement in itself was their criterion, and they attached little importance to the manner in which it was effected. In their view, incessant motion was the most fundamental trait of our epoch, and the *Sic* group perceived in the current state of unrest a signal confirmation of this theory. They were convinced that a change, a move forward, was indispensable; but the direction was of no consequence, because, as Birot himself often said, "Chercher, c'est vivre; trouver, c'est mourir."

Nord-Sud, founded in March 1917, was less exclusive in its staff and more explicit about its purpose. The mainspring of the review was Pierre Reverdy himself, but, besides him and his friends Guillaume Apollinaire and Max Jacob, there were also included in the group three men destined to play an outstanding part in the elaboration of modernistic literary doctrines: André Breton, Philippe Soupault, and Louis Aragon. The title of the review, *Nord-Sud*, was taken from the name of the underground railroad linking the two great centers of Bohemian life and vanguard literature in Paris: Montmartre and Montparnasse. Thus was illustrated in a symbolic way the fond hope of the members of the new group. They wanted to achieve a synthesis of all the ideas hitherto evolved among young writers and artists, with the avowed intention of using them as a basis for further investigation — towards the unknown.

They took as the starting-point of their search the most extreme conclusions reached so far by the Cubists: namely, that a work of art, a poem or a painting, should constitute an independent and self-contained creation. They held that the artist could borrow certain raw material, as it were, from surrounding reality; but they were opposed to his considering Nature as a model to be imitated or even interpreted. The early Cubists, it is true, even if contemptuous of the external, conventional world, had hoped to attain, through an inspired interpretation of its dislocated fragments, the view of a mystic higher reality. The later Cubists, however, repudiated as idle and vain all attempts to penetrate into a hypothetic superior realm. They insisted that a work of art should stand on its own merits without the slightest reference to any outside subject or fact, be it either material or spiritual. Pierre Reverdy expressed faithfully the opinion of his collaborators and friends in this respect when he wrote in an essay published in the fifth issue of *Nord-Sud*: "To create a work of art having its independent life, its own reality, and being to itself its own aim, seems to us more elevated than any fantastic interpretation of real life, which would be hardly less servile than a faithful imitation" (1).

But what is a work of art containing no reference whatever to any kind of reality if not a senseless divagation? The *Nord-Sud* group did not shrink before that ultimate consequence. In their view, a picture or a poem, being in itself a complete creation, does not need to present any meaning at all. It exists, and its existence constitutes both its justification and its purpose. The artist has not to describe objects, nor to grasp the essence of things, nor to express the fleeting moods of his imagination. He is a creator; he should create something new, something which by reason of its absolute newness bears no relation to anything previously seen, heard, or felt. But what is a "meaning" if not a relation between two terms, one of which, at least, is comparatively familiar? So, more and more, the young writers of the advanced school were coming to consider in all earnestness the possibility of an art and a literature utterly devoid of signification.

Thus in the year 1917 the parallel efforts of *Sic* and of

(1) Quoted by C. Sénéchal, *Les Grands Courants de la littérature française contemporaine* (Marburg: N. G. Elwert'sche Verlag, 1934), p. 381.

Nord-Sud were showing unequivocally the direction in which the newer ideas tended spontaneously to move. The need for a change was generally recognized as a vital necessity. The theories of Cubism and Futurism, though providing a convenient foundation for further research, were beginning to sink into obsolescence, at least in their most original parts. Who, indeed, was now interested in the essence or in the architecture of the universe? Of the Cubist theories there were retained only those aspects which discharged the writer from the obligation of being intelligible. These aspects, it is true, were strikingly in harmony with the dominant tendencies of the day. The world at large was revealing itself to many minds as an absurd, meaningless farce. So in literature as in life there was progressively realized the complete triumph of deliberate absurdity.

Yet the *Sic* and *Nord-Sud* groups were markedly hindered in their audacious pursuits by certain still unsevered connections with the past. They had all retained a very definite reverence for art. Most of their speculations remained purely theoretical; therefore they lacked the pungency and vigor which ideas acquire only when translated into actual fact.

The man who contributed more than anyone else to uncover the latent aspirations of the youth of his time was undoubtedly Jacques Vaché. Jacques Vaché played for the vanguard writers of the war and post-war period a rôle in many ways similar to that taken by Alfred Jarry among the Cubists. Like Jarry, he was extravagant, unbalanced, reckless; he wove openly into the pattern of his daily life the feelings of revolt and loathing toward society which were beginning to take form among the survivors of a sacrificed generation. The majority of the young men, though embittered and filled with disgust, were prevented by some remnant of common sense from giving vent to their rebellious and contemptuous sentiments otherwise than in idle conversations or ineffectual dreams. Vaché, on the contrary, did not hesitate to apply to life the ultimate conclusions of his desperate philosophy. Gradually he acquired for his contemporaries the value of a living symbol. His amazing influence was due not so much to the quality of his mind as to the natural ascendency exerted by his *daring* to assert his will over those who had not the courage to fulfill their own deep secret yearnings.

Jacques Vaché had been for some time an art student in Paris; then he had been obliged to give up this study — for which he was not, apparently, remarkably well gifted — and go to the front. At the beginning of 1916, being severely wounded in the leg, he was sent to a base hospital in Nantes. All those who came in contact with him there were struck by his original personality. In particular, André Breton, then serving as an intern at the neurological center of the same city, was perhaps the most interested observer of his character and behavior.

Vaché's sole and constant purpose seems to have been to challenge all the rules of sensible conduct. As an example of his eccentricity — when he was just out of the hospital, he took a job as a stevedore, loading and unloading coal on the wharves of Nantes harbor. Occasionally, dressed with refined elegance, he would haunt the lowest dives in the most disreputable sections of the town. He went about sometimes attired in an English uniform, at other times dressed as an officer of the French Air Force. He invented for himself and for his friends imaginary titles and unbelievable adventures. Often he introduced his new acquaintance, André Breton, much to the latter's embarrassment, as André Salmon. By telling gratuitous falsehoods on every possible occasion, and by acting in an absurdly unaccountable manner, he succeeded in creating about himself an atmosphere of complete unreality. For him, practical life with its train of conventions and obligations had ceased to exist. He was living permanently in a fictitious realm of his own imagination.

Yet his was not exactly a case of flight from an anguishing, unbearable reality into a perfect world of dreams. The fanciful world he was substituting for the actual routine of life was in no way preferable to that routine. The substitution merely implied that the present reality was so utterly devoid of importance and value that it could be abolished or replaced by something else equally bad, without affecting the general order of things. Vaché's fantastic conceptions were not a way of escape into a better and superior domain; they were but a grim form of humor intended to show that man had become absolutely indifferent to the useless and senseless display that is our existence on earth. In his view, for anyone who "knows" — that is to say, who is not content merely to look at the surface of things — life reveals itself as a ludicrous theatrical show, infinitely depressing and sad. Vaché had nothing of the elemental vitality which had conferred upon the creations of Jarry a certain jovial heartiness. His mood was uniformly disconsolate and downcast. Humor was not for him an indirect process of reaction against a hostile destiny; it was the acknowledgment, through idiotic and parodic jokes, of the cruel, irremediable imbecility of everything. As he himself said in one of his *Lettres de guerre*, humor is "un sens . . . de l'inutilité théâtrale (et sans joie) de tout, quand on sait" (2).

His mood corresponded undoubtedly to that of many men of his generation, since he soon found himself surrounded by a numerous cohort of admirers. He never composed a work of any importance: for him, literature and art were as vain and contemptible as everything else. A number of his letters,

(2) Jacques Vaché, *Lettres de guerre* (Paris: Au Sans Pareil, 1919), X. 29. 4. 17, p. 9.

in which he expressed scathing judgments upon society and life, were published only after his death; nevertheless, his influence upon young writers during his lifetime can hardly be exaggerated. Tall and handsome, with an expressive face and a crown of red hair, extremely well-informed and highly cultured, he seems to have exerted around him a magnetic fascination. André Breton went even as far as to say: "C'est à Jacques Vaché que je dois le plus. Le temps que j'ai passé avec lui à Nantes en 1916 m'apparait presque enchanté" (3). Vaché showed that a defiant rejection of all accepted rational and moral standards could result in an intoxicating feeling of total enfranchisement.

The circumstances of his death added a gruesome touch to his equivocal fame. Vaché had been for some time an opium addict. Towards the end of 1918, while still in Nantes, he apparently resolved to commit suicide by taking an overdose of the drug. This move was, after all, the normal conclusion of his nihilism and contempt for life. But, as one of his companions had evinced the curiosity to have just one experience with opium, he gave him to absorb — and he took also himself — an amount which he must have known would bring about death. This evidently was for him simply a last "funny" practical joke at the expense of his naïve friend — an ultimate derision, scoffing at the utter futility of all things.

This atrocious deed failed to arouse horror or indignation on the part of his followers. On the contrary, he was considered perhaps with increased respect. He was believed to have given the decisive proof of his complete sincerity, and to have shown that he had the courage to go to the very limit of his destructive ideas. Among the words which are used by André Breton to qualify the circumstances of his

(3) A. Breton, "La Confession dédaigneuse," *Les Pas perdus* (Paris: Nouvelle Revue Française, 1924), p. 9.

death, one finds the adjective "admirable" (4). This word does not apply, it is true, to the particularly odious aspects of Jacques Vaché's action. Yet it shows conclusively that the latter's conduct, viewed from a certain angle, was not only condoned but, in a way, admired by certain of the most intelligent representatives of the post-war generation.

Meanwhile, several new vanguard groups had already begun to take form here and there. In New York the French Cubist painter Marcel Duchamp, who had startled the artistic circles of America a few years before by his painting, "Nude Descending a Staircase," launched successively two small reviews, *Wrong Wrong* and *The Blind Man*. The Spaniard, Francis Picabia, who was to play in the post-war artistic movement a part almost comparable to that of Picasso during the Cubist period, started under the title of *291*, which later became *391*, a periodical publication containing mainly reproductions of modernistic sketches and paintings. His intentions were clearly subversive, and a grotesque, nonsensical irony constituted his avowed method of systematic destruction.

In Paris, André Breton, Philippe Soupault, Louis Aragon, Paul Eluard, Georges Ribemont-Dessaignes, Pierre Reverdy, and Blaise Cendrars had in the course of time come together. In March 1919 they found an outlet for their troubled feelings in a review ironically called *Littérature*. They had no definite program, beyond a strong leaning towards the most extreme tendencies once evinced by the now practically defunct Cubism. They felt an irrepressible disgust for the world as it had been revealed to them in the past few years, and they wanted a change at almost any price. Their anguish, as well as their sincerity, was obvious, and they received encouragement from such men as André Gide and Paul

(4) "La Confession dédaigneuse," *Les Pas perdus*, p. 23.

Valéry — the latter having even suggested, it is said, the odd, sarcastic title of their magazine.

The most important center of the new spiritual fermentation, however, was to be found in neutral Switzerland. As early as 1916, the German poet Hugo Ball, who had found military discipline in his country uncongenial, opened in Zurich a literary café which he called significantly "Cabaret Voltaire." In this cabaret congregated, among others, Richard Huelsenbeck, another German poet in exile, Hans Arp, an Alsatian wood-carver, Dr. Val Serner, fresh from the Université de Genève, and a dynamic young Rumanian named Tristan Tzara. All the members of this cosmopolitan group, uprooted from their normal environment by force of circumstances, lived in a state of perpetual excitement mainly in order to avoid a painful tête-à-tête with their own moral distress. They had very few ideas in common except the general conviction that the world which had been so harsh to them was irrevocably sinking into unfathomable imbecility.

On February 8, 1916, in the course of a tumultuous gathering held at the "Café Terrasse," they decided to adopt a name intended to show that they had given up every hope for human intelligence and were expecting still worse inanity from the future. Tristan Tzara then plunged a paper cutter at random into the pages of a *Dictionnaire Larousse*, opened the book, and read the word thus indicated: "Dada." "Dada" is a childish utterance which is supposed to stand for the difficult word "cheval." In fact, more often than not, "Dada" means nothing at all in the mind of an infant who prattles and babbles incoherently. "Dada" was hailed at once by all present as the fitting symbol of the meaningless, absurd condition of our epoch; thus was born the movement which was later to spread and to become famous under the name of Dadaism.

For the time being, the Zurich group was still very small

and practically unknown. In June 1916 a review was published, called "Cabaret Voltaire," in which the word "Dada" made its first official appearance. In June 1917 the bulletin, *Dada I, recueil d'art et de littérature,* attracted some attention, less for the intrinsic value of the articles it contained than on account of the violence of the language used. *Dada II,* which followed in the month of December of the same year, was an evidence of the persistency of the movement and of its growth. In December 1918, *Dada III* presented under the signature of Tristan Tzara a manifesto stating more or less clearly the purpose and program of the new school.

The months following the Armistice saw the fusion of the vanguard groups of New York, Paris, and Zurich, as well as the sudden, astounding expansion of the destructive tendencies which they had represented. A natural reaction, following the tenseness of the war period, loosened all the ties that had kept public morale relatively firm during the worst of the crisis. Then the abolition of censorship enabled malcontents of all sorts to voice unrestrainedly their criticisms and complaints. Everybody could now measure from the accumulated ruin the extent of the disaster visited upon western civilization. Soon the feelings of universal distress found in Dadaism a psychological outlet as well as a violent, vociferous expression.

First Francis Picabia came from New York to Switzerland and published there a few pamphlets, such as *L'Athlète des pompes funèbres, Dessins de la fille née sans mère* and *Rateliers platoniques.* His pictures made a profound impression upon Tristan Tzara and his friends on account of their elaborate and powerful absurdity. He was immediately recognized by them as the painter who had come to destroy the art of painting — the providential "anti-peintre." Meanwhile, the Zurich group and the Parisian group of *Littérature* had established definite personal relations. When the bulletin *Dada* 4-5 appeared in May 1919, the importance and variety of the contributions which had been received from all sides fully justified its new subtitle of *Anthologie Dada*. Thereupon Tristan Tzara decided to go himself to Paris, where he was at once acknowledged as a leader by all. His friend Picabia and his more recent admirer André Breton willingly admitted his strong ascendency; they strove in perfect agreement with him for the new "ideal." Tristan Tzara's prestige was due essentially to the attitude of towering superiority he affected towards one and all, to the sharp, peremptory tone he assumed on every possible occasion, and to the brutal recklessness of all his utterances. His overbearing, dictatorial manner, however trying in the long run, conferred temporarily upon the Dadaist movement an unexpected discipline and a most efficient activity.

At the close of 1919 the unsuspecting general public was invited to attend a meeting organized by the group *Littérature* in the Palais des Fêtes on the Rue Saint-Martin. Many candid men of good will flocked in, with the hope of learning at last something definite about the new trends in contemporary art. They heard André Breton comment unintelligibly upon a picture which was made by Picabia on a blackboard with a piece of chalk and whose lines were wiped off as soon as they had been drawn. Afterwards Tristan Tzara read as fast as possible several newspaper cuttings, which nobody could understand, in the midst of the din caused by Paul Eluard and one of his friends who were busily occupied striking bells with all their strength.

People went away either indignant or amused, according to their individual tempers; but all were thoroughly puzzled and disappointed. What had the grotesque manifestations they had just witnessed to do with true art? Indeed, nothing at all. The Dadaists were persuaded, as Jacques Vaché had already proclaimed, that "L'art est une sottise" (5). Dada must not be considered as a philosophical movement or as an artistic theory; it is merely an expression of collective despair and anger. This mood was felt by many young men of the post-war period who were burning with a mad desire to insult everything that was still respected and honored by the sheep-like masses. They yearned to slap the face of an inept, sanguinary world and to drag through the mud the idols of a complacent, self-satisfied society. They found in their own outrageous behavior a measure of relief for their distress, and in their blasphemies a strange, almost sadistic delight.

The only "idea" which could be discovered behind this outburst of deep-rooted rage was one of ruthless and frantic destruction. As Tristan Tzara had said, "Nous déchirons, vent furieux, le linge des nuages et des prières et préparons le grand spectacle du désastre, l'incendie, la décomposition" (6). Yet the Dadaists never attacked social institutions or intellectual standards as though they were dangerous obstacles whose resistance was to be broken by force. The very nature of their sarcasm implied that, in their view, our civilization was already in a state of total disintegration and decay. Their negations were intended to show the lack of real value, the lack of existence, as it were, of all qualities and all personalities — including our own — to which we assign a fictitious, illusory importance. That is what Georges Ribemont-Dessaignes wanted to express when he said: "What is beautiful? What is ugly? What is great, strong, weak? What is Carpentier, Renan, Foch? Don't know! What is 'I'? Don't know! Don't know, don't know, don't know!" (7)

(5) *Lettres de guerre*, 9. 5. 18, p. 20.

(6) Tristan Tzara, "Manifeste Dada," *Dada III*, Zurich, December 1918; quoted by C. Sénéchal, *Les Grands Courants de la littéraire française contemporaine*, p. 380.

(7) Quoted by A. Breton, "Pour Dada," *Les Pas perdus*, pp. 93–94.

In their negative frenzy the Dadaists spared no one, not even their own spiritual forerunners. The Symbolists and Cubists had, to various degrees and with different objectives, denied practically all intrinsic value to external reality; with that part of their doctrines the Dadaists were in thorough agreement. But both Symbolists and Cubists had retained a mystic belief in a higher essence beyond the visible terrestrial shapes. The new generation refused to go that far. Said Jacques Vaché: "We ignore Mallarmé, without hatred, because he is dead. We don't know Apollinaire any more because we suspect him of indulging in art too consciously . . ." (8); and also: ". . . Max Jacob . . . but then, you know, he has ended by taking himself seriously — grave intoxication, indeed!" (9)

The Dadaists refused to take anybody or anything seriously. According to them, even to criticize a fact in earnest would confer upon it an importance which nothing on earth can possibly deserve. The best way to denounce the absurdity of the world is to paint it, to write about it, or to describe it as a blatant absurdity. The systematic stupidity of the Dadaist productions had an intention, if not a meaning: its aim was to convey the feeling that absolutely everything is idiotic and senseless. To those who asked for explanations, the Dadaists were unable to give an intelligible response without defeating their own purpose. As a rule, they replied with obscene or sacrilegious ejaculations, adding that, if people failed to understand, they were really grasping the very spirit of Dadaism, which was, by definition, meaningless. At a public meeting organized by the Dadaists on February 5, 1920, in the Salon des Indépendants, Francis Picabia read the following typical statement: "You do not understand, of course, what we are doing! Well, my dear friends, we understand

(8) *Lettres de guerre*, 18. 8. 17, pp. 17–18.
(9) *Ibid.*, 9. 5. 18, p. 20.

it still less. How wonderful, isn't it, that you are right! . . . You don't understand? Neither do I; how sad!" (10)

Indeed, such lucubrations were profoundly sad, not only on account of their very silliness but because one could perceive in their expression the throb of a genuine pain. That a large number of young men, many of them well gifted and sincere, should have indulged in similar nonsense, conclusively shows how tragic their distress was. With all principles, all directions, and all bearings irretrievably lost, the new generation, forlorn and wretched, could at first do nothing but proclaim its agony; and its clamor, however incoherent and inarticulate, was at bottom infinitely less ridiculous than pathetic and even moving.

Moreover, there was in the very violence of their attitude a proof of insuperable vitality. If they had been really overwhelmed and crushed by their hostile environment, they would have submitted resignedly to their fate. Their vehement protestations proved that their spirit, at least, had not been destroyed. They refused categorically to accept life and the world as they were. But was there not in this refusal the implicit postulate that life and the world could be improved? They themselves offered no plan whatever for improvement, but their very revolt indicated potential hopes for a possible general transformation. For the time being, it is true, blinded by their own fury, they were not even conscious of their secret yearnings. But when the flood of their anger ebbed away, the old hopes emerged again. These aspirations showed little change since the time of Cubism and Futurism, but they were now rising in the midst of an entirely transformed moral landscape. Dadaism, like a short but furious storm, had wrecked everything in its path. Of the ancient traditional conventions, nothing had been left

(10) Quoted by E. Bouvier, *Initiation à la littérature d'aujourd'hui* (Paris: Renaissance du Livre, 1928), p. 89.

standing. The emancipated spirits found themselves with a perfectly clean slate — a consummation of their long-cherished desire.

The means by which the Dadaists effected this thorough liquidation of the past — and of the present as well — were, to say the least, disconcerting. In their writings they used incoherent vocables, just as these presented themselves to their minds, without any sort of preparation or elaboration. Their method did not differ greatly from that inaugurated by Lautréamont — the only one of their predecessors who had found grace in their eyes — but their purpose and the results which they obtained were even more stupefying. Their words were generally linked together by a fairly correct grammatical syntax, though they were sometimes interspersed with foreign locutions, senseless groups of raucous syllables, or incomprehensible, imaginary hieroglyphs, but they never offered any logical meaning whatever. In fact, the Dadaists especially rejoiced when the chance meeting of disconnected expressions suggested a burlesque association of the most heteroclitic objects or circumstances.

In painting, it was easy enough to put on a canvas irregular lines and spots of color utterly devoid of signification. Since, however, it was not always easy to distinguish such productions from the later Cubist works, the Dadaist painters systematically applied a strange and peculiar process. In the formation of a picture they deliberately used all sorts of material generally considered as foreign to the technique of the plastic arts. They would glue upon a canvas little bits of string, fragments of metal, shreds of colored paper, and, above all, large cuttings of printed text. They were not the inventors of such a method, for it had been used, though in moderation, by Picasso before the first World War, but they gave it an extension and an implication which it had not hitherto possessed. Their idea was not to find a new modality

Max Ernst: *La biciclette* [sic] *graminée garnie de grelots les grisons grivelés et les échinodermes courbants* [sic] *l'échine pour quêter des caresses* (c. 1920)
Dadaism strives after systematic absurdity

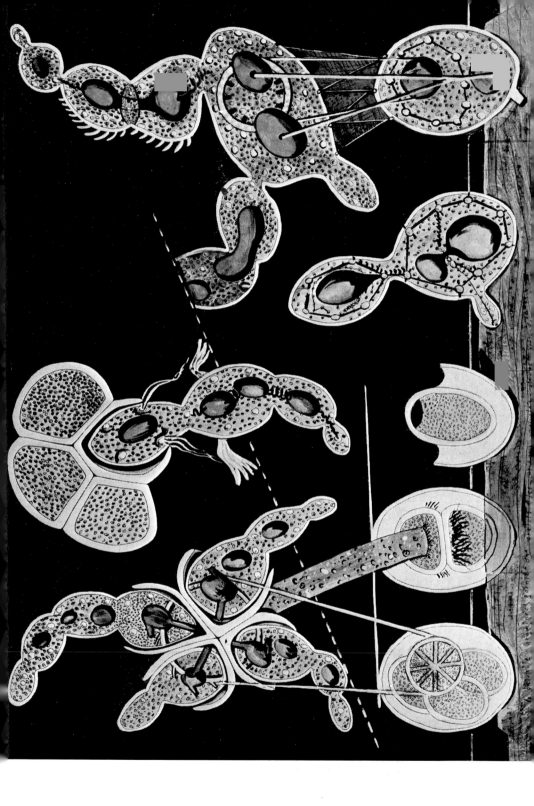

of personal expression, but simply to ruin the art of painting
itself by making their pictures a dumping ground for samples
of refuse.

They attempted to discredit musical art in a similar fashion.
Not only did Dadaist music present a hopeless potpourri of
old melodic strains and harsh dissonances, but new "instruments," such as automobile horns and typewriters, were
occasionally brought into the orchestra; their noises were
supposed to represent in a striking and up-to-date manner
the dismal voice of our contemporary era.

Outside these specific manifestations in the field of literature and art, the Dadaists took care to display on every possible occasion the most provocative behavior. They would
shout gross and gratuitous insults at the visitors who attended
their public festivals and meetings. Their avowed purpose
was to excite reactions in an otherwise indifferent and passive crowd. They very seldom failed to attain the hoped-for
result, and they considered any of their gatherings a perfect
success if it ended in a riot, with flying projectiles, and the
intervention of the police.

At the beginning of 1920 the Dadaists were forming a
resolute and bellicose cohort, with their headquarters estab-
lished at the "Café Certà." In the first rank were Tristan
Tzara, Francis Picabia, André Breton, Philippe Soupault,
Louis Aragon, Paul Eluard, Georges Ribemont-Dessaignes,
and, among the musicians, Erik Satie and Darius Milhaud.
They had the moral support and sympathy of André Lhote,
Pablo Picasso, Max Jacob, André Salmon, Pierre Reverdy,
Jean Cocteau, Blaise Cendrars, Paul Morand, and the con-
tinued approval of Paul Valéry and André Gide.

The Dadaist reviews prospered, attesting the vitality of
the movement. *Littérature* remained by far the most widely
read of them all; with the publication of the *Lettres de guerre*
of Jacques Vaché, it provided Dadaism with a basic text of

fundamental importance. *391* was still appearing intermittently, serving as a means of expression for Francis Picabia and the immediate circle of his friends. The bulletin *Dada,* which had started in Zurich and had been transferred to Paris after the Armistice, changed its name and became the *Cannibale,* remaining, however, the special organ of Tristan Tzara and his group. Finally a publishing firm, Au Sans Pareil, agreed to print and to put on the market a certain number of Dadaist "literary" productions.

The Dadaist books do not deserve more than a cursory mention. They have absolutely no plot, they contain no idea, they offer no artistic value of any kind. They generally present a string of nonsensical expressions bearing provocative but misleading or meaningless titles. The most prolific of all the Dadaist writers was undoubtedly Tristan Tzara. He has already published in Switzerland *La Première Aventure céleste de M. Antipyrine*; then appeared in Paris *Cinéma calendrier du cœur abstrait maisons, Mouchoirs de nuages,* and *Indicateur des chemins de cœur.* In the same spirit, André Breton wrote *Mont-de-Piété*, Philippe Soupault *Rose des vents*, Paul Eluard *Les Animaux et leurs hommes*, Georges Ribemont-Dessaignes *L'Œil et son œil*. All these works, however, failed to engage the attention of the general public; as a rule, they passed practically unnoticed.

The most effective means the Dadaists had of arousing curiosity was to organize public "festivals." Following the "Conférence-Manifeste" of 1919 at the Palais des Fêtes, other meetings took place during the first six months of 1920, when the Dadaist movement reached its zenith. Particularly hectic, and therefore "successful," were those held on February 5 at the Salon des Indépendants, on March 7, at the Maison de l'Œuvre, and on May 26 at the Salle Gaveau. In nearly every case, the gathering was conducted according to the same routine: challenging manifestoes were first read or recited by prominent members of the group; then a few typical Dadaist works — poems, paintings, or pieces of music — were presented more or less humorously to the audience. The audience, as if taking up a clue, would start to hiss and throw things on the stage. Insults were hurled back and forth. Generally in the end the hall had to be cleared by force.

Yet even such lively performances became in time almost monotonous: everybody knew what the regular development of the gathering and its final outcome would be. The public, which had been at first amazed and puzzled, then enraged by the taunts flung at them, now came to the meetings perfectly aware of what was to be expected and with the avowed purpose of enjoying a turbulent, but on the whole fairly safe, form of rioting. The whole thing was turning into a farce. Progressively the most earnest and sincere of the Dada sympathizers withdrew, especially those who had supported the movement only from afar. André Gide, Paul Valéry, Paul Morand, Max Jacob, André Salmon, Blaise Cendrars turned their backs discreetly upon a venture which was obviously leading nowhere. Jean Cocteau, who had never been officially a Dadaist, but who had been favorable to Dada when the movement was the fashion of the day, now broke away with such violence that he was soon looked upon as an arch enemy by the staunch members of the group. The addition of a few new recruits, such as Benjamin Péret and Jacques Rigaut, did not make up for these heavy losses; and at the end of 1920 it was evident that Dadaism could not last much longer.

The Dadaist movement had been essentially the result of temporary circumstances. The sufferings brought about by the first World War and the consequent period of morbid despair had linked together men who had no really deep affinities. The violence of their feelings of disgust had stifled for a while individual antagonisms in temperament and outlook. An overwhelming spiritual revolt, general and sincere, had brought the movement into being. But, as the conditions which had started the movement came to an end, the wave of anger subsided. Soon the different characters and personalities reappeared in their normal guise, all the more sharply defined now that they had been cleared of all the intellectual sediment formerly deposited by convention and culture.

Moreover, Dadaism had carried within itself from the very beginning the germs of its own dissolution. Dada was admittedly the negation of all possible moral or artistic doctrine. But was not such a stand the very negation of Dada itself, as a doctrine? Sooner or later the absolute nihilism of the Dadaists was bound to turn against them. Those whom they had exhorted to consider everything as a jest profited so well by the lesson that they refused to take seriously even their exhorters. Some of the most rabid Dadaists were ready to accept the consequences of that vicious circle of hopeless absurdity. But for a few of them — for the best and for the most sincere — the situation had become positively unbearable.

Above all, there was in many, after the tremendous, wanton destruction caused by the war, a secret desire to rebuild. This normal aspiration, which had been obscured during times of anguish and stress, began to make itself felt again. Art had been ridiculed, along with the rest, unmercifully; but even though joining in the derisive chorus for a while, true artists could not but suffer inwardly from such a challenge to their deeper nature. They must have realized, of course, that Dada meant for them complete emancipation from the shackles of the past. Yet their productive faculties craved expression; at the end of 1920 a marked dissatisfaction with Dada and its principle became evident almost simultaneously everywhere.

This dissatisfaction expressed itself at first by personal bickerings between the various leaders of the group. Derogatory remarks were exchanged and repeated; friction developed about insignificant trifles; anonymous letters were sent in numbers; the atmosphere once so entertaining and so friendly became charged with suspicion and intrigue. Francis Picabia was the first to retire officially from the movement and to take a stand openly against Dada's pointless sterility. André Breton followed him shortly afterwards, but maintained an attitude of diplomatic friendliness towards all his former companions.

By that time André Breton had reached the belief that a common positive element could be extracted from the confused medley of individual opinions that tended to manifest themselves among the upholders of advanced literature and art. His ambition was to bring about the clear enunciation of that constructive principle. For that purpose, he wanted all the leading Cubists, Futurists, Dadaists, etc. to meet in a "Congrès de l'Esprit Moderne" which would be held in Paris. There, official speeches would be pronounced, programs would be submitted and scrutinized, and free discussion would straighten particular difficulties. Stenographers would take down verbatim all statements made, and these statements would be published later on. Thus, thought André Breton, it would be possible to ascertain the position of everyone and to draw conclusions about any common ground which might serve as a basis for further progress.

Francis Picabia assured André Breton of his wholehearted support; when the latter approached Tristan Tzara and his followers on the subject, he received from them a disappointing, though perfectly consistent, reply. Faithful to the original destructive conception of Dadaism, they agreed to participate in the congress on one condition: that an imposing, elaborate spiritual platform be drawn up, supposedly to formulate "L'Esprit Moderne." Then, through some stratagem carefully planned in advance, the complete collapse of the whole enterprise would be brought about. Nothing would demonstrate more strikingly than such a sensational fiasco the absolute inanity of everything!

Naturally, André Breton did not want *his* congress to be a failure. He was sincere in his search for a way out of the swamps of Dadaism. He resented bitterly what he considered as a sabotage of his long-cherished plan. Soon the quarrel spread and became general. Acrimonious words were exchanged, and mutual accusations of bad faith were flung right and left. For example, André Breton said that Tristan Tzara had not really written the *Manifeste Dada* published under his signature in 1918; its veritable author was, he alleged, Val Serner. Then, adding insult to injury, he charged that Tristan Tzara was guilty of equivocal collusion with Public Enemy No. 1: Jean Cocteau! The break was now complete.

The "Congrès de l'Esprit Moderne" did not materialize, and in the midst of the heated controversies which it aroused in the course of 1921 Dada breathed its last.

V. Surrealism

The attempt of André Breton to bring about a "Congrès de l'Esprit Moderne" had been to a large extent prompted by a peculiar discovery he had made almost by chance, and which was to affect in a decisive manner the whole course of contemporary literature and art.

As early as 1919 — that is to say, in the very midst of the Dadaist turmoil — Breton had a most unusual personal experience. One evening, as he was about to fall asleep, he became aware that a sentence, grammatically correct, though preposterous from the standpoint of reason, was, according to his own expression, "knocking at the window-pane" (1) of his consciousness. The wording of that sentence, which he could not recall exactly afterwards, was something like this: "Il y eut un homme coupé en deux par une fenêtre" (2). At the same time he fancied that he saw, though very faintly, the image of a man walking erect, whose body was truncated at the waist by a large horizontal window. However surprised he must have been at the oddity of the sentence and the accompanying image, André Breton was too good a Dadaist to reject either on account of their absurdity. He therefore made a point of retaining them in his consciousness. No sooner had they taken their place in the stream of his thoughts than they were followed by another sentence and another image, both apparently unconnected with the former and equally absurd. These, having been in their turn admitted by Breton, brought in their train a series of similar phrases all appearing spontaneously and all completely irrational.

It must be said that, when all this occurred, André Breton was so miserably poor that, as he informs us himself, "Je ne

(1) A. Breton, *Manifeste du Surréalisme* (Paris: S. Kra, 1929), p. 39.
(2) *Ibid.*

mangeais pas tous les jours à cette époque" (3), and it is quite possible that sheer starvation may have been the true cause of this curious brain storm. Whatever their origin, these incomprehensible sentences obsessed him so imperiously that he felt impelled to investigate thoroughly the mysterious message they might be meant to convey.

André Breton discussed at length with his friend Philippe Soupault the phases and aspects of his psychic experience. Both decided to try to place themselves, as an experiment, in conditions which would reproduce as closely as possible the circumstances of the original phenomenon. Sitting together in a quiet room, and excluding as best they could all definite and clear ideas from their intellect, as happens naturally when we are about to fall asleep, they jotted down on paper whatever rambling thoughts came to their passive minds. At the end of one day they had each covered approximately fifty pages of fairly close writing. They then compared the results obtained. Certain similarities between their "productions" were truly striking. In both cases the writer, reading over the pages he had composed, experienced the feeling of having a text completely foreign to his own personality. He discovered elements which did not seem to belong to the Ego that he knew, elements which, in fact, surprised him as if coming from a source entirely different from his normal conscious self. Further, throbbing between the lines, there seemed to be an emotion infinitely more intense and rich than that usually evoked by the individual sentences. Finally, these pages offered, in spite of their absurdity, a wealth of imagery which neither author would have been able to produce deliberately even at the cost of long and arduous effort.

After a close study of their texts, Breton and Soupault reached the conclusion that these revealed a number of hidden spiritual qualities and facts, less obvious than the

(3) *Manifeste du Surréalisme*, p. 40.

André Masson: *Bataille de Poissons* (1927)
After automatic writing, automatic painting

properties of the material forms surrounding us, but existing really, objectively — as really and objectively as anything we can perceive. This subconscious "divulgation d'un certain nombre de propriétés et de faits non moins objectifs, en somme, que les autres" (4) is the very foundation of the movement known as Surrealism.

André Breton and Philippe Soupault had thought at first of calling "supernaturaliste" — after Gérard de Nerval — this new mode of investigation and expression. Subsequently, however, they decided to adopt the name "Surréalisme" as a homage to the memory of Guillaume Apollinaire (5). Apollinaire had used the word "Surréaliste" in connection with the attempt — not infrequent among Cubist writers — to attain a higher reality through the medium of an unbridled verbalism; but Apollinaire does not seem to have considered this process as a regular method of research, and he never propounded a systematic theory of its legitimate use. André Breton and Philippe Soupault set out to formulate a comprehensive and coherent program of studies, taking as a basic principle the possibility of the revelation of a superior, "surrealist" truth, thanks to the automatic development of man's subconscious psychic powers.

Their first step was to pursue the work of automatic writing which they had practiced originally as an experiment. In 1921 they were able to publish under the title of *Les Champs magnétiques* a small volume presenting, without correction or improvement of any sort, a number of pages composed by themselves according to the new method, while their rational minds were in a state of more or less perfect vacuity.

The example set by this book — and above all the message carried by Breton and Soupault in many animated personal

(4) *Manifeste du Surréalisme*, p. 44.
(5) *Ibid.*

conversations — aroused a vivid interest in the advanced literary circles of Paris. It was precisely the time when Dadaism was disintegrating and when many felt the urgent need of more positive, constructive efforts. The failure of the "Congrès de l'Esprit Moderne," on which not a few had pinned their hope, had shown the impossibility of a fruitful collaboration with certain irreducible extremists. Then public attention was focussed upon André Breton personally, for his attitude had been irreproachable throughout the whole affair. Thus Breton found himself at the center of a small group, enthusiastic and sincere, but composed for the most part of heterogeneous elements brought together by profoundly varying currents of thought.

Among these currents of thought, the most obvious, perhaps, was the one issuing from the old Cubist doctrine. Like the Cubists of the pre-war period, many of the younger men belonging to the new generation were anxious to reach beyond the screen of our visible universe a higher truth of an ideal nature; like the Cubists, they believed that this could be achieved only through the systematic disintegration of conventional concepts. The Dadaists had added to this a note of angry violence. After them, the destruction of the conventional concepts could be viewed only in terms of aggressive and subversive absurdity.

It has been seen how at the close of the nineteenth century scientific discoveries had provoked a grave spiritual crisis by shaking the belief in the value of the forms of reality amidst which we live. Now the latest results of scientific investigation, revealed to the general public in the years following the first World War, definitively ruined what remained of the former confidence in the value of logical reasoning. The theories about relativity, devised mainly by Einstein, left aghast those who, in spite of everything, had obstinately trusted the evidence of common sense. Was it not said that a straight line, if pursued indefinitely, would somehow return to its original starting-point? Even Time could no longer be considered as an Absolute, forever immutable and identical with itself — so that, for instance, two clocks traveling concurrently but with different speeds would, when simultaneously observed, mark different times and nevertheless both be correct. Further, Space, which it had been almost axiomatic to qualify as infinite, was in reality finite, and yet, through some bewildering antinomy, at the same time boundless!

No layman could, of course, check the accuracy of such or similar assertions. Neither was there any general speculation as to whether, from a philosophical standpoint, concepts of this kind had any bearing upon the question of the value of abstract logic or human mental categories. These astounding theories, backed as they were by the highest scientific authorities of the day, gave to the average cultured man the impression that normal, sound judgment could not be relied upon to distinguish between the possible and the preposterous. After all, the universe constituted a baffling mystery, altogether beyond the grasp of clear intelligence; one might expect even what seemed to be the craziest ideas to turn eventually into respected expressions of an incomprehensible truth. Thus the diffusion of Einstein's ideas prepared the post-war generation psychologically to accept the most disconcerting hypotheses and to follow with sympathy any unorthodox attempt to explore the ever-growing domain of the unknown.

Approximately at the same time the spread of the psychoanalytic doctrines of Freud and his associates brought about an almost complete revolution in the accepted ideas about the workings of the human mind. Certain widely known aspects of Freud's theories — for instance, those pertaining to the rôle of sex — have little to do with the development of

Surrealism. Some of his clinical principles and therapeutic methods, however, exerted a decisive influence upon the elaboration of the program of the new school. André Breton himself was a physician specializing in nervous and mental diseases, and therefore thoroughly acquainted with the medical angle of the Freudian doctrines. As a rule, the Surrealists took from psychoanalysis the general notion that the subconscious constitutes the fundamental basis, the essential reality of our mental life. The subconscious *is* the truth, a truth most of the time too crude and too potent for our shy, convention-ridden selves to bear; so clear intelligence is constantly busy disguising that truth, suppressing our instinctive, obscure cravings or giving them a fallacious, sublimated expression through symbolical ideas or imaginings. The all-important subconscious can be reached and liberated only by some method capable of eliminating intelligence temporarily from the field of man's mental activity.

The Surrealists evinced a special interest in one particular method, which is used by psychoanalysts for curative purposes, but which appeared to André Breton and his friends essentially as a means for revealing facets of human nature hitherto held inaccessible to direct observation. A subject is invited to clear his mind of any specific preoccupation and to formulate rapidly the words or sentences which may present themselves to him, without giving his intelligence an opportunity to censor or to interpret whatever surges up from the depths of his subconsciousness. In this manner, deep, genuine sentiments come to the surface which otherwise would remain concealed, unknown to the patient himself, buried in the secret recesses of his personality. Then it is sometimes possible for a competent psychoanalyst to discover a clue enabling him eventually to uproot the original cause of the patient's mental disorder.

Now the phenomenon of spontaneous verbal suggestion

which had first aroused André Breton's curiosity undoubtedly offered striking similarities to the conditions artificially and deliberately created by the psychoanalysts. The experiment in which Breton indulged subsequently with the collaboration of Philippe Soupault was, we are informed (6), directly inspired by their methods. More generally, among cultured men in France at that time, even those who were much less versed than André Breton in medical technique could not but be deeply interested in the new theories which claimed to cast a revealing light upon some of the most obscure sides of human nature. Around the years 1920–25, psychoanalysis was the great novelty, the latest vogue of the day; and even though its conclusions were not accepted by all, certain of its theses became so widely known that they influenced profoundly the views held by the public about the possibilities of mysterious revelations to be expected from the subconscious mind.

In conjunction with this renewed concern for the more hidden aspects of our spiritual life, the works of two inspired, visionary writers of a previous generation, Rimbaud and Lautréamont, rose quickly to a climax of influence and fame. Rimbaud's talent had been recognized, it is true, even during his lifetime; since then his reputation had been growing in a slow, steady manner. Admiration, however, had gone mainly in the past to the supreme artistry of his works, conjoined with an intense curiosity for the picturesque eccentricity of his career. But the *révolté* in him had received scant applause, and the esoteric prophet had been more often than not misunderstood or ignored. The modern generation, however, was better prepared to receive this particular part of his message. The Cubists already had held him in high reverence. For the post-war generation he became the great precursor and the exalted model whose ideas were to

(6) *Manifeste du Surréalisme*, p. 41.

be integrated almost in their entirety within the framework of Surrealist doctrine.

The case of Lautréamont was perhaps even more striking. For nearly half a century, he had been but little known, and he had met with scant appreciation from professional critics. No reprint of his works had been made since 1890, and his influence on literature was practically nil. Then the rebellious attitude evident in his works struck the imagination of the Dadaists. The inexhaustible flow of sentences gushing out freely from the inmost part of his subconsciousness constituted for the new school a precedent of inestimable worth. In 1920 the publishing firm, La Sirène, sponsored by André Salmon, issued a new edition of *Les Chants de Maldoror*. This book enjoyed at once such a tremendous success that within a few years five new editions were put on the market and readily absorbed by a now much interested public.

From this welter of heterogeneous movements and theories, from the conjoined influence of Cubism, Dadaism, relativity, psychoanalysis, Rimbaud, and Lautréamont, a few definite tendencies began to assert themselves, in the early 1920's, among the young men who were then surrounding André Breton. The original nucleus of common ideas within that group constituted rather a general plan for further research than a program to be carried out systematically. The essential points about which the first Surrealists found themselves in agreement were approximately as follows: they were all possessed with an almost mystic faith in the existence of a higher Reality beyond the pale of our everyday experience; their great purpose in life was to strive with all their might to grasp as much as possible of this sublime essence; they were convinced that clear reason could not help them at all in their quest; further, they felt that the data provided for man by discursive intelligence would have to be eliminated as obstructing the way towards their supreme ideal.

In their view the only means of access to Surreality was through the avenue of the subconscious mind. How to use this avenue for their search was the main problem which they hoped to solve in the course of their future investigations. They believed, however, that they had already found a first key to the enigma in the automatic development of irrational thought, springing, in certain privileged circumstances, from the depths of human consciousness.

After long and impassioned discussions, the new school came officially into being in October 1924, when André Breton published his *Manifeste du Surréalisme*. Shortly afterwards, on December 1 of the same year, appeared the review *La Révolution surréaliste*, which was to be the organ of the newly organized group. The group included a number of former Dadaists; also a few enthusiastic newcomers. The outstanding personalities were then André Breton, Philippe Soupault, Louis Aragon, Paul Eluard, Jacques Rigaut, René Crevel, Robert Desnos, and Pierre Naville. Francis Picabia expressed his formal support of the Surrealist aspirations. It is noteworthy, however, that painters at first played a rôle of minor importance in the formation of the school. Tristan Tzara and his friends remained aloof, if not hostile. The mainspring of the movement was evidently André Breton, and his leadership was openly consecrated when, after its third issue, he assumed the direction of *La Révolution surréaliste*.

The very name of *La Révolution surréaliste* — which was changed to *Le Surréalisme au service de la Révolution* in 1930 — was indicative of certain subversive trends within the Surrealist group, trends which were soon to be a cause of endless and inextricable difficulties. It must be remembered that Surrealism developed in an environment which was far from calm and happy. It was conceived in the throes of the post-war crisis, and it was born in an atmosphere of exaltation and fever. It did not spring into being *ex nihilo*, without antecedent of any kind, but succeeded directly to the frantic extravagances of the Dadaist revolt. At the origin of the Surrealist search for something more vital than the commonplace world that we know, there was a refusal to accept as inevitable its cruel and tyrannical oppression. At the basis of the contempt for clear intelligence there was a rejection of all the ancient forms of our culture founded on reason. At the bottom of the trust placed in the subconscious aspects of human thought, there was an implicit glorification of the urges and cravings which are condemned by our "conventional" moral conscience.

In short, the longing for the so-called *Surréel* was naught but the counterpart of an attitude of negation and destruction towards all the ruling standards of our life. So when Jacques Rigaut committed suicide by shooting himself in 1929, his death was greeted, as that of Jacques Vaché had been, with the reverence due to a thoroughly sincere man, almost that due to a martyr. While to an outside observer, the constructive aspirations and the feelings of revolt of the Surrealist movement appear as two complementary sides of the same complex phenomenon, for the adherents of the school themselves the coexistence of these contradictory views very soon took on most disturbing, even dramatic, implications. How was a sincere man to reconcile in practice destructive activity and creative research? If a choice had to be made, which was to take precedence over the other? Opinions, of course, were divided; hence a multiplicity of quarrels and internal polemics, which almost from the start marred the harmony and hampered the efficient work of the new Surrealist group.

Certain Surrealists held that their essential contribution lay in the field of psychology, literature, and art. They did not deny that the ultimate goal towards which all should strive was a transformation in the conditions of existence of a harried humanity. They believed, however, that a change in this regard could best be effected through alterations in the general ways of thinking, alterations which, according to them, their future discoveries would unfailingly produce within a short time. With this in mind, they concentrated their efforts upon the quest of a transcendent Surreality, persuaded that its sublime radiance would eventually illumine and regenerate the soul of desperate mankind.

Other Surrealists, reversing this order of thinking, held that it was impossible to reach any Surreality as long as mankind faced the present distressing circumstances. The most urgent task was to precipitate the general upheaval, which, according to them, was to make a clean slate for the future, with all social problems obliterated. They admitted the interest and the value of psychological researches beyond the range of clear consciousness; at the same time they asked for more direct and decisive action.

Violently tossed between these conflicting tendencies, Surrealism failed to make any marked headway during the first five years of its existence. The most striking feature of its evolution in the course of that period was the ascendency acquired by the artistic group over the literary element. At the beginning the writers had maintained, at least in the realm of theory, a position of almost undisputed leadership. As time went on, however, the painters — perhaps because, by the nature of their work, they were less directly implicated in political controversies, or perhaps because their contributions caught the public eye more aggressively — attracted increasing curiosity and aroused widespread discussion. It was essentially through their medium that the movement became known throughout France, and even eventually extended its influence abroad.

Meanwhile André Breton tried to maintain, outwardly at

least, the unity of the Surrealist group. By dint of incessant friendly negotiations, and thanks to ever-renewed diplomatic compromises, he succeeded for a while in holding together the two trends of thought, which, although originating from the same historical circumstances, were becoming more and more divergent in their practical application. Yet, in spite of all efforts at conciliation, the inevitable rupture came. Certain Surrealists, impatient with André Breton's dilatory and wavering attitude, broke away from him and devoted themselves openly to political propaganda. The most sensational instance of secession was the case of Louis Aragon, who not only deserted his old Surrealist associates but also gave up in anger the elaborate literary technique which he had formerly evolved, essentially under their influence.

Soon feeling ran high, and bitter words were exchanged; resignations and expulsions multiplied, much to the amusement of outsiders. Following Louis Aragon, for one reason or another, Philippe Soupault, Francis Picabia, Georges Ribemont-Dessaignes, Robert Desnos, Pierre Naville — that is to say, the greater part of the original Surrealist group — withdrew individually from the school. André Breton, it is true, had become reconciled with Tristan Tzara and had acquired a few new recruits, such as Georges Hugnet and René Char. But certain of these adherents were of doubtful value. When René Crevel committed suicide in 1935, there remained only Paul Eluard as outstanding poet in the group who was still faithful to the standard of the old leader. The Surrealists at this point appeared to be facing complete dissolution and rout.

Then, suddenly, powerful reinforcements coming from unexpected quarters not only enabled them to consolidate their position but even helped them to regain all the ground they had lost during the internecine feud of the past years. In its earlier days, Surrealism had crossed the frontiers of

Yves Tanguy: *Extinction des Lumières inutiles* (1927)
A suggestion of an "other" world

France and had found in Central Europe an exceptionally favorable reception. The moral and material distress prevailing there since the Armistice had created an ideal ground for the breeding of "advanced" theories in literature and art. When the Surrealist movement developed in Paris, its positive program made an enormous impression upon those artists of Central Europe who were still seeking a formula of their own. As a rule, Surrealism was not adopted by them in its entirety, but it provided them with practical guidance and with theoretical justification for their special pursuits.

When the Nazi government, however, became firmly established in Germany, all the vanguard artists were regarded with definite suspicion by the new official régime. It is said that Adolf Hitler, believing himself to be a connoisseur in art, reacted personally in the most violent manner against all types of modernistic painting. As a consequence, a mass emigration of vanguard artists was started not only from Germany but also from all the countries of Central Europe threatened by the expansion of the German system. Further, the authoritarian state sold abroad the most valuable modern pictures it possessed, thus replenishing its treasury with welcome foreign monies and also purifying its own art galleries of the taint of "degenerate" art.

The majority of the exiled artists, and many of the discarded works of art, found their way to New York, London, and Paris. In these three centers of artistic life, Surrealism, which lately had been obviously on the wane, experienced after 1936 an astonishing revival. In Paris, especially, the Surrealist recovery was spectacular. Old differences within the group were adjusted; direct political action was relegated to a secondary place; exhibitions of the new art multiplied; the general public again took notice and again began to wonder.

André Breton once more rose to a position of respected

leadership. In 1938 an exposition was held at the Galerie des Beaux-Arts in order to advertise and celebrate this renewal of Surrealist influence. Much to the visitors' surprise, there were to be seen in several rooms, hanging from the ceiling, scores of little bags all containing coal! There is in Paris a very well-known coal dealer of the name of Breton, otherwise unconnected, however, with the Surrealist writer. The unusual decoration adopted at the exposition was intended to suggest — through an easily understandable pun, typical of the Surrealists, who cherish subconscious associations of unrelated words — that the whole exposition was placed under the aegis, as it were, of "Breton."

André Breton and Paul Eluard are at present the two outstanding representatives of literary Surrealism in France. Surrealism, it is true, has made its influence felt much beyond the range of the group's own membership. From an early date the whole field of poetry has been, to an important degree, permeated with its doctrine. Nowadays the novel, too, is obliged to admit increasingly numerous elements derived from this source. Yet, though Surrealism constitutes an important factor in the development of contemporary French literature, its contributions in the domain of decoration and painting have lately attracted far more attention on the part of the general public. Indeed, the emigration which was determined by the Central European crisis and which brought about a strong revival of modernistic doctrines in Paris was of much less consequence for pure letters than for the plastic arts. Foreign vanguard authors, handicapped by the difference in language, could not affect French literary production in any perceptible manner. Foreign artists, on the contrary, could express themselves just as easily in one country as in another, and their works were to a large extent responsible for the renewed interest shown in France in the ideas presented by the Surrealists. Yet it must not be forgotten that

these ideas had originally been elaborated by the French
writers themselves. Even now, when the most arresting and
sensational manifestations of Surrealism are perhaps to be
found in the works of painters, the literary group headed by
André Breton remains still in the lead for the systematic
presentation of its theoretical principles and for the direction
of the spiritual researches which it implies.

The theoretical principles upon which the Surrealist doctrine is based form a complicated ensemble whose intricacies
still baffle the majority of the cultivated public. In order to
understand their development and their bearing, it is essential to follow the successive stages that mark, according to the
adherents of the new school, the evolution of an average
human mind from early childhood up to an adult, "reasonable" age.

The Surrealists assume that all young children live mostly
in an enchanted, miraculous world, lying halfway between
actual reality and the magic realm of dreams. The little girl
nursing a wooden doll, the little boy pretending to be a
pirate and sitting in an empty crate which for him represents
a ship on the high seas, both enjoy a state of intense exaltation which has no parallel in the experience of the adult.
These privileged moments are endowed with such rich
poetical charm that man always recalls this period of his
existence wistfully, with a sentiment of regret and loss.

It must be noted that the domain in which children move
so freely is not purely ideal. Their imagination requires a
strong and definite support based upon concrete fact. The
empty crate for the little boy, and the doll for the little girl,
play an indispensable rôle in the formal expression of their
complex piratical instincts or maternal feelings. If, on the
one hand, imagination completely transfigures for them inert
and banal playthings, on the other hand the tangible reality

of the toys themselves confers upon their fleeting turns of fancy the convincing objectiveness of actual, solid existence. Thus children find themselves at the intersection of two worlds not at all antagonistic but properly complementing each other. Children do not have to escape — as do so many adults — from an uncongenial environment into a separate and distinct realm of dreams. For them fact and fancy blend in perfect harmony; at the core of this harmony they are able to seize, all intuitively, the elusive, mysterious soul of the universe.

As the child grows up, this magic vision of the world is slowly but ineluctably obscured. The practical necessities of life and, above all, the conjoined efforts of parents, teachers, and friends tend to substitute for his direct and original perceptions a set of impersonal and ready-made ideas. Progressively, the child *learns* to see the world in a definite and conventional manner. Colors, smells, sounds which formerly spoke to him a secret and symbolic language turn into plain informative signs of usefulness, pleasure, and danger. Soon he becomes nearly incapable of any autonomous interpretation of his own surroundings. He merely repeats with fair accuracy the practical lessons impressed upon him, and, as his outlook upon life grows more and more "sensible" and stale, all the adults in his family rejoice at the wonderful progress of his education! The aim of traditional education is to awaken sound judgment and the faculty of reasoning, that is to say, to banish all nonsense and to give due recognition to actual facts. When this purpose has been achieved, the world of imagination and the world of reality are no longer inextricably interwoven. They are definitively separated, and discriminating intelligence keeps them inexorably apart in two distinct mental compartments.

For a while, however, as a rule, imagination retains a curious independent activity. It is the time of adolescence, when

young men and young women indulge in secret, wonderful
daydreams. Yet, though they may find delightful entertainment in their fancies, they know full well, deep in their
hearts, that these inventions of their mind do not correspond
in reality to anything tangible and solid. That is why daydreams, even if temporarily pleasurable, always prove in the
end to be profoundly unsatisfying.

Further, the imaginative faculties, working so to speak in a
vacuum, and lacking the substantial aliment of facts, soon fall
into a state of atrophy. After the age of twenty, very few
retain more than a dim, whimsical recollection of the fascinating realm wherein they spent their younger years. Then
nearly all possibility of intense, spontaneous enthusiasm as a
result of contact with the simplest aspects of nature is irretrievably lost. As a man grows up, he evolves into a well-
regulated automaton, whose comportment is determined by
positive material considerations and by shrewd intellectual
reasoning. At the same time, a hopeless mediocrity has
settled somehow upon all his actions and desires. Of that
condition he is only too well aware; he suffers, mourning for
the lack of any sublime inspiration in his everyday humdrum
existence. Sublime inspiration has been so well expunged
from his life by the combined pressure of practical utility
and social influence that the average adult seems condemned
to run endlessly in a maddening circle of inescapable dullness.

Yet the Surrealists believe that in most of us the capacity
for genuine enthusiasm is not altogether annihilated. Even
if we allow our lives to be ruled outwardly by a rational and
practical conventionalism, our suppressed mystic tendencies
often find a safe refuge in the depths of our subconsciousness.
Since all manifestations of their existence are prohibited by
the prevailing pattern of our material environment as well as
by the imperious consorship of our intellect, they must be

content to subsist only latently in the most remote and hidden corners of our mind. In the usual course of things, these tendencies are given no chance to play a decisive part in the motivation of our everyday behavior. They may cause in us, it is true, some indefinite restlessness; they may even arouse temporarily a nostalgic longing for the unknown; but as a rule, after a few futile attempts at self-expression, they are reduced to silence and ruthlessly driven back to their sheltering obscurity.

The purpose of Surrealism is to liberate from all shackles these supposedly rich and fecund potentialities of our inner being. We must grant them, say the Surrealists, absolute freedom and allow them to give us their message in its illuminating entirety. Further, we should deliberately help them to regain the vigor which they must have lost during years of paralyzing idleness. Through wholesome, regular exercise, the dormant forces lying in our subconsciousness will eventually get back the power which was theirs at the time of childhood. Moreover, that power will undoubtedly increase much beyond its original scope, since our adult mind, fully developed and grown, has come to possess an intrinsic strength far superior to that of our formative period. Thus it will be possible again to achieve an intense and intimate communion between the human personality and the essence of the universe. Thus human life will acquire its true, enthralling signification upon a higher transcendental plane. Thus new creative energies will be released which may be able in the end to transfigure all the forms and modes of our existence on earth.

Surrealism, nevertheless, does not advocate, as has sometimes been said, a pure and simple return to infantilism. The Surrealists believe that practical and rational education does thwart infinitely precious aptitudes which manifest themselves freely only during childhood. Yet, in their view, these aptitudes should not be merely resurrected at the elementary stage in which they are at the beginning of our life. They should be cultivated, made to unfold and expand, for probably they hold the solution to the enigma of our existence as well as the essential key to sublime happiness.

In order to achieve their aims, the Surrealists feel that they have to pursue concurrently two seemingly different objectives. First, they must break the bonds of practical and logical thinking in order to release our subconscious imagination. Second, they must devise means to enable the *Surréel* to develop and extend its empire over man's complete destiny. These two complementary aspects of Surrealism are often combined in Surrealist works; they are not easily distinguished by a casual observer. It is important, however, to separate clearly their manifestations, since they correspond to two successive stages in the development of Surrealist research.

According to the Surrealists, the liberation of our subconscious mind can best be effected through an attitude of deliberate censorship towards all the accepted forms of traditional thinking. In their view, the interpretation of the world offered by our intellect does not correspond to anything truly essential either in the deep constitution of man or in the fundamental nature of things. In truth, intellect may be compared to a screen interposed between our Ego and the radiant effulgence of the universe. Such a screen may be convenient for practical purposes, but it is decidedly an obstacle to our direct communication with the rest of the Cosmos. Therefore, all means are legitimate which might bring about its total and final disintegration. Irony, ridicule, sarcasm are our most efficient weapons in this struggle for our complete inward enfranchisement. Every fixed form of opinion or expression must be discarded as arbitrary and absurd. Every established law about aesthetics or morals must be ruthlessly swept away in order to leave room for absolute freedom.

These negative and destructive theories do not present at first sight any special feature that is original and new. It has been seen how — before the Surrealists — Rimbaud, Lautréamont, Jarry, the Cubists, and the Dadaists had set sensational precedents of revolt against the most respected traditional standards. The main contribution of the Surrealists in this respect seems to be a thorough systematization of their attacks upon these standards. For a long time before them, the indictment of the various forms of our conventional life had been a reaction of anger in the face of the imbecility or the cruelty of man's present-day surroundings. Going beyond this, the Surrealists insisted that the indictment should be more than a burst of anger; it should be a permanent, cultivated, deliberate critical attitude. Indeed conventions, intellectual or otherwise, cannot be destroyed once and for all. Under the influence of our environment they constantly tend to form and to grow again, overlaying the mind with a thick crust of artificial ideas. In order to keep our spirit perfectly lucid, we must work tirelessly to remove these adventitious formations which would otherwise develop on the surface of our personality.

Thus nearly all the Surrealist works give an important place to virulent satire. By showing on every possible occasion that all our rational conceptions about the world that we know are completely absurd, the Surrealists hope to neutralize the power that these conceptions have long held over our minds. "Humor" is the name applied — after Jarry, after the Cubists, and after the Dadaists — to this Surrealist lampooning of every notion that we have been taught to revere. Surrealist humor is a grotesque parody of all things in which the ordinary "unenlightened" man still implicitly believes. Nothing has contributed more than this challenge to common sense through absurdity to cause the misunderstanding which now exists between the general public and modernistic writers. Yet nothing, perhaps, appears more important to the modernistic writers themselves than this complete breach with what they consider remnants of an outmoded past. Thus, when André Breton tried to review the outstanding accomplishments of Surrealism, he did not fail to list in the very first place: *l'humour objectif* (7).

Indeed, when destructive humor has definitely cleared the field of all conventional obstacles, man can at last have access to the enthralling *Surréel*. In the ordinary run of daily existence, only those aspects of our character are allowed to appear which are in strict keeping with the bare pattern of standard everyday behavior. But in certain privileged moments of Surrealist transport, the unsuspected potentialities of our inmost being surge up when in contact with the elemental forces of Nature. Of course, such contact cannot take place if we look at the world analytically, breaking up its attributes into separate fragments and arranging these fragments according to an arbitrary order. We must grasp through mystic intuition the totality of energies offered to our experience. Then in a flash of supreme insight we will perceive simultaneously the depths of our own individuality and the true essence of the universal.

Thus would be resolved the age-long antagonism between the subjective and the objective. The Surrealists believe that this traditional distinction has been introduced artificially by logical intelligence. If man returns to his most spontaneous approach to life, he becomes aware that, for him as for the child, there is no clean-cut separation between his imagination and his surroundings, no irreducible opposition between his Ego and the Cosmos. The two blend and fuse, not on the

(7) A. Breton, "Limites non frontières du Surréalisme," *La Nouvelle Revue française*, February 1, 1937, p. 205.

lower level of practical activity and abstract analysis, but on the higher plane of entrancing mystic contemplation. For those who are capable of reaching this most exalted stage, the *Surréel* provides in one single, miraculous illumination the essence of our personality combined with the essence of the whole world.

It is not difficult to recognize in this magic *Surréel* a new avatar of the "other world" for which Baudelaire, Rimbaud, Mallarmé, and the Cubists had already evinced an earnest and profound yearning. The *Surréel*, however, differs markedly from its historical antecedents. Instead of being placed vaguely in a hypothetical beyond, it is definitely localized at the junction of the primal manifestations of cosmic energy and the pristine forms of subliminal thinking. The *Surréel* is not merely the expression of a fond, platonic hope. The Surrealists are convinced that it constitutes an actual domain to which we can have access if we agree to follow any of the several ways leading to its mysterious gates.

Of all the possible ways of access to the *Surréel*, the most readily practicable seems to be the one offered by imagination itself. Heretofore imagination has enjoyed, as a rule, comparatively little favor among the writers and the thinkers of France. Except during the Romantic period, when a free rein was given to all sorts of extravagant fancies, imagination has hardly ever been mentioned without a warning not to trust overmuch its alluring but deceitful suggestions. The Surrealists have undertaken to rehabilitate to the full this unduly discredited faculty. They have pointed out that the conscious mind does not possess any better instrument to effect the complete fusion of the fantastic and the real which is the avowed ultimate goal of their efforts. If we refrain from imposing a vigorous control upon our imaginative forces, both internal and external events will soon blend and merge indistinguishably one into another. Then, in the undulating reflection of a thousand combined images, we may be able to discern the outline of a supernatural pattern expressing the transcendental essence of the world. But though the Surrealists advocate the use and abuse of imagination as a means of access to a higher realm that our reason cannot penetrate, they do not seem to believe in its power to open definitely for us the inmost recesses of the unknown. Imagination, it is true, can fly well above the widest range of pedestrian intelligence. Yet on account of its ineluctable association with the familiar aspects of our daily life, it will never be able to soar absolutely freely into the forbidden domain beyond earthly experience.

Infinitely more revealing as to the true nature of Surreality seems to be the field of investigation provided by dreams. According to Surrealists, the mental phenomena occurring normally when our consciousness is overclouded by sleep correspond to the fundamental aspects of our personality. Then we catch glimpses of strange depths in our being. We grope in a vast uncertain twilight, dimly aware of the tremendous forces hidden in the secret substratum of our moral existence. If it were possible for us to get hold of these forces in their powerful totality, we would undoubtedly grasp the elemental forms of our Ego and also, through their medium, something of the essence of the universe. But, even in the most favorable cases, we can usually perceive only the upper contour of their appearance. When we come out of a dream, we retain only a pallid recollection of the mysteries we have been made to explore, and, in weary indifference, we generally disregard or despise the message that was perhaps implied in their very evocation.

In order to understand this message, the Surrealists like to dwell on the threshold of our subconscious mental activity, during those hazy moments when our spirit, half awake, half asleep, is already liberated from the influence of outer contingencies and yet not completely sunk, beyond the reach of our perceptive faculties, into total, unfathomable darkness. Nevertheless, as the Surrealists themselves are obliged to admit, the information garnered from these uncertain crepuscular hours constitutes but a very inadequate testimony of the original contents of our deeper self. Even if dreams truly hold within their meshes the fundamental secrets of Surreality, we are still almost powerless to make them deliver up their secrets.

Strangely enough, a much larger measure of mystic revelation seems to be obtainable through poetry and art. The standpoint of the Surrealists in this regard has so often been misunderstood by the general public that a clarification of their views may be deemed necessary in order to acquire a full comprehension of their objectives and their claims. A great many modernistic works, be they paintings or poems, are not only unintelligible — which might be perhaps justified or excused — but also utterly devoid of even the slightest aesthetic value. Hence the bewilderment of the bona fide lover of art who expects to find in the interplay of colors, lines, or words a measure of gratification of his own sense of the beautiful. Very soon he realizes that the Surrealists never attempt to catch and express the charm of any "thing of beauty" whatever.

Surrealism is not, properly speaking, an artistic or literary school. It is primarily a metaphysical attitude towards the whole of human existence. Art and literature are considered merely as means designed to help us to reach a superior, ideal state. Literature and art should not try to draw a faithful or attractive picture of life as it is. They should take us beyond the frontiers of this life and lead us — without any concern for the trifling accidents which are called beauty or ugliness — somewhere, very far away, on the long trail to Surrealist

Truth. As André Breton said: "On sait maintenant que la poésie doit mener quelque part" (8).

The Surrealists do not deny that certain forms of literature and art are capable of rendering with commendable accuracy the external aspects of earthly reality. For such achievements, however, they nurture an ill-concealed contempt. In their view, the genuine purpose of art is to manifest the latent spirit, the very soul of a given epoch. They believe that this spirit cannot possibly express itself within the framework of the rationalized construction which most people consider as being the only "real" world. The deepest emotions of man, collectively or individually, find an outlet essentially through fantastic creations, unsubjected to the petty carping of conventional intelligence. These fantastic symbols, all completely absurd from the standpoint of common sense, contain a message which can be deciphered only by the intuitive sympathy of a kindred mind. Their elaboration is not the work of analytical logic; it is the product of a spontaneous creative instinct having its roots at the very bottom of our inward consciousness. Thus have come into being, in the past, the great poetical myths in which has been mirrored the very soul of humanity. These myths, from the Sphinx to the Niebelungen, did not correspond to any actual creature or to any definite set of historical events. Yet in them was reflected a spiritual truth infinitely more important than the ephemeral happenings which may have occurred at a given moment throughout the development of the ages.

Similarly in our day, at a time when all our bearings have apparently been lost because abstract intellectualism has stopped the normal guiding flow of mythical invention, it behooves Surrealist literature and art to reopen the doors of spontaneous and collective fancy. Thus we shall be able at last to find our true selves, and also to discover our exact

(8) "Les Chants de Maldoror," *Les Pas perdus*, p. 80.

assigned relation to the ensemble of our epoch. Once possessing the knowledge of our proper position in the general order of the world, we shall have the power to correct the countless maladjustments coming from our present ignorance of its fundamental rhythm. Then the dream of Rimbaud, who had wanted to "changer la vie" (9), will finally come true, thanks to the Surrealist revelation of universal harmony.

One may well wonder, it is true, by what process a literary work, for instance, is capable of bringing to us such supernatural revelation. Since the time of Baudelaire, much attention has been paid to the inexplicable, miraculous power of certain words. Rimbaud showed conclusively that words possess, besides their obvious and usual signification, secret magic properties which can sometimes illumine with a sudden flash a mystic universe inaccessible to our senses. Mallarmé tried to find a rigorous method enabling the poet to make use of these properties with unerring precision. The Surrealists in their turn believe that the essential value of words lies not in their objective, trite, and worn-out meaning, but in the forces of subconscious poetical suggestion which are enclosed in the web of their syllables. How to release these forces constitutes for them the main technical literary problem. This problem they have approached with an emphatic earnestness. Only too often in the past the French have found entertainment in dexterously playing with curious vocables. According to the Surrealists, relations between words should be taken very seriously. Their fortuitous association sometimes arouses in us unexpectedly intense feelings, and in certain cases their union proves fecund in truly momentous and abiding results. André Breton could indeed affirm: "Les mots . . . ont fini de jouer. Les mots font l'amour" (10).

One of the outstanding contributions of Surrealism has

(9) "Une Saison en enfer," Œuvres, p. 279.
(10) "Les Mots sans rides," Les Pas perdus, p. 171.

been the discovery of a definite method to bring out these
latent potentialities of words. This method has had its direct
origin in the circumstances of the experiment carried out in
1919 by André Breton and Philippe Soupault. André Breton
himself has described in the following manner the practical
aspects of his new technique: "Faites-vous apporter de quoi
écrire, après vous être établi dans un lieu aussi favorable que
possible à la concentration de votre esprit sur lui-même.
Placez-vous dans l'état le plus passif ou réceptif que vous
pourrez. Faites abstraction de votre génie, de vos talents et
de ceux des autres. . . . Ecrivez vite, sans sujet préconçu,
assez vite pour ne pas vous retenir et ne pas être tenté de vous
relire" (11).

A Surrealist writer is not supposed to make any effort to
express and organize his sentiments or thoughts. He must be
content to listen to the voice of his subconsciousness — "la
voix surréaliste" — and to take down verbatim whatever that
voice may fancy to dictate. In order to receive this faint,
whispered dictation, he must shut out, as far as possible, all
disturbing outside influences. Reducing the activity of his
will power to a minimum, and putting, as it were, his faculties of critical judgment asleep, he will lapse insensibly into
a semiconscious state; then he will record automatically with
his pen absolutely every sentence that may present itself to
his indifferent mind.

Complete automatism is the condition *sine qua non* of the
successful recording of the Surrealist message. One word must
draw another word without the solicitation of any external
stimulus and without any interference on the part of discriminating intellect. Then a long train of phrases, all impregnated with the substance of the inner self, will flow
irresistibly from the very depths of subconsciousness. The
same automatism which provides the writer with an endless

(11) *Manifeste du Surréalisme*, pp. 51–52.

chain of associated vocables may offer to the painter an in-exhaustible series of loosely joined images. The artist has but to adopt an absolutely passive attitude of mind and let his brush run over the canvas without conscious control in order to obtain a juxtaposition of lines and shapes reflecting the authentic aspects of his personality. It is easy to conceive of the extension of this method to all the other forms of creative art — so much so that psychic automatism has come to be considered as the keystone of the whole structure of Surrealist method. André Breton himself has given the following cele-brated definition of Surrealism: "Automatisme psychique pur par lequel on se propose d'exprimer soit verbalement, soit par écrit, soit de toute autre manière, le fonctionnement réel de la pensée. Dictée de la pensée, en l'absence de tout contrôle exercé par la raison, en dehors de toute préoccupa-tion esthétique ou morale" (12).

The product of automatic subconscious dictation is a text of grotesque and dismaying incoherency. Such is the power of words that their sheer concatenation in an order different from the one required by our rational categories is enough to put out of gear our entire system of interpretation of the world. Indeed, most people are capable of thinking only through the intermediary of words. As long as the verbal constructions to which they have been accustomed are left rigorously intact, no expostulation can shake their confidence in the value of the principles which are supposed to stand behind them. But the framework of the fixed forms of lan-guage once destroyed, nothing can prevent the dislocation and the collapse of the readers' whole organized conception of life. They find themselves then in presence of a chaotic mass of bewildering impressions, in the midst of which they look in vain for the reassuring landmarks of a familiar reality.

(12) *Manifeste du Surréalisme*, p. 46.

Yet man is not left altogether guideless before this motley confusion of the weird and the fantastical. The bizarre images evoked by the automatic development of associated words reveal at the very core of things a certain order entirely different from that perceived by our intelligence and our senses. This new order is apprehended through obscure intuitive elements in our personality which are infinitely more delicate and subtle than our clear, common understanding. As these elements seem to be in close touch with the basic forces of Nature, one may easily see how they can grasp mysterious and yet capital relations which elude the grosser embrace of dialectical reasoning.

Nevertheless, even if uncontrolled automatism is accepted in theory as an efficient method of attaining the enigmatic *Surréel*, it must be admitted that in practice this process has only too often proved to be extremely disappointing. One may go over pages and pages of monotonous Surrealist writings and fail to discover in them — except for brief, occasional flashes — any feature of intense or compelling interest. The Surrealists themselves have become aware of this lack of human and artistic appeal in the majority of their works, and many of them have already given up the pure and simple presentation of the raw subconscious material which was considered around 1924 solely authentic and genuine. The prevailing tendency today is to allow intelligent will power a not inconsiderable measure of controlling influence. The author thus selects consciously a center of psychic resonance, and also controls undue divagations which might develop too far from its original, fundamental note. Such interference on the part of clear consciousness could ultimately open the way to a return to discipline and common sense. Yet, up to now at least, so wide a scope has still been left to the irradiation of subliminal thought that the general principles of Surrealism cannot be considered as markedly affected by this slight alteration in the practical modalities of its applied technique.

Among the guiding impulses discreetly but deliberately given by the Surrealists to the formal development of their subconsciousness, none is perhaps more illustrative of their fundamental intentions than the one oriented towards mental disorders. André Breton and Paul Eluard particularly have indulged, in that direction, in gruesome but curious personal experiments. By imitating closely the outside symptoms of, say, intermittent mania, paresis, or dementia praecox, they hoped to acquire — only temporarily, of course — the subconscious outlook of inmates of a lunatic asylum. This voluntary recourse to simulated insanity had as its purpose to destroy every vestige of the influence of reason and also to explore the strange and forbidden domains where Gérard de Nerval had once gathered marvelous flowers of "supernaturaliste" revelation. Further, the Surrealist painter Salvador Dali, in his book *La Femme visible*, has openly advocated the adoption of a delirious attitude of mind in our appraisal of the outside world. In all earnestness and without any hint of irony, he has hailed the latest aspects of modernistic art as perfect manifestations of paranoiac thought.

The results of the attempts to integrate mental alienation within the regular cycle of Surrealist research have not come up to the expectations of their authors. The book entitled *L'Immaculée Conception* in which Breton and Eluard have presented the record of their bold endeavor in this field does not differ strikingly from the previous texts obtained through the ordinary method of free, automatic dictation. Indeed, though many Surrealist works may appear to the eyes of the candid general public as stamped merely with folly, it seems very doubtful whether an average person in normal health would ever be able to force the entrance to the dismal regions of clinical irrationality.

Salvador Dali: *Endless Enigma*
Certain Surrealist creations evoke a paranoiac dream

On the whole, the capital weakness of Surrealism probably lies in the fact that, in spite of its genuinely ingenious theories, it has failed to produce so far any concrete achievement that indisputably proves its intrinsic worth. At the present moment André Breton is undeniably the outstanding representative of literary Surrealism in France. It has been seen how his work *Les Champs Magnétiques*, written in collaboration with Philippe Soupault, had marked the starting-point of the whole school. Since then his books of critical discussion of the new theories — as, for instance, *Les Pas perdus, Introduction au discours sur le peu de réalité, Les Vases communicants, Point du jour* — have established his reputation as the most fully qualified exponent of the "orthodox" Surrealist doctrine. It must be said that a large part of these studies is consecrated to the thankless task of keeping together the principle of a search for a higher reality through the medium of the subconsciousness with the Marxist program of political and social revolution. The main interest of André Breton's theoretical works, however, lies in his earnest endeavor to set on firm ground the psychological basis of modernistic literature and art. Being richly endowed with a sense of the ineffable and possessing as well a clear view of the exigencies of the mind, he knows how to present in the most convincing manner all the arguments that might induce us to relinquish this world of allegedly spurious appearances for the sake of an invisible but wonderful Surreality.

In *Poisson soluble, Clair de terre, Nadja, Le Revolver à cheveux blancs*, and *L'Amour fou*, André Breton has himself tried to evoke the *Surréel*, essentially through the power of dreams. He excels in conjuring up a turbid atmosphere of instability and incoherency in which fragmentary images coalesce and dissolve according to a law which does not belong to our tangible universe. In this dizzy mirage, no violent catastrophe ever comes to disrupt the flowing development of vague forms which melt slowly, endlessly, into one another. Nevertheless, the haunting premonition of a secret, indefinite menace seems to hover permanently about this alarming phantasmagoria. Here the plausible and the fabulous meet and unite monstrously to beget weird and uncertain hybrids which simultaneously partake of the forceful intensity of actual objects and of the disturbing inconsistency of chimerical nightmares.

Yet infinitely more penetrating and poignant is the approach to the *Surréel* presented by Paul Eluard, certainly the most richly gifted poet of the whole Surrealist group. Practically all his works, such as *Capitale de la douleur, Défense de savoir, Les Dessous d'une vie ou La Pyramide humaine, A toute épreuve, La Vie immédiate, Les Yeux fertiles,* and *Le Cours naturel,* suggest a hallucinatory vision of individual human destiny casting its reflection upon the colossal epic of universal existence. Paul Eluard's meditations gravitate spontaneously to the two opposite and yet complementary poles of solitude and love. Love is viewed by him as a mystic center of blazing forces, a fiery nucleus of passionate vibrations, diffusing energy throughout the whole world in ardent and pulsating waves. In its aura, every specific sensation loses its original distinctness and becomes identified with the spiritual Absolute. Thus love appears as a tremendous cosmic experience in which man participates anonymously through the sublime act of eternal creation. Yet if love is extended so prodigiously as to fill all the universe, its "substance" will finally dissipate itself into imperceptibility. A universe of love has as an inevitable counterpart a bleak and dismal "univers-solitude." With assumed outward impassibleness and yet with a perceptible throb of inward agony, Eluard has repeatedly conjured up its dripping silence, its icy glare, its crushing and boundless desolation. All that can be seen are atoms of suffering, particles of despair, whirling in fan-

tastic spirals, like an impalpable stellar dust in the midst of
astronomical immensities. The rest is cold, indifferent bar-
renness — hard, ascetic insensibility — oppressive and overwhelming absence.

The works of Robert Desnos, among them *La Liberté ou
l'amour* and *Corps et biens,* also mirror the supreme Surrealist
entity as viewed from the focal point of love. One would
search vainly in them, however, for the abstract metaphysical
quality which characterizes most of Eluard's productions.
Desnos seems to wallow with special predilection in the repulsive quagmire of physical eroticism. There livid, slimy forms
of sensual perversity, aroused from their heavy slumber, twist
and turn ignominiously, releasing in their convulsive spasms
an acrid and suffocating stench. The spectacle is not devoid,
it must be said, of a certain awesome grandeur. In the midst
of parched, scoriac landscapes, the sulphurous glow emanating
from this crawling accumulation of filth irresistibly conjures
up visions of those infernal haunts "where their worm dieth
not and the fire is not quenched."

When Tristan Tzara gave up the pointless extravagance of
Dadaism and decided to join the ranks of the Surrealist school,
he retained something of the tumultuous and chaotic fecun-
dity which had been the mark of his earlier period. An epic
poem, *L'Homme approximatif;* a set of lyrical pieces, *Où
boivent les loups;* a collection of essays in prose, *L'Antitête;*
and a series of more or less philosophical tales, *Grains et
issues* — all bear witness to his wild, unbounded energy and
also to his irremediable incoherence. His normal element
seems to be an atmosphere of apocalyptic disaster. In all his
works, a vortex of primal forces unleashed thrashes aimlessly
at a greyish, amorphous substance. This brutal and paroxys-
mal cosmogony unfolds blindly, with no apparent purpose,
except perhaps to suggest the tragic futility of the whole display of human life.

René Char, a former virulent adversary of Surrealism, recently converted to the ideal of this school, has produced so far only a very few works that deserve any critical consideration. Typical books of his, *L'Action de la Justice est éteinte* and *Le Tombeau des secrets* have a certain transparent hardness; it it may be questioned whether their seemingly concerted simplicity is or is not in fact the result of a definite indigence of creative inspiration.

Philippe Soupault and Louis Aragon both severed their connection with Surrealism at a comparatively early date, so only a few of their productions bear the unmistakable imprint of the technique of this school. Philippe Soupault shows in several of his *Poésies complètes* a subtle and graceful ease recalling the manner of Guillaume Apollinaire. Here a wondrous rainbow-tinted light, softened by a vague opalescent mist, suffuses the clear outline of a delicate and subtle filigree. In this enigmatical twilight, an Elysian peace seems to float over a prodigious efflorescence of inextricably intertwined festoons, blending their innumerable variegated arabesques into a chaste and subdued harmony.

If Philippe Soupault is the poet of an inward, translucid dawn, Louis Aragon is the prophet of a black, furious, crepuscular storm. With vociferous wrath, he denounces the crimes of our society and gloatingly visualizes its catastrophic collapse in a near future. In *Fin du jour, Mouvement perpétuel, La Grande Gaieté* and *Persécuté persécuteur,* a mass of gross invectives, cynical jests, and foul blasphemies gathers and rumbles ominously, ready to crush under its sheer irresistible weight a world conceived by him as a crazy jumble of tottering absurdities. Such scathing indictments are much more akin to partisan polemics than to a disinterested search for truth. Yet even now that Aragon has definitely turned away from Surrealism towards a descriptive and "proletarian" conception of literature, one can still perceive here and there in his most recent works — such as *Les Cloches de Bâle* or *Les Beaux Quartiers* — strange fulgurations coming from a deep, visionary perception of a mysterious universe.

Most of the literary productions mentioned above have been presented to the public as "poems in prose." Indeed, the Surrealist method of automatic dictation precludes the elaboration of the continuous narratives and coördinated dialogues which are required by the technique either of the novel or of the drama. Moreover, the spontaneous effusion of man's inward feelings and thoughts does possess, as a rule, a genuine poetical quality. The typical Surrealist themes — love, despair, revolt, cosmic ecstasy, thirst for the Absolute — have been treated in a variety of lyrical keys by all the great poets of all times. But, of course, there is no question of the Surrealists' complying with the intricate rules of French versification. The subconscious cannot be constrained to count the number of syllables, nor to submit to the exigencies of rhyme, nor even to follow a uniform rhythmical pace. As a consequence, the Surrealist text appears as a hybrid genre which often presents the true ring of poetry and yet lacks the indispensable support of formal poetic articulation.

This fundamental ambiguousness may have contributed to the failure of literary Surrealism to engage the abiding sympathy of the general public. It must be admitted, however, that this lack of sympathy is more easily explained by the mediocrity of the Surrealist works themselves. In order to find a few rare gems, sparkling with supraterrestrial radiance, we are only too often obliged to wade through endless swamps of depressing or disgusting absurdities. The reward seems so small in proportion to the effort involved in the search that most readers, after a half-hearted attempt, just shrug their shoulders and give up.

It is probable that literary Surrealism would have aroused only scant interest if it had not been accompanied and supported by an abundant artistic production. Though the Surrealist theories were at first elaborated essentially by writers, they have subsequently found their most adequate mode of expression in the domain of plastic art. It is certainly in the field of painting that we find the outstanding manifestations of the new school today. Indeed, the prickly and coruscating insects of Yves Tanguy; the hideous, visceral unfoldings of Max Ernst; the heavy, fabulous architectural forms of Giorgio Chirico, or his enigmatic mannequins; the sharp, geometric, crystalline vibrations of Paul Klee; the swarming, slimy larvae of André Masson; the weird nightmares of Salvador Dali, who grafts one upon another monstrous, mutilated human organs; the hairy, spidery vermicules of Joan Miró; the abstract, rigid simplifications of Francis Picabia — all these manifold examples of Surrealist hallucinatory intuition are evidently endowed with a fascinating and awe-compelling power. Yet none of these advanced artists has so far succeeded in creating an authentic, indisputable masterpiece. The Surrealists may well possess, as they claim, the secret of an epoch-making, mystic revelation, but it still remains for them to manifest this revelation through the evidence of their works.

After studying the different aspects presented by vanguard literature in France during the past half century, it seems possible to understand fairly clearly the general purpose of the modernistic movement as a whole. Yet it is doubtful whether one can always grasp the particular signification of any given work produced under its influence. Indeed, though principles and theories have changed very markedly from one period to another, a single definite tendency has asserted itself with increasing vigor throughout the evolution of the various schools, namely, the desire to rid artistic or literary works of any rigorous connection with the external reality that we perceive through reason and the senses. At the extreme limit of this tendency has even appeared the idea of a meaningless, self-contained, and self-justifying creation, absolutely unrelated to the normal concepts or shapes familiar to our experience.

It has sometimes been intimated that modernistic literature neglects the tangible and intelligible universe because of its engrossing interest in the expression of our subconscious feelings. Such a statement, though undoubtedly true, is yet somehow incomplete and even in certain respects misleading. None of the vanguard theories has ever been oriented towards pure and simple subjectivism. If our inner selves are to be brought to light, it is not because they are supposed to possess an intrinsic value of their own. Their value resides entirely in their affinity with the all-important, invisible world which, the mystics claim, exists beyond the scope of banal earthly shapes. This supreme mystic world constitutes the true goal of all the visionary artists and poets who have striven to escape from the paralyzing hold of practical conventionalism. It is because our subconscious thoughts seem to open the only possible way of access to this higher realm that they appear as endowed with inestimable worth.

To affirm that the most elementary forms of subconsciousness will eventually solve for us the baffling enigma of our destiny may seem at first sight a gratuitous and even preposterous assumption. This view, however, does not differ very much in pattern from the view that has been accepted almost unquestioningly by countless generations of strictly rational and well-balanced thinkers. The basis of rationalism itself rests upon the postulate that there is a rigorous concordance between the framework of the rational mind and the general architecture of the world. Rationalist philosophers were persuaded that by searching methodically the contents of our abstract mind we could discover the fundamental relations existing between the various attributes of external objects.

The practical attitude of those who were less philosophically inclined also implied that clear intelligence could be trusted as an adequate instrument to puzzle out the motley appearances of our universe.

When certain accidental circumstances and scientific discoveries shook the age-old belief in the correspondence between the general laws of the Cosmos and the categories of discursive reason, the men who were at the vanguard of the eternal quest for truth simply went one degree deeper in their interpretation of universal relationship. Instead of placing their confidence in clear, conscious thought, they relied upon obscure, subconscious intuitions. Instead of attempting to give an account of the visible and tangible aspects of the world, they tried to interpret a higher reality lying at the back of these allegedly superficial aspects. But with a definite, though perhaps unwilling, logical method in their apparent madness, they retained the conviction that there was between this higher reality and the subconsciousness a contact not radically different from the connection which the rationalists thought they could perceive between plain reality and the intellect.

To decide whether this "deeper" view of life is "truer" — as is claimed by all modern writers and artists — is very much a matter of intuitive feeling and personal spiritual experience. Obviously, the existence of the "other world" will never be irrefutably demonstrated. Yet so many philosophies and religions have vouched for the authenticity of some similar ideal that it is impossible to tax with extravagance those who, before the disheartening cruelty and stupidity of our world, hopefully and stubbornly believe that there must be "something else."

The methods by which certain contemporary artists and writers have tried to attain this elusive "something else" may be open, it is true, to very serious criticism. Only too often, modernistic works present grotesque and nightmarish shapes, without in any manner affording — by way of compensation — a glimpse of that "higher universe" which they are supposed to reveal. The principles from which such misshapen creations are derived may appear in theory not altogether devoid of foundation and even at times definitely impressive. Yet the works themselves have so far proved to be, almost without exception, profoundly disappointing. As Louis Aragon said: "Si vous écrivez, suivant une méthode surréaliste de tristes imbécillités, ce sont de tristes imbécillités. Sans excuses" (13).

Are we to believe, as certain adventurous minds fondly hope, that these phantasmagoric productions merely constitute prefigurations of more elaborate works of a similar kind that will develop magnificently in the years to come? Will their childish *naïveté* and all their other defects, which are so obvious at the present stage, be viewed by ulterior generations with the indulgent curiosity that we bestow now upon the "Primitifs" of past ages? Are they not, on the contrary, grave and disturbing symptoms of the moral confusion prevailing in our unbalanced epoch? In any case, it would be a mistake to consider modernistic theories either as a passing fashion or as the product of a few exceptional and pathological minds. The continuity of their development and their persistency under various forms throughout several anxious generations show conclusively that they correspond to something really deep and important in contemporary life. Starting essentially from France — though often elaborated by artists or writers of foreign origin — they have spread rapidly over the rest of Europe and America, adapting themselves here and there to the special conditions prevailing in each part of this extensive domain. In every case they have fol-

(13) Louis Aragon, *Traité du style* (Paris: Nouvelle Revue Française, 1928), p. 192.

lowed, as if on a parallel, the evolution of our social and political vicissitudes. Whatever their intrinsic worth, they express strikingly a genuinely pathetic reaction to the stress of our times.

Bibliography

I. Guillaume Apollinaire

L'Enchanteur pourrissant (Paris: Henry Kahnweiler, 1909)
La Poésie symboliste (Paris: L'Edition, 1909)
L'Hérésiarque et Cie (Paris: P. V. Stock, 1910)
Le Bestiaire ou Cortège d'Orphée (Paris: Deplanche, 1911)
Les Peintres cubistes, méditations esthétiques (Paris: E. Figuière, 1912)
Alcools (Paris: Mercure de France, 1913)
La Rome des Borgia (Paris: L'Edition, 1913)
La Fin de Babylone (Paris: L'Edition, 1913)
L'Antitradizione futurista (Milan: Direzione del Movimento Futurista, 1913)
Les Trois Don Juan (Paris: L'Edition, 1914)
Case d'armons (Aux Armées de la République, 1915)
Le Poète assassiné (Paris: L'Edition, 1916)
Vitam impendere amori (Paris: Mercure de France, 1917)
Les Mamelles de Tirésias, drame surréaliste (Paris: Editions Sic, 1918)
Calligrammes (Paris: Mercure de France, 1918)
Le Flâneur des deux rives (Paris: Editions de la Sirène, 1918)
La Femme assise (Paris: Nouvelle Revue Française, 1920)
Il y a . . . (Paris: Messein, 1925)
Anecdotiques (Paris: P. V. Stock, 1926)

II. Louis Aragon

Feu de joie (Paris: Au Sans Pareil, 1920)
Anicet ou Le Panorama (Paris: Nouvelle Revue Française, 1921)
Les Aventures de Télémaque (Paris: Nouvelle Revue Française, 1922)
Le Libertinage (Paris: Nouvelle Revue Française, 1924)
Le Mouvement perpétuel (Paris: Nouvelle Revue Française, 1926)
Le Paysan de Paris (Paris: Nouvelle Revue Française, 1926)

Traité du style (Paris: Nouvelle Revue Française, 1928)
La Grande Gaieté (Paris: Nouvelle Revue Française, 1929)
La Peinture au défi (Paris: Goemans, 1930)
Persécuté persécuteur (Paris: Editions Surréalistes, 1931)
Aux Enfants rouges (Paris: Bibliothèque Antireligieuse, 1932)
Hourra l'Oural (Paris: Denoël et Steele, 1934)
Les Cloches de Bâle (Paris: Denoël et Steele, 1934)
Pour un réalisme socialiste (Paris: Denoël et Steele, 1935)
Les Beaux Quartiers (Paris: Denoël et Steele, 1936)

III. André Breton

Mont-de-Piété (Paris: Au Sans Pareil, 1919)
Les Champs magnétiques, in collaboration with P. Soupault (Paris: Au Sans Pareil, 1921)
Clair de terre (Paris: Collection Littérature, 1923)
Les Pas perdus (Paris: Nouvelle Revue Française, 1924)
Manifeste du Surréalisme. Poisson soluble (Paris: S. Kra, 1924)
Légitime Défense (Paris: Editions Surréalistes, 1926)
Introduction au discours sur le peu de réalité (Paris: Nouvelle Revue Française, 1927)
Le Surréalisme et la peinture (Paris: Nouvelle Revue Française, 1928)
Nadja (Paris: Nouvelle Revue Française, 1928)
Manifeste du Surréalisme, nouvelle édition augmentée d'une préface et de la lettre aux voyantes (Paris: S. Kra, 1929)
Second Manifeste du Surréalisme (Paris: S. Kra, 1930)
Ralentir travaux, in collaboration with R. Char and P. Eluard (Paris: Editions Surréalistes, 1930)
L'Immaculée Conception, in collaboration with P. Eluard (Paris: Editions Surréalistes, 1930)
Misère de la poésie (Paris: Editions Surréalistes, 1932)
Le Revolver à cheveux blancs (Paris: Editions des Cahiers Libres, 1932)
Les Vases communicants (Paris: Editions des Cahiers Libres, 1932)
Qu'est-ce que le Surréalisme? (Brussels: René Henriquez, 1934)

Point du jour (Paris: Nouvelle Revue Française, 1934)
Position politique du Surréalisme (Paris: S. Kra, 1935)
Au lavoir noir (Paris: Editions G. L. M., 1935)
Notes sur la poésie, in collaboration with P. Eluard (Paris: Editions G. L. M., 1936)
L'Amour fou (Paris: Nouvelle Revue Française, 1937)
Trajectoire du rêve (Paris: Editions G. L. M., 1938)

IV. René Char

Arsenal (Paris: privately printed, 1929)
Le Tombeau des secrets (Paris: privately printed, 1930)
Artine (Paris: Editions Surréalistes, 1930)
Ralentir travaux, in collaboration with A. Breton and P. Eluard (Paris: Editions Surréalistes, 1930)
L'Action de la Justice est éteinte (Paris: Editions Surréalistes, 1931)
Hommage à D. A. F. de Sade (Paris: privately printed, 1931)
Paul Eluard (Paris: privately printed, 1931)
Le Marteau sans maître (Paris: José Corti, 1934)
Dépendance de l'adieu (Paris: Editions G. L. M., 1935)
Moulin premier (Paris: Editions G. L. M., 1936)
Placard pour un chemin des écoliers (Paris: Editions G. L. M., 1938)
Dehors la nuit est gouvernée (Paris: Editions G. L. M., 1938)

V. Jean Cocteau

La Lampe d'Aladin (Paris: Société d'Editions Bouville, 1909)
Le Prince frivole (Paris: Mercure de France, 1910)
La Danse de Sophocle (Paris: Mercure de France, 1912)
Le Coq et l'arlequin (Paris: Editions de la Sirène, 1918)
Le Potomak (Paris: Société Littéraire de France, 1919)
Le Cap de Bonne Espérance (Paris: Editions de la Sirène, 1919)
L'Ode à Picasso (Paris: F. Bernouard, 1919)
Carte blanche (Paris: Editions de la Sirène, 1920)
Poésies (Paris: Editions de la Sirène, 1920)
Escales (Paris: Editions de la Sirène, 1920)

La Noce massacrée. Visite à Barrès (Paris: Editions de la Sirène, 1921)

Le Secret professionnel (Paris: P. V. Stock, 1922)

Vocabulaire (Paris: Editions de la Sirène, 1922)

La Rose de François (Paris: F. Bernouard, 1923)

Thomas l'Imposteur (Paris: Nouvelle Revue Française, 1923)

Le Grand Ecart (Paris: P. V. Stock, 1923)

Dessins (Paris: P. V. Stock, 1923)

Plain-Chant (Paris: P. V. Stock, 1923)

Les Mariés de la Tour Eiffel (Paris: Nouvelle Revue Française, 1923)

Picasso (Paris: P. V. Stock, 1923)

Les Biches, in collaboration with Darius Milhaud (Paris: Editions des Quatre Chemins, 1924)

Les Fâcheux, in collaboration with Louis Laloy (Paris: Editions des Quatre Chemins, 1924)

Le Mystère de l'oiseleur (Paris: H. Champion, 1925)

Prière mutilée (Paris: Editions des Cahiers Libres, 1925)

Maison de santé (Paris: Editions Briant-Robert, 1926)

L'Ange Heurtebise (Paris: P. V. Stock, 1926)

Lettre à Jacques Maritain (Paris: P. V. Stock, 1926)

Roméo et Juliette (Paris: Au Sans Pareil, 1926)

Le Rappel à l'ordre (Paris: P. V. Stock, 1926)

Orphée (Paris: P. V. Stock, 1927)

Opéra (Paris: P. V. Stock, 1927)

Antigone (Paris: Nouvelle Revue Française, 1927)

Œdipe-Roi (Paris: Plon, 1928)

Le Mystère laïc (Paris: Editions des Quatre Chemins, 1928)

Les Enfants terribles (Paris: B. Grasset, 1929)

La Voix humaine (Paris: P. V. Stock, 1930)

Opium, journal d'une désintoxication (Paris: P. V. Stock, 1930)

Le Livre blanc (Paris: Editions du Signe, 1930)

Carnet de l'amiral (Paris: B. Grasset, 1930)

La Machine infernale (Paris: B. Grasset, 1934)

Mythologie (Paris: Editions des Quatre Chemins, 1934)

Portraits-Souvenirs (Paris: B. Grasset, 1935)

Mon premier voyage (Paris: Nouvelle Revue Française, 1936)

Les *Chevaliers de la Table Ronde* (Paris: Nouvelle Revue Française, 1937)
Les *Parents terribles* (Paris: Nouvelle Revue Française, 1938)

VI. René Crevel

Détours (Paris: Nouvelle Revue Française, 1924)
Mon Corps et moi (Paris: S. Kra, 1925)
La Mort difficile (Paris: S. Kra, 1926)
Babylone (Paris: S. Kra, 1927)
L'Esprit contre la raison (Marseille: Cahiers du Sud, 1928)
Etes-vous fou? (Paris: Nouvelle Revue Française, 1929)
Paul Klee (Paris: Nouvelle Revue Française, 1930)
Salvador Dali ou l'anti-obscurantisme (Paris: Editions Surréalistes, 1931)
Le Clavecin de Diderot (Paris: Editions Surréalistes, 1932)
Les Pieds dans le plat (Paris: S. Kra, 1932)

VII. Salvador Dali

La Femme visible (Paris: Editions Surréalistes, 1930)
L'Amour et ma mémoire (Paris: Editions Surréalistes, 1931)
Babaouo (Paris: Editions des Cahiers Libres, 1932)
La Conquète de l'irrationnel (Paris: Editions Surréalistes, 1936)
Métamorphose de Narcisse (Paris: Editions Surréalistes, 1937)

VIII. Robert Desnos

Corps et biens (Paris: Nouvelle Revue Française, 1930)
La Liberté ou l'amour (Paris: S. Kra, 1931)

IX. Marcel Duchamp

La Mariée mise à nu par ses célibataires même (Paris: Editions Rrose Sélavy, 1934)
Rrose Sélavy (Paris: Editions G. L. M., 1937)

X. Paul Eluard

Le Devoir et l'inquiétude (Paris: Gonon, 1917)
Poèmes pour la paix (Mantes: Imprimerie du Petit Mantais, 1918)

Les Animaux et leurs hommes (Paris: Au Sans Pareil, 1920)

Les Nécessités de la vie et les conséquences des rêves (Paris: Au Sans Pareil, 1921)

Répétitions (Paris: Au Sans Pareil, 1922)

Les Malheurs des immortels, in collaboration with Max Ernst (Paris: Librairie Six, 1922)

Mourir de ne pas mourir (Paris: Nouvelle Revue Française, 1924)

152 proverbes mis au goût du jour, in collaboration with B. Péret (Paris: Editions Surréalistes, 1925)

Capitale de la douleur (Paris: Nouvelle Revue Française, 1926)

Les Dessous d'une vie ou La Pyramide humaine (Marseille: Cahiers du Sud, 1926)

Défense de savoir (Paris: Editions Surréalistes, 1928)

L'Amour, la poésie (Paris: Nouvelle Revue Française, 1929)

Ralentir travaux, in collaboration with A. Breton and R. Char (Paris: Editions Surréalistes, 1930)

A toute épreuve (Paris: Editions Surréalistes, 1930)

L'Immaculée Conception, in collaboration with A. Breton (Paris: Editions Surréalistes, 1930)

Dors (Paris: privately printed, 1931)

La Vie immédiate (Paris: Editions des Cahiers Libres, 1932)

Comme deux gouttes d'eau (Paris: Editions Surréalistes, 1933)

La Rose publique (Paris: Nouvelle Revue Française, 1934)

Facile (Paris: Editions G. L. M., 1935)

Nuits partagées (Paris: Editions G. L. M., 1935)

Notes sur la poésie, in collaboration with A. Breton (Paris: Editions G. L. M., 1936)

Les Yeux fertiles (Paris: Editions G. L. M., 1936)

Cours naturel (Paris: S. Kra, 1938)

Quelques uns des mots qui jusqu'ici m'étaient mystérieusement interdits, in collaboration with Man Ray (Paris: Editions G. L. M., 1938)

Chanson complète (Paris: Nouvelle Revue Française, 1939)

Donner à voir (Paris: Nouvelle Revue Française, 1939)

40 poésies de Stanislas Boutemer (Paris: Théophile Briant, 1928)
Le Droit de varech (Paris: Editions de la Montagne, 1930)
Ombres portées (Paris: Editions de la Montagne, 1932)
Enfances (Paris: Editions Cahiers d'Art, 1933)
La Belle en dormant (Paris: Editions des Cahiers Libres, 1933)
Onan (Paris: Editions Surréalistes, 1934)
La Hampe de l'imaginaire (Paris: Editions G. L. M., 1935)
La Septième Face du dé (Paris: Jeanne Bucher, 1936)

XII. Max Jacob

Le Roi Kaboul et le marmiton Gauvin (Paris: Picard et Kahn, 1904)
Le Géant du soleil (Paris: Librairie Générale, 1904)
Saint Matorel (Paris: Henry Kahnweiler, 1909)
Les Œuvres mystiques et burlesques de Frère Matorel, mort au couvent de Barcelone (Paris: Henry Kahnweiler, 1911)
Le Siège de Jérusalem (Paris: Henry Kahnweiler, 1912)
La Côte (Paris: privately printed, 1913; G. Crès, 1927)
Les Alliés sont en Arménie (Paris: privately printed, 1916)
Le Cornet à dés (Paris: privately printed, 1917; P. V. Stock, 1923)
Le Phanérogame (Paris: privately printed, 1918)
La Défense de Tartufe; extases, remords, visions, prières, poèmes et méditations d'un Juif converti (Paris: Société Littéraire de France, 1919)
Le Cinématoma (Paris: Editions de la Sirène, 1920)
Ne coupez pas, mademoiselle (Paris: Galerie Simon, 1921)
Dos d'arlequin (Paris: S. Kra, 1921)
Matorel en province (Paris: Vogel, 1921)
Le Laboratoire central (Paris: Au Sans Pareil, 1921)
Le Roi de Béotie (Paris: Nouvelle Revue Française, 1922)
Art poétique (Paris: Emile-Paul, 1922)
Le Cabinet noir (Paris: Nouvelle Revue Française, 1922)
Le Terrain Bouchaballe (Paris: Emile-Paul, 1922)
Filibuth ou la montre en or (Paris: Nouvelle Revue Française, 1923)

Les Visions infernales (Paris: Nouvelle Revue Française, 1924)
L'Homme de chair et l'homme reflet (Paris: S. Kra, 1924)
Les Pénitents en maillots roses (Paris: S. Kra, 1925)
Le Fond de l'eau (Toulouse: L'Horloge, 1927)
La Couronne de Vulcain (Paris: Galerie Simon, 1928)
Visions des souffrances et de la mort de Jésus, fils de Dieu (Paris: Editions des Quatre Chemins, 1928)
Tableau de la bourgeoisie (Paris: Nouvelle Revue Française, 1930)
Fable sans moralité (Paris: Maurice Senart, 1931)
Le Bal masqué (Paris: Rouart, Lerolle & Cie, 1932)
Cinq Poèmes (Paris: Rouart, Lerolle & Cie, 1932)
Bourgeois de France et d'ailleurs (Paris: Nouvelle Revue Française, 1932)
Rivage (Paris: Editions des Cahiers Libres, 1934)
Chemin de Croix infernal (Paris: Editions G. L. M., 1935)
Ballades (Paris: Debresse, 1938)

XIII. Alfred Jarry

Les Minutes de sable mémorial (Paris: Mercure de France, 1894)
César-Antéchrist (Paris: Mercure de France, 1895)
Ubu-Roi (Paris: Mercure de France, 1896)
Les Jours et les nuits (Paris: Mercure de France, 1897)
L'Amour absolu (Paris: mimeographed, 1898; Seheur, 1933)
L'Amour en visites (Paris: P. Fort, 1898)
Ubu-Enchainé (Paris: Revue Blanche, 1900)
Messaline (Paris: Revue Blanche, 1901)
Le Surmâle (Paris: Revue Blanche, 1902)
Ubu sur la butte (Paris: Sansot, 1906)
Albert Samain (Paris: Lemasle, 1907)
Le Moutardier du pape (Paris: Mercure de France, 1907)
La Papesse Jeanne, translation of a Greek novel by E. Rhoides (Paris: Fasquelle, 1908)
Gestes et opinions du Dr. Faustroll, pataphysicien (Paris: Fasquelle, 1911)
Gestes; Paralipomènes d'Ubu (Paris, S. Kra, 1921)

Les Chants de Maldoror, chant premier (Paris: Balitout, Questroy & Cie, 1868)

Les Chants de Maldoror. Chants I, II, III, IV, V, VI (Paris: A. Lacroix, 1869; not placed on the market until 1879)

Préface aux Poésies (Paris: Librairie Gabrie, 1870)

Les Chants de Maldoror (Paris: L. Genonceaux, 1890)

XV. Benjamin Péret

Le Passager du transatlantique (Paris: Au Sans Pareil, 1921)

Au 125 du Boulevard Saint-Germain (Paris: Editions Littérature, 1923)

Immortelle Maladie (Paris: Editions Littérature, 1924)

152 proverbes mis au goût du jour, in collaboration with P. Eluard (Paris: Editions Surréalistes, 1925)

Il était une boulangère (Paris: S. Kra, 1925)

Dormir, dormir dans les pierres (Paris: Editions Surréalistes, 1927)

Le Grand Jeu (Paris: Nouvelle Revue Française, 1928)

Et les seins mouraient (Marseille: Cahiers du Sud, 1928)

De derrière les fagots (Paris: Editions Surréalistes, 1934)

Trois cerises et une sardine (Paris: Editions Surréalistes, 1935)

XVI. Pierre Reverdy

Poèmes en prose (Paris: Editions Nord-Sud, 1915)

La Lucarne ovale (Paris: Editions Nord-Sud, 1916)

Quelques Poèmes (Paris: Editions Nord-Sud, 1916)

Le Voleur de Talan (Paris: Editions Nord-Sud, 1917)

Les Ardoises du toit (Paris: Editions Nord-Sud, 1918)

Les Jockeys camouflés et période hors texte (Paris: F. Bernouard, 1918)

La Guitare endormie (Paris: Editions Nord-Sud, 1919)

Self Defense (Paris: Editions Nord-Sud, 1919)

Etoiles peintes (Paris: S. Kra, 1921)

Cœur de chêne (Paris: Galerie Simon, 1921)

Cravates de chanvre (Paris: Editions Nord-Sud, 1922)

Epaves du ciel (Paris: Nouvelle Revue Française, 1924)

Ecumes de la mer (Paris: Nouvelle Revue Française, 1925)

Grande Nature (Paris: Editions des Cahiers Libres, 1926)

La Peau de l'homme (Paris: Nouvelle Revue Française, 1926)

Le Gant de crin (Paris: Plon, 1926)

Pablo Picasso (Paris: Nouvelle Revue Française, 1929)

Sources du vent (Carcassonne: Collection des Ecrivains Audois, 1930)

Pierres blanches (Carcassonne: Collection des Ecrivains Audois, 1931)

Risques et périls (Paris: Nouvelle Revue Française, 1931)

Ferraille (Brussels: Cahiers du Journal des Poètes, 1937)

XVII. André Salmon

Ames en peine et corps sans âme (Paris: Vers et Prose, 1905)

Les Féeries (Paris: Vers et Prose, 1907)

Le Calumet (Paris: Falque, 1910)

La Jeune Peinture française (Paris: Messein, 1912)

Tendres Canailles (Paris: Ollendorff, 1913)

Le Chass'bi. Notes de campagne en Artois et en Argonne (Paris: Perrin, 1915)

Histoires de Boches (Paris: Société Littéraire de France, 1917)

Monstres choisis (Paris: Nouvelle Revue Française, 1918)

La Jeune Sculpture française (Paris: Messein, 1919)

Mœurs de la famille Poivre (Genève: Kundig, 1919)

Prikaz (Paris: Editions de la Sirène, 1919)

L'Amant des Amazones (Paris: Editions Banderole, 1920)

L'Art vivant (Paris: G. Crès, 1920)

Bob et Bobette en ménage (Paris: Michel, 1920)

C'est une belle fille (Paris: Michel, 1920)

Emile Othon Friez (Paris: Nouvelle Revue Française, 1920)

Le Livre et la bouteille (Paris: Bloch, 1920)

Le Manuscrit trouvé dans un chapeau (Paris: Société Littéraire de France, 1920)

La Négresse du Sacré-Cœur (Paris: Nouvelle Revue Française, 1920)

Ventes d'amour (Paris: F. Bernouard, 1921)

Peindre (Paris: Editions de la Sirène, 1921)

L'Entrepreneur d'illuminations (Paris: Nouvelle Revue Française, 1921)

L'Age de l'humanité (Paris: Nouvelle Revue Française, 1921)

Natchalo, in collaboration with R. Saunier (Paris: Petite Illustration, 1922)

Propos d'atelier (Paris: G. Crès, 1923)

Archives du Club des Onze (Paris: Mornay, 1924)

Alfred Jarry ou le Père Ubu en liberté (Paris: G. Crès, 1924)

Créances (Paris: Nouvelle Revue Française, 1926)

Modigliani, sa vie et son œuvre (Paris: Editions des Quatre Chemins, 1926)

Vénus dans la balance (Paris: Editions des Quatre Chemins, 1926)

Henri Rousseau dit le douanier (Paris: G. Crès, 1927)

Le Drapeau noir (Paris: Cité des Livres, 1927)

Gouaches d'Utrillo (Paris: Dumoulin, 1928)

Max Jacob, poète, peintre mystique et homme de qualité (Paris: R. Girard, 1928)

Tout l'or du monde (Paris: S. Kra, 1928)

André Derain (Paris: Nouvelle Revue Française, 1929)

Carreaux (Paris: Nouvelle Revue Française, 1929)

Chagall (Paris: Grande Librairie Universelle, 1929)

Comme un homme; Faust à Montparnasse (Paris: E. Figuière, 1931)

L'Erotisme dans l'art contemporain (Paris: Calavas, 1931)

Voyage au pays des voyantes (Paris: Editions des Portiques, 1931)

L'Affaire Dreyfus (Paris: Emile-Paul, 1934)

Le Secret de Barataud (Paris: Emile-Paul, 1934)

Troubles en Chine (Paris: Debresse, 1935)

Saint André (Paris: Nouvelle Revue Française, 1936)

XVIII. Philippe Soupault

Aquarium (Paris: Au Sans Pareil, 1917)

Rose des vents (Paris: Au Sans Pareil, 1920)

Les Champs magnétiques, in collaboration with A. Breton (Paris: Au Sans Pareil, 1921)

Westwego (Paris: Au Sans Pareil, 1922)

Le Bon Apôtre (Paris: S. Kra, 1923)

Le Bar de l'amour (Paris: Emile-Paul, 1925)

Georgia (Paris: Au Sans Pareil, 1926)

En joue (Paris: B. Grasset, 1926)

Corps perdu (Paris: Au Sans Pareil, 1926)

Henri Rousseau, le douanier (Paris: Editions des Quatre Chemins, 1927)

Le Cœur d'or (Paris: B. Grasset, 1927)

Le Nègre (Paris: S. Kra, 1927)

Histoire d'un blanc (Paris: Au Sans Pareil, 1927)

Guillaume Apollinaire ou Reflets de l'incendie (Marseille: Cahiers du Sud, 1927)

Lautréamont (Paris: Editions des Cahiers Libres, 1927)

Terpsichore (Paris: Hazan, 1929)

Paolo Ucello (Paris: Rieder, 1930)

Jean Lurcat (Paris: Editions Cahiers d'Art, 1930)

Baudelaire (Paris: Rieder, 1931)

Charlot (Paris: Plon, 1931)

Les Moribonds (Paris: Rieder, 1934)

Il y a un océan (Paris: Editions G. L. M., 1936)

Poésies complètes (Paris: Editions G. L. M., 1937)

Dubout (Paris: Ullmann, 1938)

XIX. Tristan Tzara

La Première Aventure céleste de M. Antipyrine (Zurich: Collection Dada, 1916)

Vingt-cinq Poèmes (Zurich: Collection Dada, 1918)

Cinéma calendrier du cœur abstrait maisons (Paris: Au Sans Pareil, 1920)

Sept Manifestes Dada (Paris: Jean Budry, 1924)

Mouchoirs de nuages (Paris: Galerie Simon, 1925)

Indicateurs des chemins de cœur (Paris: Jeanne Bucher, 1928)

De nos oiseaux (Paris: S. Kra, 1929)

L'Homme approximatif (Paris: Fourcade, 1930)

L'Arbre des voyageurs (Paris: Editions de la Montagne, 1930)
Où boivent les loups (Paris: Editions des Cahiers Libres, 1933)
L'Antitête (Paris: Editions des Cahiers Libres, 1933)
Grains et issues (Paris: Denoël et Steele, 1935)
La Main passe (Paris: Editions G. L. M., 1935)
Ramures (Paris: Editions G. L. M., 1935)

XX. Jacques Vaché

Lettres de guerre (Paris: Au Sans Pareil, 1919)

Works of Criticism

I. Books and Pamphlets

Aegerter, Emmanuel: *Guillaume Apollinaire et les destins de la poésie* (Paris: Haleva, 1937)
Apollinaire, Guillaume: *Les Peintres cubistes, méditations esthétiques* (Paris: E. Figuière, 1912)
————: *Il y a . . .* (Paris: Messein, 1925)
Aragon, Louis: *Traité du style* (Paris: Nouvelle Revue Française, 1928)
————: *La Peinture au défi* (Paris: Galerie Goemans, 1930)
Bachelard, Gaston: *Lautréamont* (Paris: José Corti, 1939)
Baldensperger, Fernand: *La Littérature française entre les deux guerres, 1919–1939* (Los Angeles: Lymanhouse, 1941)
Berge, André: *L'Esprit de la littérature moderne* (Paris: Perrin, 1930)
Bertram, Anthony: *Pablo Picasso* (New York: Studio, 1934)
Billy, André: *Apollinaire vivant* (Paris: Editions de la Sirène, 1923)
————: *La Littérature française contemporaine* (Paris: Armand Colin, 1927)
Blanche, Jacques-Emile: *Les Arts plastiques de 1870 à nos jours* (Paris: Editions de France, 1932)
Bouvier, Emile: *Initiation à la littérature d'aujourd'hui* (Paris: Renaissance du Livre, 1928)

232

Breton, André: *Les Pas perdus* (Paris: Nouvelle Revue Française, 1924)

——: *Manifeste du Surréalisme* (Paris: S. Kra, 1924)

——: *Introduction au discours sur le peu de réalité* (Paris: Nouvelle Revue Française, 1927)

——: *Le Surréalisme et la peinture* (Paris: Nouvelle Revue Française, 1928)

——: *Manifeste du Surréalisme, nouvelle édition augmentée d'une préface et de la lettre aux voyantes* (Paris: S. Kra, 1929)

——: *Second Manifeste du Surréalisme* (Paris: S. Kra, 1930)

——: *Qu'est-ce que le Surréalisme?* (Brussels: René Henriquez, 1934)

——: *Position politique du Surréalisme* (Paris: S. Kra, 1935)

Cahun, Claude: *Les paris sont ouverts* (Paris: José Corti, 1934)

Carco, Francis: *De Montmartre au quartier latin* (Paris: Albin Michel, 1927)

Cassou, Jean: *Marcoussis* (Paris: Nouvelle Revue Française, 1930)

——: *Pour la poésie* (Paris: R.-A. Corrêa, 1935)

Cazaux, Jean: *Surréalisme et psychologie* (Paris: José Corti, 1938)

Chassé, Charles: *Sous le masque d'Alfred Jarry; les sources d'Ubu-Roi* (Paris: Floury, 1921)

Chauveau, Paul: *Alfred Jarry ou la naissance, la vie et la mort du Père Ubu* (Paris: Mercure de France, 1923)

Clouard, Henri: *La Poésie française moderne* (Paris: Gauthier-Villars, 1924)

Courthion, Pierre: *Panorama de la peinture française contemporaine* (Paris: S. Kra, 1927)

Cubism and abstract art, ed. by Alfred H. Barr Jr. (New York: The Museum of Modern Art, 1936)

Dale, Maud: *Modern Art: Picasso* (New York: Knopf, 1930)

Dubech, Lucien: *Les Chefs de file de la jeune génération* (Paris: Plon, 1925)

Du Colombier, P. et R. Manuel: *Les Arts* (Paris: Denoël et Steele, 1933)

Eddy, Arthur: *Cubists and Post-Impressionism* (Chicago: McClurg, 1919)

European Caravan, ed. by Samuel Putnam (New York: Harcourt Brace, 1931)

Fabureau, Hubert: *Guillaume Apollinaire, son œuvre* (Paris: Nouvelle Revue Critique, 1932)

———: *Max Jacob, son œuvre* (Paris: Nouvelle Revue Critique, 1935)

Fantastic Art Dada Surrealism, ed. by Alfred H. Barr Jr. (New York: The Museum of Modern Art, 1936)

Faÿ, Bernard: *Panorama de la littérature française contemporaine* (Paris: S. Kra, 1927)

Fettweis, Christian: *Apollinaire en Ardenne* (Brussels: René Henriquez, 1934)

Gascoyne, David: *A Short Survey of Surrealism* (London: Cobden-Sanderson, 1935)

Giedion, Sigfried: *Space, Time and Architecture; The Growth of a New Tradition* (Cambridge: Harvard University Press, 1941)

Gleizes, Albert et Jean Metzinger: *Du Cubisme* (Paris: E. Figuière, 1912)

Gleizes, Albert: *Du Cubisme et des moyens de le comprendre* (Paris: Editions La Cible, 1920)

———: *La Mission créatrice de l'homme dans le domaine plastique* (Paris: J. Povolozky, 1922)

———: *Traditions et Cubisme; vers une conscience plastique* (Paris: J. Povolozky, 1927)

———: *La Signification humaine du Cubisme* (Sablons: Moly Sabata, 1938)

Gordon, Jan: *Modern French Painters* (New York: Dodd, Mead & Co., 1923)

Grey, Roch: *Guillaume Apollinaire* (Paris: Editions Sic, 1918)

Horter, Earl: *Picasso, Matisse, Derain, Modigliani* (Philadelphia: H. C. Perlenberg, 1930)

Huyghe, René: *Histoire de l'art contemporain. La Peinture* (Paris: Alcan, 1935)

Jacob, Max: *Art poétique* (Paris: Emile-Paul, 1922)

Janis, Sidney: *They Taught Themselves: American Primitive Painters of the 20th Century* (New York: Dial Press, 1941)

Lalou, René: *Histoire de la littérature française contemporaine* (Paris: Presses Universitaires de France, 1939)

Lefèvre, Frédéric: *Une heure avec . . . Deuxième Série (Max Jacob)* (Paris: Nouvelle Revue Francaise, 1924)

Level, André: *Picasso* (Paris: G. Crès, 1928)

Levy, Julien: *Surrealism* (New York: The Black Sun Press, 1936)

Lhote, André: *La Peinture; le cœur et l'esprit* (Paris: Denoël et Steele, 1933)

Lot, Fernand: *Alfred Jarry, son œuvre* (Paris: Nouvelle Revue Critique, 1934)

Mabille, Pierre: *Le Miroir du merveilleux* (Paris: S. Kra, 1940)

Mangeot, Guy: *Histoire du Surréalisme* (Brussels: René Henriquez, 1934)

Marinetti, E. T.: *Le Futurisme* (Paris: Sansot, 1911)

Mariott, Charles: *Modern Movements in Painting* (London: Chapman & Hall, 1920)

Maritain, Jacques et Raïssa: *Situation de la poésie* (Paris: Desclée de Brouwer, 1938)

Maublanc, Jean-Daniel: *Surréalisme romantique* (Paris: Editions de la Pipe en Ecume, 1934)

Neuhuys, Paul: *Poètes d'aujourd'hui* (Antwerp: Editions Ça Ira, 1922)

Olivier, Fernande: *Picasso et ses amis* (Paris: Delamain et Boutelleau, 1933)

Ozenfant, Amédée et Charles-Edouard Jeanneret: *Après le Cubisme* (Paris: Editions des Commentaires, 1918)

Pach, Walter: *The Masters of Modern Art* (New York: B. Huebsch, 1934)

Petite Anthologie poétique du Surréalisme, ed. by Georges Hugnet (Paris: Jeanne Bucher, 1934)

Picasso: Forty Years of His Art, ed. by Alfred H. Barr, Jr. (New York: The Museum of Modern Art, 1939)

Pierre-Quint, Léon: *Le Comte de Lautréamont et Dieu* (Marseille: Cahiers du Sud, 1929)

Rachilde: *Alfred Jarry ou Le Surmâle de lettres* (Paris: B. Grasset, 1928)

Ramsden, E. H.: *An Introduction to Modern Art* (London: Oxford University Press, 1940)

Raymond, Marcel: *De Baudelaire au Surréalisme* (Paris: R.-A. Corrêa, 1933)

Raynal, Maurice: *Juan Gris* (Paris: L'Effort Moderne, 1920)

———: *Picasso* (Paris: G. Crès, 1922)

———: *Anthologie de la peinture en France de 1906 à nos jours* (Paris: Editions Montaigne, 1927)

Read, Herbert: *Art Now; An Introduction to the Theory of Modern Painting and Sculpture* (New York: Harcourt Brace, 1934)

Rolland de Renéville, A.: *L'Expérience poétique* (Paris: Nouvelle Revue Française, 1938)

Rosenberg, Léonce: *Cubisme et tradition* (Paris: L'Effort moderne, 1920)

———: *Cubisme et empirisme* (Paris: L'Effort moderne, 1921)

Rothschild, Edward: *The Meaning of Unintelligibility in Modern Art* (Chicago: University of Chicago Press, 1931)

Rouveyre, André: *Souvenirs de mon commerce. Au bras de Guillaume Apollinaire* (Paris: G. Crès, 1920)

Rutter, Frank: *Evolution in Modern Art* (London: G. C. Harrap, 1926)

Salmon, André: *La Jeune Peinture française* (Paris: Messein, 1912)

———: *La Jeune Sculpture française* (Paris: Messein, 1919)

———: *L'Art vivant* (Paris: G. Crès, 1920)

———: *Alfred Jarry ou le Père Ubu en liberté* (Paris: G. Crès, 1924)

———: *Max Jacob, poète, peintre mystique et homme de qualité* (Paris: R. Girard, 1927)

Sénéchal, Christian: *Les Grands Courants de la littérature française contemporaine* (Marburg: N. G. Elwert'sche Verlag, 1934)

Severini, Gino: *Du Cubisme au Classicisme* (Paris: J. Povolozky, 1921)

Soby, James T.: *After Picasso* (New York: Dodd, Mead & Co., 1935)

Soupault, Philippe: *Guillaume Apollinaire ou Reflets de l'incendie* (Marseille: Cahiers du Sud, 1927)
——: *Lautréamont* (Paris: Editions des Cahiers Libres, 1927)
Stein, Gertrude: *Dix portraits* (Paris: Editions de la Montagne, 1930)
——: *The Autobiography of Alice B. Toklas* (New York: Harcourt Brace, 1933)
——: *Picasso* (Paris: Floury, 1938; New York: Scribner's, 1939)
——: *Paris, France* (New York: Scribner's, 1940)
Surrealism, ed. by Herbert Read (London: Faber & Faber, 1936)
Sweeney, James J.: *Plastic Redirections in 20th Century Painting* (Chicago: University of Chicago Press, 1934)
Taupin, R. et L. Zukofsky: *Le Style Apollinaire* (Paris: Presses Modernes, 1934)
Topass, Jan: *La Pensée en révolte. Essai sur le Surréalisme* (Brussels: René Henriquez, 1935)
Uhde, W.: *Picasso et la tradition française* (Paris: Editions des Quatre Chemins, 1928)
Vitrac, Roger: *Georges de Chirico* (Paris: Nouvelle Revue Française, 1927)
Wilenski, Reginald H.: *The Modern Movement in Art* (New York: Stokes, 1927)
——: *French Painting* (Boston: Hale, Cushman & Flint, 1931)
——: *Modern French Painters* (New York: Reynal & Hitchcock, 1940)
Wright, Willard H.: *Modern Painting, Its Tendency and Meaning* (New York: Dodd, Mead & Co., 1926)

II. Articles in Periodicals

Apollinaire, Guillaume: "L'Esprit nouveau et les poètes," *Le Mercure de France* (Paris), December 1, 1918, pp. 384–396.
Bounoure, Gabriel: "La Grande Gaieté de Louis Aragon," *La Nouvelle Revue française* (Paris), March 1, 1931, pp. 455–456.
——: "La Poésie," *La Nouvelle Revue française* (Paris), July 1, 1934, pp. 109–118.
Breton, André: "Limites non frontières du Surréalisme," *La*

Nouvelle Revue française (Paris), February 1, 1937, pp. 200–215.

Byrne, B.: "Surrealism Passes," *Commonweal* (New York), July 2, 1937, pp. 262–263.

Caspers, F.: "Surrealism in Overalls," *Scribner's Magazine* (New York), August 1938, pp. 17–21.

Cassou, Jean: "Max Jacob et la liberté," *La Nouvelle Revue française* (Paris), April 1, 1928, pp. 454–463.

Charlot, J.: "The Reason for Unreason," *American Scholar*, April 1938, pp. 230–242.

Chauveau, Paul: "Notes sur Alfred Jarry," *Le Mercure de France* (Paris), November 1, 1926, pp. 581–599.

———: "Les Derniers Jours d'Alfred Jarry," *Le Mercure de France* (Paris), February 15, 1933, pp. 77–86.

Contreras, F.: "L'Origine du Comte de Lautréamont," *Le Mercure de France* (Paris), July 15, 1927, pp. 474–478.

Cowley, Malcolm: "The Religion of Art; a Discourse over the Grave of Dada," *The New Republic* (New York), January 10, 1934, pp. 246–249.

———: "The Religion of Art; the Death of a Religion," *The New Republic* (New York), January 17, 1934, pp. 272–275.

———: "Louis Aragon," *The New Republic* (New York), October 7, 1936, p. 258.

Crastre, Victor: "Sur le suicide de Jacques Rigaut," *La Nouvelle Revue française* (Paris), August 1, 1930, pp. 251–255.

Daumal, Paul: "Le Comte de Lautréamont et la critique," *La Nouvelle Revue Française* (Paris), November 1, 1930, pp. 738–745.

Ferguson, C. W.: "Art for Our Sake," *Harper's Magazine* (New York), July 1937, pp. 218–220.

Guiette, Robert: "Vie de Max Jacob," *La Nouvelle Revue française* (Paris), July 1, 1934, pp. 5–19 and August 1, 1934, pp. 348–359.

Horter, Earl: "Abstract Painting, a Visit to Braque," *Pennsylvania Museum Bulletin* (Philadelphia), vol. 29, 1934, pp. 62–64.

Hugnet, Georges: "L'Esprit Dada dans la peinture," *Cahiers d'art* (Paris), vol. VII, 1932, no. 1–2, pp. 57–65; no. 6–7, pp. 281–285; no. 8–10, pp. 358–364. Vol. IX, 1934, no. 1–4, pp. 109–114.

Jaloux, Edmond: "Etes-vous fou?" *Les Nouvelles Littéraires* (Paris), September 28, 1929.

King, B. M.: "First Venture into Surrealism," *School Arts* (Worcester, Mass.), March 1940, p. 222.

Lanoe, Julien: "Sources du Vent . . . par Pierre Reverdy," *La Nouvelle Revue française* (Paris), November 1, 1931, pp. 811–814.

Lerch, J.: "New Paintings for Connoisseurs; Interview with J. Levy," *Country Life* (New York), February 1938, pp. 48–49.

Lhote, André: "Irréalisme et Surréalisme," *La Nouvelle Revue française* (Paris), August 1, 1933, pp. 307–309.

——: "Les Créateurs du Cubisme," *La Nouvelle Revue française* (Paris), May 1, 1935, pp. 785–789.

——: "Surréalisme," *La Nouvelle Revue française* (Paris), May 1, 1938, pp. 859–861.

Lloyd, Peter: "Max Ernst and Surrealism," *Creative Art* (New York), vol. XI, 1932, pp. 214–216.

Loeb, Janice: "Surrealism," *Vassar Review* (Poughkeepsie), February 1935, pp. 5–12, 22–25.

McGavick, A.: "Weird Worlds," *Commonweal* (New York), April 1, 1938, p. 631.

Mortimer, R.: "The Art of Displeasing," *The Living Age* (New York), August 1936, pp. 329–332.

Pearson, R. M.: "Artist's Point of View," *Forum* (New York), March 1937, p. 181.

Pierre-Quint, Léon: "Lautréamont vu en 1938," *Revue de Paris* (Paris), November 1, 1938, pp. 202–210.

Rhodes, S. A.: "Lautréamont redivivus," *Romanic Review* (New York), October–December 1931, pp. 285–290.

——: "Candles for Isis," *Sewanee Review* (Sewanee), April–June 1933, pp. 212–224, and July–September, 1933, pp. 286–300.

——: "Poetical Affiliations of Gérard de Nerval," *Publications of the Modern Language Association of America*, December 1938, pp. 1157–1171.

Ribemont-Dessaignes, Georges: "Histoire de Dada," *La Nouvelle Revue française* (Paris), June 1, 1931, pp. 867–879, and July 1, 1931, pp. 39–52.

Rolland de Renéville, A.: "Dernier Etat de la poésie surréaliste," *La Nouvelle Revue française* (Paris), February 1, 1932, pp. 284–293.

———: "Le Surréalisme et la poésie," *La Nouvelle Revue française* (Paris), October 1, 1933, pp. 614–618.

———: "Du temps que les Surréalistes avaient raison," *La Nouvelle Revue française* (Paris), October 1, 1935, pp. 610–612.

———: "Le Surréalisme en 1938," *La Nouvelle Revue française* (Paris), September 1, 1938, pp. 302–306.

Rousseaux, André: "Jean ou l'intelligence pervertie," *Le Correspondant* (Paris), March 25, 1931, pp. 820–829.

Rouveyre, André: "Apollinarianes," *La Nouvelle Revue française* (Paris), December 1, 1938, pp. 905–940.

Royère, Jean: "Sur Guillaume Apollinaire," *Le Mercure de France* (Paris), Nov. 15, 1923, pp. 97–105.

Stein, Gertrude: "Pablo Picasso," *Camera Work* (New York), 1912, Special Number, pp. 29–30.

———: "The Life of Juan Gris; the Life and Death of Juan Gris," *Transition* (New York), no. 7, 1927, pp. 160–162.

Wolf, E. M.: "Apollinaire en Rhénanie et les Rhénanes d'Alcools," *Le Mercure de France* (Paris), August 1, 1933, pp. 590–608.

———: "Le Séjour d'Apollinaire en Rhénanie," *Le Mercure de France* (Paris), June 15, 1938, pp. 615–623.

Zimmermann, C.: "L'Art et le Surréalisme," *Le Mercure de France* (Paris), October 15, 1938, pp. 326–339.

III. Special Numbers of Reviews

L'Amour de l'art (Paris), March 1934. Special number on "La Nouvelle Subjectivité."

Cahiers d'art (Paris), no. 5–6, 1935, and no. 1–2, 1936. Special numbers on "Surréalisme."

Cahiers du Sud (Marseille), December 1929. Special number on "La Poésie et la Critique."

Disque vert (Paris and Brussels), November 1923. Special number on "Max Jacob."

Documents 34 (Brussels), May 1934. Special number on "Intervention surréaliste."

Mail (Paris), April 1928. Special number on "Max Jacob."

Minotaure (Paris), June 1933, December 1933, May 1934, and June 1936. Special numbers on "Surréalisme."

This Quarter (Paris), September 1932. Special "Surrealist Number."

Variétés (Paris), June 1929. Special number on "Le Surréalisme en 1929."

Vient de paraître (Paris), November 1923. Special number on "Hommage à Guillaume Apollinaire."

A toute épreuve, 210
Absolute, search for, by Romantics, 21–23, 25–28; Baudelaire's, 30–31; Rimbaud's, 34–35; Mallarmé's, 42–43; by Cubists, 80, 139–140, 145–146, 152–153; by Futurists, 149–151; by Surrealists, 186–187, 215
Action de la Justice est éteinte, L', 212
Africa, 55
Alcools, 105, 117
Algeria, 106
America, 15, 165, 217
Amour absolu, L', 61
Amour en visites, L', 61
Amour fou, L', 209
Amsterdam, Rue d', 73
Animaux et leurs hommes, Les, 174
Anthologie Dada, 168
Antitête, L', 211
Antitradizione futurista, L', 111, 149
Apollinaire, Guillaume (Kostrowitzki, Wilhelm Apollinaris de), 93–121; and Jarry, 61, 65, 97; and H. Rousseau, 70; and Picasso, 73ff; portrait by Metzinger, 78; early life, 94–97; travels, 97; Bohemian life, 98–99; and Cubism, 79, 86, 93–94, 100–103, 104ff; on goal of modern art, 82; and theft of "Mona Lisa," 103–104; and first World War, 105–107, 158; death, 107; personal characteristics, 101–102; conception of art, 107–109; literary technique, 110–117; prose, 118–119; mystic message, 119–121; and Salmon, 137; supports Futurism, 148; contributes to *Nord-Sud*, 159; Vaché on, 170; and Surrealism, 106, 181; mentioned, 125, 130, 131, 136, 138, 212
Arabian Nights, 122
Aragon, Louis, and *Nord-Sud* group, 159; and *Littérature* group, 165; among ranking Dadaists, 173; and Surrealist school, 187, 190, 212, 217
Archives du Club des Onze, 139

Ardoises du toit, Les, 143
Arp, Hans, 166
Art, and literature, 15–16, 192–193; Baudelaire on, 32–33; Rimbaud on, 35–36; as incantation, 85–86; Dadaists on, 159–161, 168–170; Surrealist views on, 202–205
Art poétique, 130
Artois, 138
Athlète des pompes funèbres, L', 167
Aurélia, 25
Automatism, 113–114, 180–181, 184–185, 205–206, 213

Ball, Hugo, 166
Balzac, Honoré de, 23, 139
Barcelona, 72
Bateau ivre, 35
Bateau-lavoir, and Cubism, 71–75; mentioned, 80, 93, 125, 138, 142
Baudelaire, Charles, inner conflict, 29–30; value of symbols, 31–33; V. Hugo on, 40; and Symbolism, 41; mystic transports, 52; and Cubism, 81, 153; poems in prose, 135; search for Absolute, 200; and Surrealism, 204
Beaux Quartiers, Les, 213
Beethoven, Ludwig van, 123
Belgium, 97
Bergson, Henri, 53–55, 88
Berthe la Bourguignonne, 75
Bertrand, Aloysius, 23, 135
Billy, André, 105
Birot, Pierre-Albert, 158, 159
Black Forest, 97
Blind Man, The, 165
Boccioni, Umberto, 148
Bohemia, 97
Bonaparte, Louis-Napoleon, 26
Bourbon, Duc de, 24
Braque, Georges, in Montmartre, 71; first Cubist pictures, 77–78; abstract view of Cubism, 90
Breton, André, and *Nord-Sud* group,

159; and J. Vaché, 162, 164; and *Littérature* group, 165; and Dadaism, 168, 173, 174; "Congrès de l'Esprit Moderne," 177–178; first Surrealist experience, 179–181; and Surrealism, 182–193, 199; and psychoanalysis, 184–185; on poetry, 203; on words, 204; on Surrealism, 205, 206; and mental disease, 208; literary productions, 209

Brittany, 56, 121

Brussels, 79

Calligrammes, 107, 117

Calumet, Le, 138

Cannes, 96

Cannibale, 174

Capitale de la douleur, 210

Cassette, Rue, 62, 63

C'est une belle fille, 139

Cendrars, Blaise, and Futurism, 151, 152; and *Littérature* group, 165; and Dadaism, 173, 175

Cézanne, Paul, 66, 67, 70

Champs magnétiques, Les, 181, 209

Chants de Maldoror, Les, 37, 38, 186

Char, René, 190, 212

Charleville, 33

Childhood, world of, 193–195

Chimères, Les, 25

Chirico, Giorgio, 214

Cinéma calendrier du cœur abstrait maisons, 174

Cinématoma, Le, 130

Clair de terre, 209

Cloches de Bâle, Les, 213

Cocteau, Jean, early career, 147; and Cubism, 147–148; and first World War, 158; and Dadaism, 173, 175, 178

Collage, 172

Colon, Jenny, 24

Columbus, Christopher, 111

Congo, 76

Congrès de l'Esprit Moderne, 177–178; relation to Surrealism, 179; consequences of failure, 182

Corbeil, 61, 63

Cornet à dés, Le, 129

Corps et biens, 211

Côte, La, 129

Cours naturel, Le, 210

Crevel, René, 187, 190

Cubism, setting and social background, 15, 16, 20, 71–75; fusion of literary and artistic groups, 74; origin and early development, 72–79; aims, 79–82, 84, 152; and primitivism, 75–77; pictorial method, 77–78, 80–83, 84; and decorative art, 85–86, 92–93; types of, 87–88; French influences, 89–90; Spanish influences, 90–91; decline, 91–92, 161; literary aspects, 93–94, 100–101, 105, 107–109, 118–119, 121, 131, 134–135; relation to Futurism, 148–152; partial failure, 153; a precedent for Dadaism, 157, 158; and *Littérature* group, 165–166; persistence of aspirations, 171; influence on Surrealists, 186. *See also* Apollinaire; Jacob; Salmon; Reverdy; Picasso; Gris; Braque; Rousseau; Cocteau

Dada, 167, 168, 174

Dadaism, influences M. Jacob, 130; outgrowth of first World War, 155–157; *Sic* and *Nord-Sud*, 158–161; and J. Vaché, 161–165; origin of name, 166; development, 167–169, 173–175; characteristics, 169–172; methods, 172–173; reviews, 173–174; books, 174; "festivals," 174–175; decline and fall, 175–178; mentioned, 16, 20, 186, 211

Dakar, 77

Dali, Salvador, 208, 214

Dalize, René (Dupuy, René), 95, 99, 105

Da Vinci, Leonardo, *see* Vinci

Decorative art, Cubism and, 85–86, 92–93

Défense de savoir, 210

Défense de Tartufe, La, 129

De la Fresnaye, Roger, *see* La Fresnaye

Delaunay, Robert, 92

De Lautréamont, Comte, *see* Lautréamont
De Nerval, Gérard, *see* Nerval
Democratie sociale, La, 98
Derain, André, 67
Desnos, Robert, 187, 190, 211
Dessins de la fille née sans mère, 167
Dessous d'une vie ou la Pyramide humaine, Les, 210
Dieu, 28
Dreams, 134–135, 201–202
Ducasse, Isidore, *see* Lautréamont, Comte de
Duchamp, Marcel, 165
Dupuy, René, *see* Dalize, René

Ecumes de la mer, 144
Einstein, Albert, 182, 183
Eluard, Paul, and *Littérature* group, 165; and Dadaism, 168, 173, 174; and Surrealism, 187, 190, 192; interest in mental diseases, 208; literary works, 210, 211
Enchanteur pourrissant, L', 118
Entrepreneur d'illuminations, L', 139
Epaves du Ciel, 143, 145
Ermenonville, 22, 23
Ernst, Max, 214

Facts, cult of, 140–141; opposition to, 145
Faustroll, Dr., 65
Fauves, revolt against tradition, 56, 57–68; limitations, 69; decline, 75; and Cubism, 77, 78
Fauvism, *see* Fauves
Féeries, 138
Femme assise, La, 107, 118
Femme visible, La, 208
Festin d'Esope, Le, 98, 137
Feuchères, Baronne de, 24
Filibuth ou la montre en or, 130
Fin de Babylone, 99
Fin de Satan, La, 28
Fin du jour, 212
France, rationalism in, 19–23, 200; Romanticism in, 21–23; and Symbolism, 41; influence of Bergson, 53–55; and Negro art, 76; and

Cubism, 89–90, 93, 148; and good taste, 109; and Futurism, 151; effect of first World War, 157–158; and Surrealism, 190–191; and imagination, 200; as cradle of modernist doctrines, 15, 217; mentioned, 97, 117, 130, 139, 185, 189, 192, 209
Frédé, Père, 74
French Revolution, 22
Freud, Sigmund, 183
Futurism, and French thought, 15, 151–152; social background, 16, 20; origins, 148–149; theories of, 149–152; and Cubism, 149, 152–153; obsolescence, 161; persistence of aspirations, 171

Gant de crin, Le, 144
Gaul, 141
Gaveau, salle, 174
Géant du soleil, Le, 128
Genève, 166
Germany, 97, 191
Géry, 103
Gestes et opinions du Dr. Faustroll, 63
Gide, André, and *Littérature* group, 165; and Dadaists, 173, 175
Gill, André, 74
Gleizes, Albert, 90
Grains et Issues, 211
Grande Gaieté, La, 212
Grande Nature, 144
Greece, 96, 120
Gris, Juan, 71, 142; and Cubism, 89
Guitare endormie, La, 143

Heb, Le Père, 56, 57, 58
Hébert, 56
Hercules, 140
Hérésiarque et Cie, L', 103, 118
Hitler, Adolf, 191
Hoffman, E. T. A., 122
Holland, 97
Holterhoff-Milhau, Viscountess von, 97
Homme approximatif, L', 211
Homme de chair et l'homme reflet, L', 131
Honnef, 97

Huelsenbeck, Richard, 166
Hugnet, Georges, 190
Hugo, Adèle, 27
Hugo, Eugène, 27
Hugo, Léopoldine, 26
Hugo, Victor, 23, 26–28, 33; on Baudelaire, 40; as forerunner of Cubism, 153

Illuminations, Les, 53
Imagination, and reality, 193–198; rehabilitation of, 200–201
Immaculée Conception, L', 208
Impressionism, and nature, 46; pictorial technique, 47; general influence, 48, 66
Indicateur des chemins de cœur, 174
Industry, modern, glorification of, 150
Introduction au discours sur le peu de réalité, 209
Introspection, 146–147
Intuition, 54–55, 81–82, 149
Italy, 148
Ivory Coast, 76

Jacob, Max, and Jarry, 61, 65; and Picasso, 73, 124–125; and Cubism, 79, 125–127, 129, 131–136; early life, 121–123; conversion to Catholicism, 127–129; characteristics, 131–136; and Salmon, 138; and Dadaists, 139, 173, 175; collaborates in Nord-Sud, 159; Vaché on, 170; mentioned, 71, 77, 143, 144, 158
Jarry, Alfred, early life, 56–57; personal characteristics, 57–58, 61, 73; Ubu-Roi, 59–60; influence, 61; later life, 61–63; view of the world, 64–65; and H. Rousseau, 69–70, 75; and Negro art, 76; and Apollinaire, 97, 98, 101–102, 106, 115; and Dadaism, 157; and Vaché, 161, 163; mentioned, 93, 137, 198
Jersey, 26
Jupiter, 35

Kerensky, 139
Klee, Paul, 214

Kostrowitzki, Jacqueline de, 107
Kostrowitzki, Madame de, 94
Kostrowitzki, Wilhelm Apollinaris de, see Apollinaire, Guillaume

Laboratoire central, Le, 130
La Fresnaye, Roger de, 89
Language, see Words
Lautréamont, Comte de (Ducasse, Isidore), mysterious personality, 36; extreme révolté, 37–38, 40; literary characteristics, 38–40, 58; and Dadaism, 172, 186; and Surrealism, 185, 186; mentioned, 29, 102, 153
Larousse, Dictionnaire, 166
Laurencin, Marie, 89, 102
Laval, 56, 63
Léautaud, Paul, 103
Le Fauconnier, 89
Léger, Fernand, 92
Lettres de guerre, 163, 173
Lhote, André, 89, 173
Liberté ou l'amour, La, 211
Literature, and art, 15–16, 65, 191–192; and social background, 16; Surrealist views on, 202–205
Littérature, 165, 167, 168, 173
Livre et la Bouteille, Le, 138, 139
London, 191
Louvre, 103, 104
Lucarne ovale, La, 143
Lugné-Poe, 60
Lyons, 96

Malaga, 72
Maldoror, 37, 38, 39
Mallarmé, Stéphane, inner conflict, 41–42; on the power of words, 43–46, 86, 204; influence on Jarry, 61, 65; and Cubists, 86; and Apollinaire, 113; Vaché on, 170; mentioned, 52, 137, 153, 200
Mamelles de Tirésias, Les, 106
Manifeste Dada, 178
Manifeste du Surréalisme, 187
Marcoussis, 90
Marinetti, E. T., 148–151
Marne, 61
Masson, André, 214

Mathematics, and Cubism, 80–81, 85–87, 89–92
Matisse, Henri, 67, 78
Meaning, denial of, 159–161, 166, 169–171
Mediterranean, 96, 97
Mental disease, 208
Mercure de France, 57, 103, 106, 107
Messaline, 61, 62
Metzinger, Jean, 78, 89
Michelangelo, 87
Milan, 149
Milhaud, Darius, 173
Minutes de sable mémorial, Les, 61
Miró, Joan, 214
"Mona Lisa," theft of, 103–104
Monaco, 95
Mont-de-Piété, 174
Montevideo, 36
Montmartre, cradle of Cubism, 15, 71, 73, 159; deserted by artists, 93–94, 142; mentioned, 125, 127, 129, 131, 138
Montparnasse, and literary Cubism, 15, 93–94; mentioned, 129, 159
Morand, Paul, and Futurism, 151–152; and Dadaism, 173, 175
Mormons, Les, 118
Mortefontaine, 23, 24
Movement, worship of, 150–151, 158–159
Mouchoirs de nuages, 174
Mouvement perpétuel, 212
Music, Dadaist, 173

Nadja, 209
Nantes, 162, 164
Napoleon, 22, 23
Narbonne, 141
Nature, as seen by Impressionists, 46; as seen by Futurists, 149–150; as seen by Cubists, 159–160
Naville, Pierre, 187, 190
Négresse du Sacre-Cœur, La, 139
Negroes, primitivism, 55; influence on Cubism, 76–77, 79, 80–81
Nerval, Gérard de, 23–26, 52; and modern theories, 33, 153; and Surrealism, 181, 208

Neu Glück, 97
New York, 165, 167, 191
Niebelungen, 203
Nodier, Charles, 23
Nord-Sud, 158, 159, 160–161
Notre-Dame, 22

Œil et son œil, L', 174
Œuvres mystiques et burlesques de Frère Matorel, 129
Oran, 106
Orléans, 130
Orpheus, 87
Où boivent les loups, 211

Painting, influence, 192, 214; technique, 46–48, 66, 68, 75; Cubist, 76–78, 82–83, 89–91; Futurist, 151; Dadaist, 172–173; Surrealist, 214
Palais des Fêtes, 174
Paris, literary Bohemia of, 57, 62, 71, 73–75, 93–94, 124–125; first Futurist exhibition, 148; publication of *Nord-Sud*, 159; and *Littérature* group, 165; center of Dadaism, 174; and Surrealism, 182, 191–192
Pas perdus, Les, 209
Pan, 36
Péret, Benjamin, 175
Persécuté persécuteur, 212
Petite Auto, La, 117
Petrograd, 139
Pfeipfer, Madame, 124
Phalanstère, 61, 62
Picabia, Francis, in New York, 165; in Switzerland, 167–168; and Dadaism, 168, 170, 173, 174, 177; and Surrealism, 187, 190, 214
Picasso, Pablo, life, 72–73; and Cubism, 73–74, 77, 89, 90; and M. Jacob, 124–125, 126, 129; use of collage, 172; supports Dadaists, 173; mentioned, 61, 71, 99, 104, 148
Poe, Edgar Allan, 122
Poèmes en prose, 143
Poésies complètes, 212
Poète assassiné, Le, 118
Poetic technique, of Apollinaire, 115–117; of Jacob, 135; of Surrealists, 213

Point du jour, 209
Poisson soluble, 209
Polonais, Les, 57, 58
Prague, 97
Première Aventure céleste de M. Antipyrine, La, 174
Princet, 80
Prometheus, 35, 37
Primitivism, 55, 69–70, 75–77
Prose, Cubist, 118–119, 135, 139; Dadaist, 172, 174; Surrealist, 213
Psychoanalysis, influence, 183–185, 186

Quimper, 121, 122, 126

Rabelais, François, 59
Raphael, 87
Rateliers platoniques, 167
Rationalism, in France, 19–22; opposition to, 53–55, 72, 84, 108–109, 133, 139–140, 149, 186–188, 193–200; basis of, 200–201
Ravignan, Rue, home of Cubism, 74–75; mentioned, 71–137, *passim*
Realism, 134. *See also* Rationalism
Relativity, 182–183, 186
Renaissance, 51, 67, 84
Rennes, 56
Reverdy, Pierre, and Cubism, 136, 142–143, 144–145; early life, 141–142; and Surrealism, 143, 146; conception of the world, 145–146; characteristics, 146–147; as a founder of *Nord-Sud*, 159–160; and *Littérature* group, 165; and Dadaists, 173; mentioned, 158, 171
Rêveries du promeneur solitaire, Les, 21
Révolution surréaliste, La, 187
Revolver à cheveux blancs, Le, 209
Rheinland, 97
Ribemont-Dessaignes, Georges, and *Littérature* group, 165; and Dadaism, 169, 173, 174; and Surrealism, 190
Rigaut, Jacques, and Dadaism, 175; and Surrealism, 187; commits suicide, 188
Rimbaud, Arthur, early life, 33; revolt, 29, 33, 198; literary theories, 34–35; literary characteristics, 36; and Symbolism, 41; and Cubism, 81, 153; poems in prose, 135; and Surrealism, 185–186, 204; mentioned, 52, 64, 200
Risques et périls, 144
Riviera, French, 94, 96, 101
Roi Kaboul et le marmiton Gauvin, Le, 128
Romantic period, characteristics, 22–23; poems in prose, 135; vogue of imagination, 200. *See also* Romanticism
Romanticism, 22–23; criticized by M. Jacob, 133
Rome, 94, 96
Rome des Borgia, La, 99
Rose des vents, 174
Rousseau, Henri, 69–70, 75
Rousseau, Jean-Jacques, 21–22, 33
Russia, 137

Saint-Benoît-sur-Loire, 130
Saint-Charles, college, 95
Saint-Germain, boulevard, 57
Saint-Martin, rue, 168
Saint Matorel, 128
St. Petersburg, 137
Sainte-Beuve, 23
Salmon, André, life and character, 136–141; and the *Festin d'Esope*, 98, 137; and *Les Soirées de Paris*, 105; friendship with M. Jacob, 125, 138; and Cubism, 136, 138, 139–140, 144; the poetry of facts, 140; influence of journalism, 141; contrasted with Reverdy, 144–145; and Dadaism, 173, 175; mentioned, 61, 65, 71, 162, 186
Satie, Erik, 173
Satire, 59–60, 131–132; Surrealist use of 198–199
Saunier, H., 138
Science, possibilities, 29; reaction against, 40–41, 53–54; disturbing influence, 51–53, 182–184
Seine, 94
Sénégal, 77

Serner, Val, 166, 178
Severini, Gino, 148, 158
Sic, 158–161
Siège de Jérusalem, Le, 129
Soirées de Paris, Les, 105
Solesmes, Abbey of, 144
Soupault, Philippe, and *Nord-Sud* group, 159; and *Littérature* group, 165; and Dadaism, 173, 174; collaboration with A. Breton, 180–181, 185, 205; and Surrealism, 187, 190, 212
Sources du vent, 144
Spain, 73, 124
Spaniards, influence on Cubism, 90–91
Speed, worship of, 151–153
Sphinx, 203
Subconscious, literary use of, 145–146, 179–181, 184–185, 187; Surrealist views on, 195–198, 203–204, 215–216. *See also* Dreams
Sudan, 77
Surmâle, Le, 61
Surrealism, originally conceived by Apollinaire, 106; Salmon and Breton, 179–182; origin of name, 181; and relativity, 182–183; and Freudian theories, 183–185; aims, 186–187, 196–198; conflicting tendencies, 187–190; diffusion, 190–193; theoretical principles, 193–196; "humor," 198–199; the Surreal, 199–202; as a philosophy of life, 202–203; literary method, 204–209; literary productions, 209–213; in art, 214; mentioned, 15, 16, 20, 49, 93
Surréalisme au service de la Révolution, Le, 187
Surreality, *see* Surrealism
Sylvie, 25
Symbolism, origin, 40–41; and Impressionism, 46; Jacob on, 133; influence on A. Salmon, 136. *See also* Mallarmé, Stéphane
Symbols, Baudelaire on, 31–33. *See also* Surrealism
Switzerland, 166, 167

Tanguy, Yves, 214
Tarbes, 36
Terrain Bouchaballe, Le, 130
Tombeau des secrets, Le, 212
Toulouse, 141
Trernec'k de Coutouly, 56
Typography, as a poetic device, 117
Tzara, Tristan, and Dadaism, 166–168, 173, 174; view of life, 169; opposition to Congrès de l'Esprit Moderne, 177–178; quarrel with A. Breton, 178, 190; and Surrealist group, 187; works, 174

Ubu, 59, 60, 61, 65
Ubu-Enchaîné, 61
Ubu-Roi, 59–60

Vaché, Jacques, life and character, 161–165; on art, 168–169; on Mallarmé, Apollinaire, and Jacob, 170; and Dadaism, 173; mentioned, 188
Valéry, Paul, and *Littérature* group, 166; and Dadaism, 173, 175
Vallette, Alfred, 57, 61
Vases communicants, Les, 209
Vaucelles, Louis, 78
Vers et Prose, 137
Vie immédiate, La, 210
Vinci, Leonardo da, 87
Visions infernales, 131
Vlaminck, Maurice, 67

Waterloo, 22
Weill, Alexandre, 26
Words, power of, 43–46, 49, 86, 112–113, 204–206; use of, 132–133
World War, influence, 91, 105–106, 155–157, 158, 175–176
Wrong Wrong, 165

Yeux fertiles, Les, 210

Zurich, 166, 167, 174